Scenes of a Reclusive Writer & Reader of Mumbai

Scenes of a Reclusive Writer & Reader of Mumbai

ESSAYS

Fiza Pathan

Fiza Pathan Publishing OPC Private Limited

Mumbai, INDIA

Imprint. Freedom With Pluralism®
Fiza Pathan Publishing OPC Private Limited
2 Symbol Apts., Tertullian Rd, Off Dr. Peter Dias Road
Bandra West, Mumbai 400050, INDIA
Email. fizapathan@fizapathanpublishing.com
Website. https://fizapathanpublishing.us/

Editor. Kimberly Catanzarite.
Proofreader. Shelagh Aitken.
Cover illustration by Farzana Cooper. Image is copyrighted. © 2019
Cover art and design: LLPix Photography & Design.

Author's Note: This is a work of nonfiction. I have tried to recreate events, locales, and conversation from my memories of them. I recognize that the memories of people described in this book may be different from my own. It is also possible that my recollection and interpretation of events may not be entirely objective. In order to maintain their anonymity, in some instances I have omitted mention of names of individuals as my intention was not to hurt them. This book should be treated as a combination of facts about my life and certain embellishments. It is not my intention to malign any person or institution. The book also contains reviews of books which have influenced me and my thinking and have benefitted me. I have not been paid to review any book, and the thoughts, feelings, and experiences of the author are purely subjective, and are not to be considered as advice or suggestions to be acted upon. The author is not responsible for any loss or damage incurred through acting on these suggestions. The reader should not consider this book anything other than a work of literature.

Book Title/Author. Scenes of a Reclusive Writer & Reader of Mumbai: Essays. Pathan, Fiza -- 1st ed

ISBN 978-8-1940558-0-8 Hardcover
ISBN 978-8-1940558-1-5 Paperback
ISBN 978-8-1940558-2-2 E-book

Contents

For Nana

Between the pages of a book is a lovely place to be.

–ANONYMOUS

ESSAY 1

Introduction

I AM A RECLUSE and I love books more than I love people.

If, however, you do happen to find me in conversation, you can be sure that I am doing so to study the person with whom I'm speaking for a book that I am writing. People are interesting, but books are even better. I'd always rather read than be around people. Really, that's the truth.

I have been like this ever since I learned that my father had abandoned me as a baby because I was a girl. Mama brought me up alone. I have no brothers or sisters, and I live with my maternal family in my grandmother's home.

Grandmother, or Nana, was educated only through the third grade. But she was very independently minded and told my father off for doing what he did.

She gave me, then a four-month-old, a roof over my head. She is no more. I am ever so grateful for her kindness.

I've never known my father nor what it means to have a father in one's life.

When I went to school, I knew that because I didn't have a father and because I was from a middle-class family, I was considered different from the affluent, elite students who studied with me from kindergarten through tenth grade.

Although I studied at Bombay Scottish School (BSS), I never made friends there. The school is located in the Mahim area of Mumbai. It is one of the best Indian Certificate of Secondary Education (ICSE) schools in Mumbai. I got in almost free because Mama was a teacher there. Built by Scottish missionaries, it was founded in 1847, ten years before the Indian Mutiny of 1857, or as we Indians are proud to call it, India's First War of Independence 1857.

The school once housed European orphans and was known as Bombay Scottish School Orphanage Society. Today, no orphans live there, and only regular school-going affluent kids and loner bookworms like me attended in 1993.

I spent all my time in the school library reading. Those books were my father. They taught me things that a father might have done. I'm ever thankful to have had such a wonderful school library.

Students were scared of Mama, so they didn't want to converse with me. For all my twelve years of study at BSS, no one wanted to play with me. So I took to reading. Now, at age twenty-nine, books are still my only friends and the father-figure in my life.

In this book of essays, I'm going to analyze the books, bookshops, libraries, and reading haunts that played a considerable part in making me the person I am today – a reclusive, bookish introvert.

I will also dwell on certain social issues and discrimination in society that I personally have faced from the very moment I was born to the present date as a twenty-nine-year-old multiple award-winning author, teacher, and director of Fiza Pathan Publishing. Some of these issues have molded my life into a bizarre shape that many people find uncanny – but not me.

I am happy being a recluse and far from the madding crowd.

I don't like people, but I love my plant and animal friends. I find children tolerable, but only to a certain extent. I find it more comfortable to be around them than adults or young adults my age, and I'm not ashamed to say so. Children are far smarter than adults. I've found most of the adults in my life to be stupid, vindictive, and paradoxical; that's why I've chosen to stay away from them as much as possible. I live to read and write. If there were no books in this world, I might not have lived long enough to write these lines on my Dell laptop.

And today is a beautiful winter's day in January. The taste of my morning coffee is still fresh in my mouth, and I can't wait to get started conversing with you, dear reader, about books, authors, libraries, bookshops, and myself via this book of essays.

If you have your cup of tea or coffee by your side and have almost finished it, then it's time for you to enter my world – a solitary world where I worship books and where I have lived my scenes knowingly or unknowingly as a book lover.

Mama always said that, before I could talk, I wrote cursive and before I could read, I told stories. Reminds me of ABBA's lyrics in *Thank You for the Music*; one of Mama's favorite songs. Where Papa was concerned, he didn't feel a girl child would amount to much. Well, Papa, maybe I haven't amounted to much, but I do like to keep an account of things.

These are the scenes.

Live them with me once more, evermore!

Love to every one of my readers. Love you all the way to the bookstore and back!

Fiza Pathan

3rd of January, 2019.

ESSAY 2

I Am a Girl Child, Live with It

MY FATHER DIDN'T WANT ME because I was a girl.

I was born at Mandar Maternity Hospital, Bandra (West), on the 19th of March, 1989. Mama was thirty-nine years old when she had me. She went into dry labor without informing my father.

During the dry labor, I stopped moving, and Mama asked for a C-section to be done at once. Yes, she knew Papa's orthodox Sunni Muslim family wanted a normal delivery, but she wanted a living child, not a dead baby.

So the caesarean operation was done without my father's knowledge. My Aunt Rita, who I just call Rita, said that my cry was like that of a girl. Aunt Mercia, who I call Mechu, stopped reciting the rosary, which she had started chanting the moment my mama's water bag was burst, when she heard my cry.

I arrived, a healthy nine-pound baby girl, soon wrapped in pristine white cloth, and with a whole lot of hair, all curly raven black.

When I was brought to Mama's side, she was still reeling from the anaesthesia. She looked at me, and I looked at her. It was love at first sight. Truly it was.

I snuggled closer to her, and she saw that I, like her, had inherited the maternal family dimple on only one cheek, the right cheek.

I was healthy, adorable, and full of life, or so I'm told.

But my Papa didn't want me. His family, my paternal family, did not want me either; I was a girl. Too bad I couldn't have been a boy; after all, I was the eldest child and firstborn.

Mama knew Papa didn't want me. She wanted to come back to Nana but my uncle, who is also my godfather, and whom I call Blaise or Blazy, said that my mama should give the marriage a chance. So Mama, after her ritual forty-day stay at Nana's, went to live at her in-laws.

Mama was a staunch Catholic. Papa was a staunch Muslim. What more can I say? It was a no-go from that point of view alone.

My paternal grandfather was a nice man. He ran a stationery store that sold schoolbooks, textbooks, fiction and nonfiction books, book bags, pens and pencils, examination boards, et al. His name was Ibrahim, and I have no memory of what he looked like.

I just call him Ibrahim. He was uneducated but could speak English.

It was he who whispered the *kalma* in my ear as well as my name, Fiza, which in Urdu means "the atmosphere."

Mama took me to Papa's home, knowing I wouldn't be welcomed. She looked at our painting of the Sacred Heart of Jesus in the common bedroom and begged him to send her back to Nana. She had seen the way my father beat and physically abused his younger, unmarried sisters because they wanted to study and go to college. Mama was scared.

Blaise says that while Mama was recuperating from the delivery at Nana's place, I used to spend most of my time staring at the picture of the Sacred Heart of Jesus.

I loved looking at that picture and playing with Nana's blue rosary beads.

But if I was to be brought up at Papa's place, I would be a Muslim. Mama was afraid to go back to her in-laws, but circumstances that even after twenty-nine years are not clear to me because no one wants to talk about them, caused me to reside for four months at my papa's home in Byculla, the Muslim area of a once-Christian area in the main city of Mumbai.

My papa's family were clear under which conditions they were willing to accept a girl child. My mama would have to stop teaching at BSS and stay at home and look after me herself. None of my unmarried paternal aunts, nor my vicious paternal grandmother, whom I call Khadijah, were willing to care for me. My mama refused to comply, naturally, as Papa was being paid a pittance by his father.

When Mama informed them that she would continue to work, all hell broke loose.

Papa kept telling my mother that his family would try to kill me while she was not home. They would drop me down the heritage building stairs, or drop me to the floor, or crush my neck to make it seem like an accident.

At first Mama didn't believe him. But then things started to happen.

I'm not sure about the facts of the matter because no one in my maternal family wants to talk about it. They are unnaturally silent on this part of my history. Furthermore, there are no photographs of me as an infant; the earliest photos of me are of my first birthday.

As I said, things started happening. There were the taunts and the squabbling. Mama would come back home to find me lying on a mat in the one-room apartment that they had, crying, my nappy reeking of urine and a rash covering all my body. I was not being fed sometimes. One day Mama came home earlier than usual. When she opened the door, to her horror, she found my paternal aunt about to trip over my tiny head. She would have crushed me, but Mama was there just in time.

There were fights and the vilest things were said about me being a girl. Ibrahim ordered my mama to leave his home and come back when things settled down.

"Leave with Fiza?" asked Mama.

"Yes, she is the cause of all this unrest in my happy home," Ibrahim said, lying on the bed looking into the distance.

I was a five-month-old baby, and I was the cause of my Mama's marriage breaking.

I ruined her marriage because I was a girl.

"Are you seriously telling me to go just because she is a girl?" my mama said, exasperated. "And remember, sir, if I go today from your house, I will never again come back."

Ibrahim did not reply. He was confident that my mama would come back; where else would she go? He was hoping, however, that she would return without me. I was the problem, not Mama.

My Mama left with me. Nana took her back and gave me a roof over my head.

"She is my grandchild," said Nana proudly. "She will live with me."

Blaise, Rita, David uncle, and Mechu were overjoyed! Blaise brought me back to the common bedroom. It seems when I saw the picture of the Sacred Heart, I squealed happily.

Papa came to visit after a very long while.

He had come to take Mama back to his home.

"And your daughter?" asked my nana, folding her hands, looking sternly at Papa, as the family matriarch.

"Er ... her too I guess," said my papa, and my nana did not like the hesitation.

"Look, Iqbal," said Nana, "My daughter is not a puppet on a string that you'll send her from here to there and there to here throughout her life. I'm sorry, but just leave. We will look after your responsibility."

"But ...," my spineless papa stammered.

"Leave, Iqbal, just go."

That was my nana's final word on the matter.

And Papa never came to take me back. My paternal family never came to visit. Well, except for Raju, my father's younger brother who had taken a shine to me, but he was Papa's brother so I still didn't like him.

I hated Papa. I hated myself for being a girl and for ruining my mama's marriage.

I know it's juvenile and not so "Me, too" to think like this. But for a greater part of my life, this has been my truth – that I ruined my mama's marriage.

And so, what happened? During my childhood, I was always fearful and apprehensive. I was young and didn't know what to think.

The events of my young life became the groundwork for the lifetime of self-loathing and mental torture that I would live with for years to come.

And what acted as a balm for these invisible wounds in footsteps I have since taken toward my real self? Books, of course!

ESSAY 3

In the Beginning Was the Word

I WAS BAPTIZED AT AGE TWO at Mount Mary's Basilica, Bandra. I was named Fiza Josephine Pathan.

I was lucky, for normally baptisms do not take place at such important basilicas.

I was brought up a Roman Catholic and I was spoiled silly by my nana, Mama, and mama's sisters and brothers.

I was fascinated with books and writing from the time I could crawl, and I loved watching people write. To imitate them, I used my Macintosh as paper and, with a sketch pen, I tried to "write" in cursive. I could spend hours playing with my sketch pen. The first letter I learned how to write was the small letter *e* and the big letter *N*. Other letters which I learned randomly were *c*, *C*, *D*, *F*, *G*, *k*, *j*, *M*, *o*, *O*, *T*, and *x*. And I used to string them together and pretend to be writing something significant.

I can still remember the way I learned at age two to join *e* and *c* and write them together.

These days when I see the awful handwriting of my students, I tend to believe the rumor that says that adults will one day use cursive writing as some sort of secret code! That would be quite a lark, wouldn't it?

Both Mama and Blaise read to me as a child. As a toddler, I listened every night to Blaise read stories. He loved Hans Christian Anderson more than the Grimm Brothers, for reasons that I would later discover when I became a teacher myself. Mechu told me Bible stories; after all, she was my godmother. I was taken to church every day, something I wish I could continue to do today, but I'm just too busy with work.

Religious writings, especially Catholic religious writings, have been a huge part of my reading material ever since I was a child (more on this in a later essay). I have been in love with St. Francis for the longest time. I invoke his spirit when I write, and he is my God, apart from books. What I like about these Franciscan works is the eccentric way in which the saint interpreted life and the importance he gave to self-sacrifice and ecology. That's because I am a die-hard lover of nature myself. All denizens of the animal world seem to be attracted to me.

Which brings me to another story of my childhood. I was once almost killed by one of these overfriendly denizens.

I was three years old, and it was an evening in November. I was digging a hole at the back of our apartment building, and I was singing a song from *Snow White and the Seven Dwarfs* to myself, when I struck something soft.

I put my hand into the hole and felt something move. I looked inside and realized immediately that it was a cobra.

A poisonous king cobra, and I had dug into his lair while he slept.

I threw the stick I'd used to dig with and ran indoors, into the common bedroom. I was shivering and my stomach churned. That was the first time I can remember feeling fear. Later in the week, the Wadi men killed the king cobra, and when I heard about it I was glad, and yet I felt strange.

The snake episode would remain in my memory forever, giving me a dreadful fear of snakes. In time, with my leaning towards Franciscan literature, I've become more adaptable, but I still flinch when mention of a snake is made.

When I was a child, I read many of the books printed by the publisher Ladybird; someone had purchased a whole bunch of them. Probably Blaise. I liked Peter and his sister, Jane, but I always liked Peter more. I loved his nurturing nature and his sinewy body in the illustrations. I loved when they spent time at the beach or at the park.

I had Disney books too. My favorites were *The Little Mermaid, The Sorcerer's Apprentice,* and *Pinocchio.*

Around this same time, I used Mama's dark pink or maroon lipstick to write on the walls. I wrote like a teacher – letters, words, and numbers. My favorite numbers were 0, 4, 2, and 100. Mama thought I would do well in math at school, but that was not meant to be.

I was better at English, history, and Hindi, my three favorite subjects then and now.

I preferred books about history and the Bible stories. I loved the story of Moses and the burning bush, the story of Noah's ark, and the story of the Passion of Christ.

As a child, I couldn't grasp what *resurrection* meant.

Silly little me used to think that after Jesus died, he went to heaven and then he went to a higher heaven. I couldn't for the life of me comprehend the idea of a resurrection.

The death on the cross part was easier to understand. Jesus died because of our sins – simple and comprehensible. I even colored Jesus's pictures with a red crayon to show the blood pouring from his wounds.

I would, as an adult, read more about the life of Jesus the Christ, both theological works and esoteric texts.

The very first word I spoke and understood was *Rita,* which I used to gurgle out as *taa.* She is Mama's younger, unmarried sister, who loves reading Bollywood gossip magazines and used to spend a lot of time with me. Then I learned the names of my other maternal family members in quick succession: Date (David uncle), Mechu (Mercia), Blaze (Blaise), Mama, and Nana.

I learned to say Papa last. I was always mixing it up with *dada* or *dad*, but my mama didn't want me to call my papa by those endearments.

As a toddler, I felt the absence of my father. I also was very lonely, spending most of my time playing with my toys and books. I drew and colored a lot, but my love was writing, that was clear. I had a firm grip on the pen, pencil, and crayon but not on the chalk. It was very difficult to hold a chalk and write on a slate. I just hated it, but I didn't mind the pencil or pen.

I never went to a play school. At home, I would sit in a cupboard, green bucket, on my red potty, or on my red cycle (anywhere comfy), and I would write over my storybooks or read from them. Blaise used to visit the circulating library near our home, called Step-In, and he brought home a lot of *Archie* comics for me to read. I would read them sitting on my potty or inside Blaise's cupboard.

I loved Big Ethel best and found Betty to be such a nice girl and Veronica such a brat.

I couldn't read at that time. Instead, I would make up what I thought the characters must be saying. When I learned how to read and write, I realized what rubbish I used to make up in my head about them all!

I also used to page through the *Katy Keene* comics as well as *The Phantom* and *Mandrake the Magician,* which were in abundance at Step-In.

The owner of Step-In was a Sindhi gentleman called Prakash and Blaise, who was thirty-two at that time, used to carry me to the library to visit him after church.

I didn't understand the concept of a library yet. Even though I had a shelf of books to myself at home, it didn't click that they were my library of books and comics.

I loved my children's Bible, though I loved the New Testament better than the Old Testament back then. Now it's the opposite; I prefer the Old Testament to the New, especially the Pentateuch and the Historical Books, the Psalms and the books of the Prophets.

And then one day, I learned to spell my name.

I still remember that "aha" moment.

It was after a long afternoon nap, when I slid down the mattresses piled one on top of the other (*Princess and the Pea* style) that I pulled out a dark pink lipstick of Mama's from the nearby jewelry box.

I rolled out the stick of lip paint and wrote the letter *F* in capitals on a nearby wall.

"What comes after that Fiza?" said someone, I think it was Mama, but it could have been my imagination.

I seemed to know what came after *F*.

I wrote an *i* then quickly a *z*. The last letter made me think really hard and I thought I was stumped. But wait a minute, there it came! I crunched up my face wrote *a* and then very quickly, in cursive, followed with *Pathan*.

"That's me," I said triumphantly to myself. "I am Fiza Pathan. This is me. This is my name."

I closed the lid of the dark pink lipstick and pulled out a yellow-colored pencil from a nearby table. An *Archie* comic lay face down on the common bed where old Nana slept the sleep of a dementia patient. The smell of her powder and soap filled the room with the comforting perfume, one of the most memorable smells of my childhood.

The *Archie* comic pages crinkled in the breeze.

I lifted up my hand and wrote the word *GIRL* in capitals next to my name.

Girl. The word was *girl*.

ESSAY 4

God's Pauper: St. Francis of Assisi by Nikos Kazantzakis

MY NAME IS FIZA JOSEPHINE PATHAN. I was born on the nineteenth of March, 1989, and I am a Catholic. My patron saint is supposed to be St. Joseph, the foster-father of Jesus.

But for me, my true patron saint is St. Francis of Assisi or, as described by the venerable writer Nikos Kazantzakis, "God's Pauper."

When I went as a toddler, my parish church happened to be St. Francis of Assisi Church (Bandra West). I did all of the things a person does at church – kneel and pray – and I also used to dance around the place and climb the altar, distracting the congregation. But nobody seemed to mind. I guess I was just too cute.

One day, my eyes fell on the statue of St. Francis of Assisi helping Jesus off the cross.

"Mama, who's that man in brown?" I asked before mass began.

Mama was deep in prayer, but she looked in the direction of my gaze.

"He is St. Francis of Assisi. He's a saint and a good man," she answered.

"He helped Jesus down from the cross?" I asked.

Mama was stumped.

"Not really. Not exactly ..." she mumbled.

"Is he Simon of Cyrene?" I asked. I was an expert in the children's Bible. Unfortunately, some adults don't have even that much expertise in their Catholic faith.

Mama ignored me and continued to pray. I continued to watch this "good man" who seemed to be helping Jesus down from the cross.

But how could that be? Jesus wasn't helped down from the cross; he died there. And he was wrapped in sheets and placed in the tomb from where he rose again. Wasn't that the way it went?

Then who was this "good man"? What was he doing and where did he come from?

Was he the Good Samaritan that Mechu, my godmother, spoke about? Was he a traveler or a gypsy?

This question was answered for me later in life, but at that age I was naïve where this statue of the Pauper saint and Jesus Christ were concerned. I was really baffled until I read a book about saints and their lives, and until Blaise told me the story of St. Francis of Assisi and his chant "Make Me a Channel of Your Peace."

I would go on to love St. Francis and read a lot about him. But it wasn't until I read Nikos Kazantzakis's book *God's Pauper* that I really got to know St. Francis. I picked up this book at Kitab Khana (Flora Fountain) when I was twenty-one. It was the first Kazantzakis book I ever read, and I loved his prose. *God's Pauper* mesmerized me. Kazantzakis brought out the battle between the flesh and the spirit of goodness in this book. I loved the way Brother Leo (Leone) was been depicted in the book and couldn't imagine why the Catholic church would want to ban such a beautiful book and the works of such a wonderful writer! The story is beautifully researched and presented.

By the time I was in college, I was reading the authoritative biographies of St. Francis of Assisi, but for a beginner to his life and mysticism Kazantzakis' novel is a good introduction.

When I read this book again during the winter of 2011, I was struggling with teaching and writing. I was not finding a publisher for my first book, and the teaching part of my life was becoming taxing.

Kazantzakis's book gave me spiritual comfort that year.

The drama of this saint of the soil of Assisi is like a ballad, especially now that materialism is at its peak and the ecology is in peril.

To me, as a child, St. Francis of Assisi was a good man who helped Jesus down from the cross. Later I would realize that he was much more than that – he would take the burden of the whole church upon his head. This rock of a pauper, Francis, was going to build His church for the future. We can see that now, in the personage of Pope Francis and the problems His holiness is facing because of the clergy that are not following the tenets of pauperism, let alone Christianity!

As a toddler, I used to walk back from church hand-in-hand with Blaise or Mama, and I'd think a lot about St. Francis of Assisi. Sometimes we would take a right at the junction road and stop by at Step-In and borrow yet another *Archie* or *Jughead* comic. By then I was borrowing small booklets of condensed classics for children.

I couldn't read or write, but I thumbed through the pages of those well-worn and well-used classics that smelled of old books and ink. I remember learning the titles of only two of those books. One was *Heart of Darkness* by Joseph Conrad and the other was *The Black Arrow* by Robert Louis Stevenson. I can still remember their cheap, bright red, blue and black covers. They were printed in the USSR.

I was a child of the 1990s, and so my world was not yet completely overtaken by artificial intelligence and high-tech devices. If I ever did play, it was by pretending to be poor, like St. Francis.

I used to pretend I lived in a hut with a bedridden Nana (who was really sick) and a lot of stray animals whom I had to feed; that was my favorite game – to play the pauper.

By the time I grew up, St. Francis of Assisi Church had become a home for me. I taught Sunday school there, conducted Communion classes, became a lector, worked for the youth group, and played the keyboard occasionally for important masses. I was enamoured by the saint and adored him. I still do.

I would recommend Kazantzakis's book to anyone interested in the history of the saint in question and in the times he lived in (the late thirteenth century A.D.). Anyone interested from a literary perspective can try a read at this, though if you want to study Kazantzakis as a literature or MFA student, I think you should start with *Zorba the Greek* or *The Last Temptation of Christ*.

I read *Zorba the Greek* right after *God's Pauper: Saint Francis of Assisi* and loved both books. I read *The Last Temptation of Christ* recently and am now looking forward to reading his biography in letters.

St. Francis of Assisi has become a great part of my life.

These days I don't exactly pray to him, but I like to think that he is in some way with me wherever I go. He has been with me for the longest time. He has been blessing me with ideas for books and with some money to buy the books I need to read from time to time.

I like his style and when I read about his stigmata in Kazantzakis's work, I fall to pieces. There can never be a greater love for God in the middle ages in Europe than St. Francis of Assisi's love for his God, Lord Jesus Christ.

When I started to read books on theosophy and the esoteric arts, I came to know that this saint in my life was once St. John the Evangelist in a previous birth, and, in a later birth, Mughal Emperor Shah Jahan himself, the king who loved his wife Mumtaz Mahal so much that he built the Taj Mahal for her.

I saw you my love when I saw your mahal,
The Taj Mahal bestows your shadow kiss upon my serenity;
I saw you my love when I saw your mahal,
Queen of Love your tomb till eternity.

Nowadays it seems he is going by the title of Kuthumi. But to little old me, he's my Francesco, the "good man" who has shown me the love of a peepal leaf when its dew falls upon the earth as mercifully as compassion for other men who don't like daughters.

I once wanted to join the Third Order of Saint Francis, but I'm too worldly for that. One can't help but think lofty thoughts about a man who scorned the riches of the world for something that, even today, no one is completely sure of.

ESSAY 5

Step-In Circulating Library

NEAR THE JUNCTION OF all the main roads near my home, in a humbler part of Bandra West, lies the Step-In Circulating Library.

It is run, with good humor, by a Sindhi gentleman called Prakash, who has been catering to the needs of the readers in our area for many years. It was a bigger library a long time ago when Blaise was in his early thirties and I was a toddler and schoolchild. But now it has sadly dwindled in size, and the gentleman's stock has reduced dramatically.

As I understand it, this happened because of the 2005 Mumbai floods that destroyed most of his precious stock. The 2005 Mumbai floods ruined the hardiest of businessmen. Mechu's home in Malad was flooded by four feet of water, and poor Mechu and her husband lost most of their personal belongings and money that day in the terrible floods of the twenty-sixth of July, 2005.

But now, back to a time when I was a toddler, quite a plump rascal who loved picking a new book to read at Prakash uncle's place. I loved the comics and books I used to find there. Later, when I was in the seventh grade, I read most of the *Fear Street* books by R. L. Stine, murder and horror books, along with a good dose of Roald Dahl, including *The Witches* and *Matilda,* plus Wodehouse, and a lot of Dover classics like *Frankenstein, The Hunchback of Notre Dame, Treasure Island, The Coral Island, Kidnapped,* and of course, *My Family and Other Animals.*

Where comics were concerned, I read them on the potty when I was a toddler and then on the "throne" when I grew up. I, for some disgusting reason, loved to read while doing my big job; can't even fathom the reason why! *Archie* was a favorite on the potty. *Phantom* and *Mandrake the Magician* were other favorites.

I was introduced to Tintin as well as dear old Asterix. Blaise introduced me to graphic comic series because he loved them himself. I read most of the issues at Step-In until I could afford (sort of) to own copies of my own. Blaise likes *Asterix the Gaul* best, but I love *Tintin* more.

By the time I was four years old and ready to go to school, my papa had become a fill-in-the-blank in my otherwise solitary life. But I had other men in my life!

Yes, and they were Parsi men. According to Rita, one day I had come back from church and was standing on the new Rexine sofa with my shoes on, flexing my muscles, when in came Blaise's best friend from his bank, Ratan Panthaki, a thirty-two-year-old Parsi bachelor with a long raven beard and a love for Tintin and Asterix.

We saw each other. It was love at first sight – as much as that's possible for a four-year-old.

He started coming every week to pay, not his best friend Blaise, a visit – but little old me. Ratan uncle, like the stereotypical Parsi, has a wonderful sense of humor and a very strong sense of family bonding. I'm quite well aware of that, because in no time at all, his younger brother in his late twenties came along another Sunday.

His name was Minoo, and he didn't have a raven black beard but a charcoal black moustache and looked very handsome. He had an even better sense of humor than Ratan uncle and was very modern.

We looked at each other. He made a funny face and I chortled till I was out of breath.

Yet again, it was love at first sight! Now Minoo also started visiting every week along with Ratan uncle.

I call them Ratan uncle and Minoo uncle. Because I was only four years old and had no manners, I gave them the titles of Rabbit and Wolf respectively. Ratan uncle worked at the Bank of India as a head clerk, and Minoo uncle worked at Godrej as a manager. Minoo uncle was always going to foreign places and then coming back to tell me of his adventures. Later in life he taught me engineering drawing.

Ratan uncle was a real whiz in math and whenever I was in the soup at school, he would try to teach me mathematics.

Ratan uncle and Minoo uncle were the only male figures in my life outside of Blaise and David uncle.

They both loved *The Adventures of Tintin* and *Asterix* comics, and Ratan uncle looked like Captain Haddock!

But when these two wonderful men were not around to entertain, Step-In was.

I remember once being lent by Prakash uncle, for the entire Diwali vacations, a whole stack of *Phantom* and *Mandrake the Magician* comics ... a whole stack!

"Prakash uncle, this is too much!" I said, totally excited.

He wouldn't let me say anything more. I spent a wonderful Diwali reading those comics on the mat in the hall while colorful rockets lit up the dark night sky.

I was borrowing comics and books from Prakash uncle during my whole life at school, a whole twelve years. I continued to do so for a while at college, but then the stock decreased. The variety of comic books decreased, and I was getting my own cash to buy my own books at a shop called Crossword. So one day I stopped borrowing comics and books from Prakash uncle.

Blaise was crestfallen, because it was he who used to choose books or comics for me. Now he wouldn't be able to do so. He is still very close friends with Prakash uncle.

Blaise, Ratan uncle, and Minoo uncle. The best young men I've ever met.

To this day, we have such good times together; it doesn't even seem like we are not of one blood or the same religious community. We are family. That's it. Ratan uncle and Minoo uncle are closer to me than my papa has ever been.

Papa was, as I said, a non-entity in my life. I did not know what to make of him. He was such a queer chap. Whenever he used to come to visit, I would think, "Ugh, whatever did Mama see in this leech!"

Blaise, Ratan uncle, and Minoo uncle knew I abhorred my papa. They also knew that Mama was forcing herself to smile when he was around.

They took it nicely. They are nice men; Papa would be just a few years older than they were, but they were much more mature and cultured than Papa could ever be.

Papa was a leech, a bloodsucker, and very indifferent. He used to make a big show that he was indeed my father and Mama's husband. At parties and dances, he did not dance or sing. He used to sit in a corner and make gruff sounds as if he were about to puke or spit. He would keep me sitting next to him all the bloody time; he never spoke to guests, he never played games, he never joked. He was not human!

I wondered why he bothered to come over to Nana's house. With his odd behavior, why did everyone tolerate him?

One day, I asked Mechu.

"Why does he come here, anyway?" I said.

"Who?"

"Papa, that's who!"

"He's your father, dolly girl. Of course, he has to come and see you."

"But aren't he and Mama divorced? Isn't he supposed to not see me?"

"But – they aren't divorced," Mechu yelped, holding her heaving chest in shock. "Whatever gave you that idea, dolly girl?"

I had read about such a thing in comics and seen it in a few movies on the VCR, but I avoided that part of the conversation and continued, "If they are not divorced, then why doesn't he live with us?" I spitefully thought to myself, *not that I want him to, yuck!*

"They are separated. That's all."

"Meaning they are divorced?"

"No."

"Meaning they are not allowed to live together?"

"No."

"Then what is it?" I whined like the broken tape recorder that I was.

This was the pits. They were just living separately; they were not divorced. My life would have been quite different if they had done the decent thing and been divorced, because the moment it was time to go to school, life was going to get nasty. And only one thing would see me through it all. Not Mama, and not Papa – just books.

ESSAY 6

The Tintin Series

THE FIRST TINTIN graphic novel I read was *The Cigars of the Pharaoh*. I was hooked.

Today, in the hall of my home, there hangs a framed poster of Tintin and Snowy, his "dog Friday" and trustworthy companion. Tintin is trying to balance a whole stack of *The Adventures of Tintin* comic hardbacks in his young arms, some of which are about to fall on the perturbed Snowy.

This poster is one of the first things you will see when you enter my home, along with many other curiosities and bric-a-brac of bookish and sometimes garden-related items.

I was introduced to Tintin by Blaise when he borrowed *The Cigars of the Pharaoh* from Step-In. I loved the adventure, colorful drawings, and the crazy and eccentric behavior of Dr. Sarcophagus, who leads Tintin, the young Belgian reporter, on an epic adventure of sorts.

I finished the graphic novel in two days' time and demanded another Tintin adventure. Excited that a new member to the Tintin fraternity had been born, Blaise rushed to Prakash uncle and returned with *The Crab with the Golden Claws*.

I started reading Tintin in 1995, when I was very much a kid in junior school and already a loner left to my own devices. For some reason, we were not allowed to carry graphic novels or comics to school, so every *Tintin* I read was at home or on my BSA purple cycle as I rambled around the compound of my building on my own.

I equate Tintin to that time in my life when I realized I would always be alone ... and yet, not completely alone.

Tintin was a great companion for a child forced to become silent and contemplative. His adventures and misadventures with the wily Snowy the dog, the ready-for-action Captain Haddock, the always hard-of-hearing Professor Calculus, the silly but at-your-service Thompson twins, and so many other unforgettable characters woven expertly by the brush and mind of Hergé, the creator of the Tintin series, the creator of so many happy but solitary moments during my childhood days.

I was an expert on Tintin by the end of the 1990s. Ratan uncle and Minoo uncle were, along with Blaise, diehard fans of the same series, which would soon become a series on Cartoon Network.

"Ha. That's not Tintin," Ratan uncle would say as he drank his evening tea with us. "They are ruining it. The books are the original thing, I tell you. You kids are being made dummkopfs by seeing this series on TV."

I, too, used to be wanting more from the series on TV, but I wasn't averse to whatever they managed to adapt to the screen. I remember Blaise buying the whole VCR collection and then, in the early years of the twenty-first century, the whole VCD and DVD collection of the Tintin series.

Minoo uncle too bought the VCD and DVD collection, and we would share with each other what we had watched last whenever the Parsi brothers came to visit.

"Dummkopfs all of you!" Ratan uncle would declare, and Blaise would laugh his high-pitched, youthful laughter as he chugged down his milky white Tata tea.

I was mesmerized by the world of Tintin. But to be truthful, I was also mesmerized and comforted by the life such different characters lived under the same roof at Marlinspike Hall in the comic.

Marlinspike Hall was Captain Haddock's ancestral home which, thanks to Tintin's cleverness, he was able to take possession of quite late in life.

There, he lived with Nestor (his dutiful butler), Tintin, Snowy, Professor Calculus and (whenever they were in town), the Thompson twins and Signora Bianca Castafiore.

Seeing these people, not related by blood, living amicably together made me feel a bit less odd.

In my world of a little child, mamas had to live with papas or things were very odd indeed. I did not understand why things were happening the way they were within my family. No one at home was willing to tell me exactly what had happened, which made me unsure about my identity.

Tintin came to my rescue, as did other graphic comics. I felt more at home at Marlinspike Hall than in my own home, and certainly than in my own mind.

In fact, my mind couldn't fathom it all. If Papa was not to live with us, then why did he have to come to see us? Why was Papa so peculiar? Why couldn't Mama and Papa divorce? And, most importantly, why did *I* have to talk to him? We were as different from each other as jade and ivory!

I read *Red Rackham's Treasure* and laughed my head off. It was a masterpiece of adventure, jokes, humorous antics, and a lot of puzzles that kept me turning page after page with abandon.

My papa didn't understand my love for Tintin; in fact, I don't even remember him ever referring to it.

He just wasn't bothered about what I cared for.

And he was jealous of Blaise and the Parsi brothers, and how much I worshipped them and abhorred him.

There was a lot more to abhor about Papa than there was to like.

Mama never seemed to see that I didn't want to be with Papa. I guess she had other worries as a single parent which she had to deal with, as well as her career but, yes, I was hurting inside.

One day I was busy reading yet another Tintin comic. I remember it was *Tintin in America*. I was on the piled-up mattresses in the common bedroom, and Mama walked in to get something.

I told her, “Tell Papa not to come here anymore.”

She didn’t look at me.

“I said, I don’t want Papa to come here anymore. I hate him.”

Mama didn’t say a word. When I pestered her, she shot back angry words that felt worse than a slap on my cheek. “Don’t act strange. He is your father, and can’t you see I’m busy cleaning the house?”

“Blaise is my papa.”

“No. And don’t say that in front of Blaise. He’ll not like it.”

“But I don’t like Papa.”

Mama ignored me, picked up what she was looking for, and left the room.

I withdrew into a corner, which to this day I haven’t got out from, and turned the Tintin comic to a new page.

Papa would keep on coming. He would keep on calling. He would wear a smug face every time he did, because he was the proud father of a smart little girl and the husband of an educated wife.

The orthodox Muslim in him was showing day by painful day, and my mama couldn’t see me retreating into myself. It was a pain to converse with someone who thought that women were the chattels of men. That’s my papa for you. To date, he has a very sexist and gender-biased idea of women, I wanted to beat that idea to death at one time during my childhood.

But things like that don’t die so easily. He was my father. He hadn’t divorced my mama. He continued to come from Byculla to Bandra to eat my brains out.

And I withdrew, along with my Tintin comics, further and further away from my circumstances.

It was terrible to be told that you are the child of someone so worthy of hate.

But Hergé was a proxy father of sorts. His world of his Belgian reporter, Tintin, made me see something that would later influence a large part of my thinking and my lifestyle choices.

One of them was independence.

None of the Tintin characters were related to each other by blood, and none were needy or dependent on the other. Those who acted needy, like Jolyon Wagg and Prince Abdullah, were painted as disturbed characters and freeloaders.

I liked that Tintin didn't have a wife or a girlfriend. He didn't have responsibilities and was a free soul.

I wanted to be like Tintin. I wanted to be free and independent, not obliged to any one person in this world.

What had relationships given me but discomfort and pain?

No, I wouldn't make the mistake my mama made.

I would not allow another Papa to enter my world of books, writing, teaching, and Tintin comics.

Tintin remains part and parcel of my everyday existence even today. I studied Hergé's writing style and the way he presented his graphic novels. I was fascinated with his concentration on characters. Their unusual habits, their eccentricities, their loves, their vices – all of it appealed to me. Today, in my fiction, I focus more on people and their thoughts and actions rather than their symbology. I am not an MFA or literature student, so I don't know whether that is a shortcoming, but I still enjoy it all.

My favorite Tintin graphic novel has got to be *King Ottokar's Sceptre*. It's an odd choice, but it defines my sensibilities for adventure, humor, and scholarship to a tee. I love the Haddock and Calculus books as well, but I like the older graphic novels more, where Snowy was more of a nuisance and Tintin more human and less asexual.

I have a fixation for the Tintin comics where Tintin alone tackles spies, villains, hoodlums, et al. In a word, I am enamoured by the Belgian detective, even without the wonderful characters that replaced Snowy the dog as exceedingly silly or overenthusiastic adventurers.

It would be the year 2007 when the older Tintin books would become available in India. I'm referring to the collectable items like *Tintin in Russia, Tintin in the Congo,* and *Tintin and Modern Art.* It's understandable that when India was closely associated with USSR, the earlier Tintin comics were banned. Books are always banned in India at the drop of a hat – it's nothing new – but it is irksome for a compulsive reader like me.

After the dissolution of the USSR, it took a while, but the rare Tintin collectables arrived after a decade of waiting, and I took great pride in spending my hard-earned tuition money to purchase them. I loved *Tintin in Russia.* I find it to be very true reportage. *Tintin in the Congo* is racist, but I still enjoy the art of the story.

My favorite remains *King Ottokar's Sceptre.* When I go through my Tintin comics during a free moment, that is the graphic novel that draws my attention.

As stated earlier, I couldn't read comics in school. In college, however, I gorged myself on Tintin during free periods and snack breaks. The college boys thought I was a weirdo. The girls thought I was a lesbian. Whatever makes everybody happy, I guess, let it be – they don't know the magic of a Tintin comic more than a dinosaur does.

I recommend Tintin to anybody and everybody; just get the comics, people, there's enough magic in those adventures to last you a lifetime. I recommend reading *The Cigars of the Pharaoh* first, then *The Blue Lotus* – and then you can take it from there.

ESSAY 7

The *Archie* Comics

PRAKASH UNCLE (FROM STEP-IN) AND BLAISE fed me all the best of the best *Archie* comics in the whole wide world. I was reading them even before I could read.

I loved Archie Andrews, that average kid from Riverdale who had two girlfriends, Betty the sweet blonde and Veronica the obnoxious snob. I loved Jughead, who was Archie's best friend, and his overeating along with some really witty one-liners that I would only understand when I reached middle school – and some only in college!

Archie and his huge cluster of friends attended Riverdale High School. As I have said before, I adored Ethel (or Big Ethel as she was called in most of the comics) and wanted to read more about her.

"Fiza," Blaise said one day when I was sitting on the Rexine sofa with a Betty and Veronica double digest in my pudgy tiny-tot hands, "whom do you prefer – Betty or Veronica?"

Blaise was wondering whether I was on his side – he liked Betty – but me being me, I answered, "They should bring out a double digest for Ethel, you know."

Blaise was stumped. For once he was really stumped. He later went over to Prakash uncle to see if there was a Big Ethel digest, let alone a double digest. Prakash uncle unearthed a few Delton digests and a few Reggie digests, but alas no Big Ethel. Blaise made do by bringing home a stack of Jughead comics that were sure to have Big Ethel in them, as she was having a one-sided love affair with Jughead.

I was envious of the Riverdale crowd; they had each other, so many friends, and I had not even one.

In my little-girl mind, I pondered what was wrong with me? Why did no one like me? Why did no student at school want to associate with me?

I was lonely, terribly sad and silent. Silence became a part of me; it has remained with me to this day.

I had too many questions I wanted to ask that no one wanted to answer. There was so much I really wanted to say, but nobody wanted to listen. Archie had none of the problems I had. He had Jughead, Betty, Veronica, Delton, Big Moose, and Reggie all ready and willing to give him a listening ear. I was alone, and the silence echoed through my being. Little as I was, I was so melancholic. I couldn't understand things. I wanted to understand and I wanted a best friend; everyone is entitled to a best friend!

But no, no one wanted to be my friend, let alone *best* friend. I was too different from them, maybe. I was in the wrong place at the wrong time. School was a very lonely time for me until I realized there was a library I could retreat to. There is nothing more painful than for a kid to be made to feel that she is of no consequence. That's what my peers at school made me feel, that I was not wanted. I was just there, an acne mark on a fair woman's face, which everyone preferred not to notice.

But does it go away?

I used to sit in Blaise's cupboard after school when he was at the bank. I would sit there with an Archie and Jughead digest on my sweaty lap in a summer frock. I used to wrap myself in Blaise's home lungi and wear his oversize Bata slippers, and I used to cry. I cried because I thought he wouldn't come back. That silly little-kid brain of mine used to think that he would go away one day and never come back. Never come back to take me to Prakash uncle, never come back to tell me a bedtime story, never come back to tie my shoelaces to go to school, never bring me Archie comics to decipher the rules of high school for myself, never ...

For Archie every day is a Sunday. He is wanted by his pals. How could I compare myself with him, when my own papa didn't want me? And now, even students at school didn't want me. They thought me strange.

It was then, in Blaise's cupboard, I used to wonder: Would my life have been different if I had been a boy child, like Archie Andrews from Riverdale? What would my name have been? Feroze, Faiz, Faisal, Farhan, Farooq? Would I have had friends then? Would other boys have become my best buddies and played cricket with me or a bit of baseball like Archie played? Soccer?

As it was, I was rejected twice in a very short span of time: first by my father because of my gender, and second by my peers because of my existence. But between gender and existence, I found a life. It's a solitary one, but it's there. It's beautiful like a butterfly on a white penta flower.

And Blaise always came back, his office bag filled with the *Archie* comics I loved. I especially loved to read Betty's diary. She taught me how to keep a diary, and I keep one to this day.

Betty's diary was always an interesting read, especially the parts about her older sister, who was a journalist living in a flat on her own in a big city. I liked to think of the time I would have a job like Betty's big sis and live in an apartment of my own and, most importantly, have a whole room full of books of my very own. I've since got that wish half fulfilled, but more of that later.

I loved the older Archie characters too: Pop Tate, Mr. Lodge, Mr. Andrews, Principal Waldo Weatherbee, Miss Grundy the teacher, et al. I loved Pop Tate best because he seemed cool with kids and always ready to dish out some great advice along with a banana split ice cream shake.

These characters filled the gaps in my silent life with laughter, chortling, and, yes, a teardrop or two, especially when all the old folks of the fictitious town Riverdale saved up their cash and time to save old Pop Tate's Chock'lit Shoppe from closing.

"What's AIDS, Mama?" I once asked while on the red potty.

Mama flinched; I was only five years old.

She gasped. "Who-who told you about AIDS?"

"This *Archie* comic." I held up my reading proudly. "The comic says that kids with AIDS are not to be treated as abnormal and are allowed to kiss, drink water from the water fountain, and ..."

Mama immediately confiscated the comic, but after a talk with Blaise it was returned to me, a gleeful tot. Yes, *Archie* comics had these social and community awareness ads in them that had a big effect on me. I learned that you can be cool without taking drugs – just say no to drugs! I learned that differently abled kids should be integrated into everyday school life – everyone is special! I learned that, just like our home, we must keep the outside environment clean – use a dustbin when necessary! These social messages stuck with me. I've been a better person by following the comics' advice.

I feel everyone should be brought up with *Archie* comics. I hear they have reinvented or upgraded Archie to fit in with twenty-first century kids and teenagers. I've personally not come across these versions, and I hope I don't, because for me, the Archie of the 1990s is the Archie I want to remember till the day I close my eyes for good.

I've even heard that Veronica was the one Archie chose to marry when they graduated from school. I'm okay with that. Betty doesn't need an Archie or any other man in her life; she can go the distance and have more of a decent life without him.

If you haven't read *Archie* comics, this is a shout out to you to do so. *Archie* comics are forever. The many vibrant characters and their capers are just too funny to miss.

ESSAY 8

School Time and School Library

I'M NOT HERE TO SAY THAT there was something wrong with my school, Bombay Scottish School, that turned me into a solitary introvert. Rather I'm here to say that certain circumstances define a four-year-old kid's life – my circumstances were not the best.

As I said before, and I maintain, I had no friends at school and no one cared a hang about me.

I took it badly and withdrew into myself. I've still not come out, and I don't want to. It's cozy in here.

On the other hand, I'm here to say that the best part about school was the fantastic library.

I went to school at age four in the year 1993, in the month of June, just after the summer holidays. Mama was a junior academic coordinator and teacher of the first and second graders. She was vibrant, full of life, optimistic, dedicated, strict, lovable, famous (among BSS students), and envied. I was nothing. Just the daughter who got into all this by mistake. And for a long while I believed a mistake had really been made. Why was no one wanting to play with me? Why did kids think me weird? Why was I not taken seriously? Why was everyone ignoring me? What did I do wrong?

"You were a girl," said a voice that sounded like a robot in my head. "That was the first mistake you made. Also, you stayed alive, and that was the second mistake."

I lived like this, in silence, for a long while. I used to draw and color in my rough book. I loved drawing cartoons and caricatures. I was fond of making pen-and-ink drawings of Winnie-the-Pooh, Tweety Bird, Bugs Bunny, Scooby-Doo, Jerry the mouse (of *Tom and Jerry*), Peter Pan, Alice in Wonderland, Goofy, and a lot more. I gave all of that up after I discovered the BSS library.

In the third grade, we started having a library period at school. They would lead us to the library, where we had to choose a book from a large table in front of the arts and crafts section. We were told to read it thrice and then to write a book review in our library notebooks (which I'd decorated with stickers) about the book we had just read.

On that first day, everyone in my grade got to work except for puzzled me. I didn't pay attention to the instructions or even look at our library teacher. I was busy staring at the ceiling-high bookshelves with my mouth open, gaping like a roasted pig stuffed with prunes!

The BSS library was not only beautiful but stocked with books from the nineteenth century on. It had floor-to-ceiling shelves about twenty feet high. For an impressionable kid like me, it was like the library in the animated Disney cartoon *Beauty and the Beast* – the Beast's library.

By the time the other kids had chosen their books and settled down to read, I was still standing there in the middle of the library all by myself in a daydream – the place was a wonderland of books.

"What happened to you, now?" came a stern but compassionate voice. "Didn't you hear the instructions? Why are you without a book?"

I turned around and looked up. A woman in a silk-printed saree stood towering over tiny me. She was coffee-brown skinned, tall, as I've already mentioned, bespectacled, with pepper-gray hair and a nasal voice that I would learn to love. She was Mrs. Ratnaswami, our library teacher, or to be more accurate, the head and senior librarian of the BSS library. The goddess of books!

"Where is your attention, child?" she scolded little, plump me. Oh, how I loved the way she uttered the word *child* as if she were trying to talk a tired Labrador puppy into playing a game. "Child, where is your book?"

I looked from her face to my hands. Then I looked at my classmates, who were busy reading silently. I looked back at my hands again. Empty, like my empty, lonely life of solitude and private contemplations.

And that's when the tears fell from my eyes. Hot tears like huge blobs of salty water tumbling down my cheeks into empty palms. It occurred to me at the moment, I'm not sure why, that I had not hugged anyone in the longest while.

Slowly, almost magically, a handkerchief materialized from somewhere, maybe my pocket, and my cheeks were wiped, and my snotty little nose blown. A rough, brown hand held mine, drawing me to the table of books mentioned earlier. I looked at the wonderful books spread before me, all of them in dazzling colors and shapes and sizes.

"Child!" came the voice of the lady who held my hand. I looked up and saw for the first time the friendly face of Mrs. Ratnaswami.

She chuckled. "Child, child, now don't waste time. Go ahead and choose a book. Then go back to your bench, read it thrice, and do the book review."

"Huh?"

"Child," said Mrs. Ratnaswami shaking her head from side to side in astonishment. "Pick a book to read, please!"

I looked at those marvelous books on the table. I searched for a red cover, red being my favorite. I picked one and read the title aloud but softly so that only Mrs. Ratnaswami could hear. The title of the book was *Mithu and the Mango*, I remember it even after all these long, lonely but bookish years – the red book with a green parrot, feasting on a golden yellow mango on a tree in the grove, on its cover. Mithu was the parrot.

"Now," she took me once again by the hand and led me to my bench. "You read *Mithu and the Mango* three times. How many times?"

"Three times," I repeated shyly.

"Good girl," she said, lifting me onto the high bench. "Then, after you've read it thrice and know the story almost by heart, you can write a book review of it in your library book." She looked around my desk. "Where is your library book?"

I was so bedazzled by the book in my hands that she repeated the question thrice before I realized I had forgotten to bring my library notebook to the BSS library. I felt so ashamed. Now I would not get to review *Mithu and the Mango*. Hot tears flowed like rivulets in the middle of a mud land.

"This child cries too easily," declared Mrs. Ratnaswami as she dried my tears again, this time with the palms of her rough hands. "So what if you've forgotten it? Just relax, child, and read, and I'll give you a foolscap sheet to write your review. Fine? Child now get to reading. It's not rocket science, believe me."

And she went back to her desk. Some of the students had already finished reading their book. They were now in the process of writing the review. I dried the last of my hot tears and opened the book in front of me. I read and I read and I read.

After I dutifully finished reading the book three times, I raised my chubby little hand. Mrs. Ratnaswami came to me, foolscap sheet in hand. She silently placed the sheet in front of me.

I looked at the typed questions on the sheet:

1. What is the title of your book?
2. Who is the main character of the story?
3. Describe the main character of the story in four sentences of your own.
4. What did you learn from this story?

I diligently wrote all the answers with my Natraj pencil and then went to join a long line of Grade 3E students standing at Mrs. Ratnaswami's desk for submission.

My turn arrived after a long while; I was as a matter of fact, the last to join the line. Mrs. Ratnaswami chuckled when she ticked with a red ballpoint pen the answer to the last question.

Q. What did you learn from this story?

My answer: I learned that I love to read in the school library.

"I'm giving you a star," said Mrs. Ratnaswami. "You would have got one more if you had brought your own library book. Now, child, go."

I stood, puzzled.

"Well, child," Mrs. Ratnaswami said with a chuckle, "it doesn't end here, you know. There are more books to read, so go and read. Go on now, child. CHILD GO!"

I scooted away like a huge bursting bundle of joy. I went up to the table. Some of the girls were choosing along with me. They were surrounding the table so I couldn't get enough space to choose leisurely.

"Hey, move, move," came a loud voice behind me.

I turned back quickly. A tiny mite of a woman was pushing some of the bigger girls away to make room – for me!

After clearing enough space to fit in an elephant, the tiny woman said in English, with an accent, "Go now, pick – read."

She was Aruna, the support staff of the library. She was the one who looked after the books, the cataloging, the dusting, mending of broken spines, etc. She was the only one who could do so because, of all the women helpers in the support staff of the school, she had gone to school and could read and write fluently. She made me comfortable at the book table and went to dust another shelf.

I rummaged through the pile of books. I found a book about a girl and her love for a red balloon whose title today I cannot recall.

From that day onward, the library became my second home. Mrs. Ratnaswami and Aruna became my trusted friends and comrades. I had a special spot in the library where I used to sit and read. I read the books all children read when they are young – The Hardy Boys,

Nancy Drew, R. L. Stine's Goosebumps, Judy Blume books, abridged classics, the children's encyclopedia, puzzle books, abridged biographies for children, stories from the Bible, and so much more.

I spent all my free classes there as well as a larger part of my snack and lunch breaks ... and sometimes, I would sneak and hide in the library during the PT period, especially during the games' session.

No one missed me because no one wanted to play with me in the first place. I used to get so bored during the games' session, just standing around doing nothing at all in the hot sun or being the butt of the rude jokes the boys in my class made about my physique.

So, I used to sneak away to the library to do, what else but read, of course, and browse through the many massive and old late nineteenth-century and early twentieth-century books of the library.

"This child only reads the whole day," Mrs. Ratnaswami said as she switched on the fan and tube lights around where I was lost in an abridged classic.

"You don't bother about what she says," Aruna told me. "You read however much you want. Girls should read. See, because I can read English, I can work in the library today. Read, go on reading. Plenty of books for everyone."

Mama never knew what was going on in my life. She was busy with schoolwork and school problems. I was in the eighth grade when she came to know that I had no friends, never spoke a word in class, and was always by myself. I don't blame her. It's not easy handling a career and being a single mother; I will never be able to handle such a situation. At least Mama was brave enough to try.

I loved the BSS library to tears. I loved browsing through its mighty shelves and feeling the spine of a leather hardback. The BSS library had a beautiful smell, the smell of vanilla, old paper, and calf leather – I've never smelled anything else like it ever in my life.

Aruna taught me the ways of the library the same way Baloo the bear taught Mowgli the ways of the jungle in Kipling's *The Jungle Book*. She taught me how to fix a spine, make a library card pocket, stamp a card, catalog books, how to shelf books using the Dewy Decimal System, how to read an ISBN number, and so much else right from third grade till the tenth.

"What do you do at school most of the time?" asked Mama one day. "Your friends tell me you don't talk to them."

"What friends?" I snapped. I was mean back then.

"Your friends at school," Mama yelled as I turned the page of my latest Goosebumps story.

"I don't have friends, and no one talks to me."

"Why? What did you do wrong?" Mama sounded quite annoyed with me.

How could I tell her that being her daughter was the biggest mistake I had ever made in my life? If I was a boy, we would have lived with Papa, I would have gone to a Muslim school and learned Urdu, I would have been a Muslim, I would have gone to the mosque, said the Muslim prayers, learned the family business from my father, paternal uncle and grandfather and so on.

But, no, I made the mistake of being a girl. I'm guilty of XX in the first degree. No mercy. No talking. Silence forever. Only the sound of pages turning.

"Why are you reading Hardy Boys so much, child!" Mrs. Ratnaswami was exasperated as she corrected my ninth book review about a Hardy Boys adventure in a matter of three weeks. "Read something else, please. Go to the classic section, child, and pick a classic to read."

On summer holidays, I was carted to school with Mama to spend time there, but more of that later. I remember going to the library on the first day and going into the classics section. I was in the third grade. Unfortunately, or fortunately, I went to the adult unabridged classic section instead of the abridged classics children's section. I wanted to read a scary book. Everyone was doing that back then, and everyone was raving about a certain horror classic. It was Bram Stoker's *Dracula*.

While I colored a still life painting all alone at a table, I had overheard male peers rave to each other about the vampire, his long teeth, the blood he drank, the way he preyed on innocent women.

The story sounded great to me, so I memorized the name Dracula. To be doubly sure I wouldn't forget, I wrote the name *Dracula* in my school calendar.

That summer, I found the unabridged version of *Dracula* to read.

I read the whole thing in a matter of seven hours. I understood everything. I was a new person.

"Did you enjoy it?" Mrs. Ratnaswami asked me skeptically as I returned the book.

"Yes," I said. "The good parts were very good, and the bad parts were very bad."

I was never the same after that day.

From then on, I would read as much as I could, practically all the time. I spoke to no one at school. I avoided extracurricular activities and never played a sport. I was the silent one, the one who wouldn't open her mouth to speak but who always had a book to read.

"Child," Mrs. Ratnaswami scolded me whenever I was reading a book with small print. "Child, you are reading books with such small print that you will be wearing glasses soon."

But I never listened. I didn't get glasses. Not then, not even now. Strange.

I read indiscriminately from grade three to grade ten: Bram Stoker, Mary Shelley, O. Henry, Saki, R. L. Stevenson, P. G. Wodehouse, Charles Dickens, Terry Pratchett, H. G. Wells, Jules Verne, Rabindranath Tagore, Robin Cook, Arthur Hailey, Graham Greene, Thomas Hardy, Oscar Wilde, Maxim Gorky, Shakespeare, Rudyard Kipling, Alexander Dumas, Edgar Allan Poe, Mark Twain, Agatha Christie, Richard Bach, Anne Frank, L. M. Montgomery, Ruskin Bond, R. L. Stine, and a host of nonfiction books!

Mrs. Ratnaswami never got in my way nor did she humiliate me. I will be grateful to her for the rest for my life for her kindness and compassion. She never questioned my extraordinary appetite for books. In fact, she encouraged it.

"Fiza, child," she once told me, "don't you know that you can use mummy's card to take home any number of books for as long as you wish to keep them?"

This was manna from heaven.

"Yes, child, yes," said dear Mrs. Ratnaswami as I leaped up in the air for sheer joy. "And you can write mummy's name in the card which you give to me. Just make sure to return them before the school closes for summer so that mummy can get her salary."

This was the best thing that had ever happened to me! With my student card, I could only borrow two books at a time and return them in less than two weeks' time.

Now I could have any number of books. For any length of time. Oh boy, oh boy, oh boy!

"Mummy anyways hasn't read a book in all the twenty-seven years she's been teaching here," said Mrs. Ratnaswami as she stirred her hot, milky tea in her special cup. "Go ahead and read, child. New books have come to the library just yesterday. Select what you want and read quietly."

I repeat, manna from heaven!

I gave Aruna a hug. She smelled of jasmine and roses and leather books. Her fingers were covered with dried Joker's gum and she was dusting the shelves in the inner sanctum of the library with an old rag.

"So much love all of a sudden?" she asked as she dusted away. I was beside myself with joy. School had been misery but now salvation was at hand, given to me by a kind-hearted librarian with strict principles and a staff worker who taught me the value of being educated.

My journey into the school library had only just begun.

ESSAY 9

Dracula by Bram Stoker

I READ *DRACULA* BY BRAM STOKER in the unabridged version in the year 1997 when I was in the third grade. I finished reading the book in seven hours' time, but I'm not yet done with the book any more than I'm done with reading as a way of life and the reason for life!

When I went into the adult classics section to find the book, numerous versions sat upon the shelf. I picked the one with the pretty cover, black leather with golden pages, with the golden and red motifs of a tiny coffin, cross and rose as the image at the center of the book. The title was etched in gold as well.

I checked out the book and went to a classroom next to the library to read. I would have read in the library but high school students were having classes there. Basically, the place was packed and I loved reading in silence, so I went to a nearby classroom.

I sat alone in the dark classroom. I backed against a nearby wall, hugged my Barbie backpack close to me, and opened the book.

It's been twenty-two years since that fateful day when I made the acquaintance with the most diabolical of villains in literature, Count Dracula. Today I have reread the book at least forty-four times and certain parts of the text more times than I can account for. Bram

Stoker opened my mind to reading good literature and left me unforgettable characters that have been engrained into my subconscious.

To many, *Dracula* is not the ideal read. Many kids of my class preferred abridged classics like Louisa May Alcott's *Little Women*, Kenneth Grahame's *The Wind in The Willows*, Robert Louis Stevenson's *Treasure Island*, Mark Twain's *The Adventures of Tom Sawyer*, and so forth. But I loved *Dracula*; its adventure, thrills, horror, morals, and every element that made me a fan of horror books.

The unique story of Jonathan Harker's stay at Castle Dracula has molded the horror and paranormal literature of today. There is no story as dramatic and horrific to me as the tale of the vampire Dracula who was out to establish a home in Victorian England from which to prey on the innocent, the helpless, and the beautiful.

Dracula became the reason I started to read the classics en masse. *Dracula* is also the reason I started reading horror and paranormal fiction and nonfiction which was surprisingly plentiful at the BSS library. I gorged on *Dracula* the way he gorged on the blood of his victims. When tough days came my way at school, when people ridiculed me in public and I had no private place to shed my tears, Bram Stoker's words were my solace. His character was my companion, comrade, a dear friend.

Bram Stoker, may he rest in eternal peace. Since 1997, I've been thinking of him and wondering whether I'll meet him some day in the afterlife. I'd like to tell him how his vampire was my succor for a lifetime of school. Maybe I'll give him a hug and then it will be said that an author starts a story, but a reader completes it.

The book *Dracula* and its fight of good versus evil continues to hold me, so much so that I want to contribute to the vampire lore by creating my own fiend of the night in letters. But not so soon; I still need to master the craft of writing a bit more before I'll succeed in my efforts. I hope it shall be my magnum opus of sorts and, like Dracula, his three brides, and Bram Stoker, I shall go to my rest in a coffin, sealed tight perhaps with a golden crucifix of Van Helsing upon it.

The story of Dracula completes me. After reading the unabridged classic, I looked for another classic that might have an equal effect on me. I read many, but for me, nothing surpasses the hold *Dracula* had on me, strong as his steel-like iron grip on Jonathan Harker's wrist.

I have Count Dracula running through my veins. I am more his seed than my papa's. The Count was well-read, nocturnal, solitary, cunning, and hardworking. I think I am indeed all of these. The book has gotten into my system, and yet, even after all these years, I am still chilled to the bone when I read of the sighting of Lucy Westenra near her tomb, the innocent victim of Count Dracula's sharp teeth.

I recommend this book to anyone and everyone who likes good literature and a bit of good versus evil. To all readers of paranormal and horror books, if you have not yet read *Dracula*, what have you been doing all this time, eh? Go to your nearest library and get down to reading it.

For those who are "faint of heart," as the old Victorian saying goes, don't read this book. It's very scary and can give you the creeps! If you recall from my earlier writings, I was reading the book alone in that classroom and believe me, I was terrified to bits – but I liked it.

For those of you who want an introduction to Gothic fiction, horror, or vampire stories, read this book first.

The plot is enticing, the characters are lovable, and the ending takes your breath away. It is sad that Bram Stoker did not see the success of his book in his own lifetime. Reminds me of Jesus's saying, "I sent you to reap what you have not worked for. Others have done the hard work, and you have reaped the benefits of their labor." Today I am reaping the benefit of reading Bram Stoker's *Dracula* as a writer, teacher, and publisher – if it weren't for *Dracula* in 1997, the latter would never have taken place.

"Why do you always read this creepy book?" one of my classmates at BSS asked, disapproval and disgust written all over his face. "Are you planning a homicide?"

Everyone at school found my fascination with the classic morbidly funny. I was the butt of jokes because I kept a copy on my lap practically all through tenth grade, my crucial board exam year. To be frank, I was going berserk due to all the exams and only *Dracula* made me feel okay.

I was sick with erosions in my alimentary canal. Reason: anxiety, bad eating habits, and sadness, said the doctor who did my endoscopy.

I was sick throughout the ninth and tenth grades when I had to study for the board exams that would determine my future for college. By then I was not only ignored by my peers but, because of my voracious reading, I was thought to be a weirdo, someone the kids didn't want to be near. Teachers were no better. Only Mrs. Ratnaswami and Aruna were my friends back at BSS.

I was so alone – so totally alone and I was in pain. I was hurting, and only the books witnessed my forlorn state.

ESSAY 10

Ruskin Bond Books

AT BSS, EVERY SUMMER VACATION we were compelled to read a book. We were given a list of three books from which to choose, and the teachers would test us on the book we had read.

In the third grade I was given a choice from the following list:

1. *Grandfather's Tales* by Ruskin Bond
2. *Water Babies* by Charles Kingsley
3. *The Wonderful Wizard of Oz* by L. F. Baum

Blaise went to a bookshop and got me *Grandfather's Tales* by Ruskin Bond. I remember reading it on our bed, in my summer frock, under which my red undershorts were on display; it was a really hot summer you know, and the magic of Ruskin Bond entered my world.

To many, Ruskin Bond is the writer from the hills and is often today termed India's favorite writer. To me, Ruskin Bond is the writer whose stories made up not only school reading but leisure reading and was a part and parcel of my life growing up as a child and avid reader in the late 1990s and early 2000s.

I don't remember taking the test, but I remember the wonderful stories of Grandfather Bond's pet python, who scared Aunt Mabel to a faint; Ruskin's pet squirrel, Chips, who hid safely in the writer's pocket; Grandmother Bond's pet parrot, who was suspicious of train hawkers and conductors; Ruskin's lazy Uncle Ken, who was chased by a hive of bees into a pool; Ruskin's banyan tree, from where he saw a showdown between a black cobra and a wiry mongoose; Grandfather's pet tiger, Timothy, who slept with the cook; Ruskin's glass jug of frogs, and so much more and more and more!

"All aboard," says Grandmother Bond's parrot in one of the many stories I read as a child on that bed.

"Ruskin Bond had so many pets. Can't we get a goldfish?" I pleaded with Blaise and Mama, to no avail. When I went to college, Blaise brought a bowl of goldfish home, but the next day our efficient maid decided to clean the ceiling, which hadn't been cleaned since the stone age, and the dust entered the bowl and killed the fish. Sounds like a Ruskin Bond story.

"How could the chap have so many animals as pets?" Blaise mused.

Rita was more practical. "It's only tall tales to entertain the children," she said as she stirred the batter in a pot to bake a cake for me.

Mechu didn't mind snakes as pets so long as there were no cats. When I told her Ruskin Bond had a tiger, Mechu with all solemnity stated, "Tigers are decent. They are more like dogs. You can reason with bigger animals. They have bigger brains."

Mechu has abhorred cats ever since she was a little girl.

"Can Papa get me a cat?" I asked Mama as she was giving tuition. Mama scowled.

"He has not paid a penny for your upkeep, and you expect him of all people to give you a cat! Buy your own house when you grow up and then keep as many pets as you want," roared my mama like she always did.

Even today, I'm not allowed to bring pets into the house. I have to entertain all my animal, bird, and reptile friends outside.

Ruskin Bond was just pulling our legs of course, but I loved his short stories and his novels and novellas. I used to borrow them often from the school library and would like to write book reviews on them. Ruskin Bond made me the nature lover and enthusiast I am in a small modest way.

I read *Grandfather's Tales* in one week. Later on, during the library period in school, I would read the collected stories of Ruskin Bond.

"So much Ruskin Bond all the time!" Mrs. Ratnaswami scolded me as she went through my library notebook. "Child, read some classics or a biography."

Aruna would roll her eyes and then give me the smile which indirectly said, "Take it in one ear and out the other."

Ruskin Bond became a part of my lonely childhood. In his books, I read that he, too, loved to read; in fact, he was the only boy who loved reading books in the library. This was observed by his librarian and so he gave Bond the keys to the library so that he could go in whenever he wanted. ... I envy Ruskin Bond!

Seeing my love for Ruskin Bond, Mrs. Ratnaswami directed me to read his first novel, *The Room on the Roof*. I read the book in the fourth grade, sitting in my usual place while Aruna cleaned the early twentieth-century ceiling fans in the library, and Mrs. Ratnaswami drank her hot milky tea as she spoke with senior students who only came to the library for previous years' school exam papers.

"This child, I think, is always in the library but has never once asked for past years papers," Mrs. Ratnaswami would shake her head as she checked out another Ruskin Bond book for me. She would sign her name and then the bell would ring.

"Go to class now, before they catch you. Scoot!"

I would say goodbye to Aruna and run back to class.

I loved reading the Rusty stories of Ruskin Bond. I loved *The Room on the Roof* but would only read the sequel to it which was *Vagrants in the Valley* as a young adult, when I was just starting out as a writer.

The Rusty series was full of tales of friendship, escapades at school and the mountains, beautiful love stories that ended on bittersweet notes. They were about going away and coming back to one's friends ... and all of them made me feel melancholic. I had no friends. If it were not for books and the BSS library, I don't know what would have become of me.

But Ruskin Bond became my friend through his stories. I loved the story of the poor hill girls and boys in his tales, who used to work so hard to get to school. I loved his cherry tree, the one he planted on a whim. It is a healthy full-grown tree now in Landour, Mussoorie, where Ruskin Bond resides with his adopted family. I have not grown any cherry trees to date, but I have grown neem trees. I love neem trees and so do my cats, who keep on eating the leaves.

Yes, Ruskin Bond became a friend if only in book form. The best part of him was that he wrote practically all manner of genres: essays, short stories, novels, novellas, poems, ghost stories, nature stories, humorous stories, character sketches, diary entries, travelogues, thrillers. Every one of his books is written with charming sentences that have delighted me, a loner in a lonely world of book dust and silver fish.

To date, Ruskin Bond remains my second favorite writer. He is still alive, and one day I hope to touch his feet and meet his adopted family members, who made a home not only for him but for a solitary soul like me.

Ruskin Bond's books are interesting, evergreen, and soothing to the soul. Once you start reading him, you will be compelled to reread his works. As the cliché goes, he writes from the heart and not the mind.

At school, Ruskin Bond stories made up some of our literature lessons and comprehension passages. I remember studying *The Eyes Have It,* which is one of the most memorable of Bond's works. We also studied *The Blue Umbrella*, in an abridged form of course, though I read the unabridged version from the BSS library.

My school life as a reader in the 1990s and early 2000s was ruled by Ruskin Bond; it was impossible not to be influenced in some way by him. Like him, I too dreamed of being a writer, although I wanted to be a teacher first.

Like Ruskin Bond, I want to be one with nature. I grow a number of trees and plants in my modest garden. I love my modest garden. Mama always told me that the day I earned my own money I could have my own garden. That dream came true in 2016 when I potted my first china grass plant shoots. Now my modest garden boasts philodendrons, pink syngoniums, green and white syngoniums, yellow ixoras, pink pentas, white pentas, purple butterfly catchers, aralias, china grass, neem trees in abundance, a drumstick tree, all varieties of money plants, a ginger plant, an overpopulation of cacti, white flowered euphorbia, dark pink euphorbia, white ixoras, a white-and-pink bougainvillea, white-yellow scented magnolias and much more.

My cats are my pride (hey, that was a pun), and birds love spending time in my garden. I used to have a pet snail in my office-cum-writing hut. The snail's name was Snailey Wailey, and he was one of my best animal friends who loved to gorge on leaves and travel about the writing hut. He passed away lately, leaving his shell behind. I miss him.

Animals, birds, reptiles, and plants are my only true friends. They don't ask questions; they love you without reason.

Today, I still find peace reading a Ruskin Bond book. He is the only writer whose books I buy without looking at the synopsis first. His photograph rests on a shelf in my office-cum-writing hut. He is always there for me, even as I move from my twenties into my thirties.

Ruskin Bond's books are treasures of literature and of a side of India that we normally do not get to see, the hills of India. Ruskin Bond has spent more than seventy years living in these hills, and my dream is to retire to the hills when I am done with city life, earning money, and living the rat race.

Yes, one day I will go to the hills. I love the hills thanks to Ruskin Bond's books. I would love to spend the rest of my life there, far away, in a land I have never visited in person but which I have always known in spirit.

"You must be mad," said Mama the other day when I said I wanted to retire to the hills. "In the hills there are panthers and leopards. You will be eaten up."

Panthers and leopards, oh what a lark! I love cats, big and small. Besides, the further I'm away from the sea, the better I will be. I can't stand water; it ruins books, you know!

These days, I read Ruskin Bond's books whenever I feel the need to charge up my writing batteries. I also read him when I am tired of a long week of teaching at my tutorial. I usually read his essays more than anything else; he has a surreal way of penning essays, and I love it. I read his essays on my recliner in my office-cum-writing hut, my abode of bliss and solitude, with only the sounds of the Wadi people in the background, living their daily lives: talking, cooking, filling water, gathering wood for fuel, etc.

I love everything Ruskin Bond has ever written. But the essays I like best are the essays of his relationship with his father. When I was young, tears used to fill my eyes when I read about Bond's last meeting with his Royal Air Force father. I wished my papa was as good a man as Mr. Bond senior, who was not so picky; who loved collecting stamps, winding the handle of the gramophone, and watching Laurel and Hardy movies.

Papa could never be Ruskin Bond's father, not even in a million years. Ruskin Bond, I envy you for the papa you had.

I recommend all of Ruskin Bond's books to anyone and everyone. He is a gem of an author to have in your library, and his books are an experience in literature. I recommend his children's books of hill children, leopard sightings, forests, blue umbrellas, etc. to all young children; his humor is contagious. If you would like a more specific book recommendation, I will recommend *The Room on the Roof,* his very first novel. And don't wait long to read the sequel, *Vagrants in the Valley.* Do it quickly and then go on to read the following:

1. *The Sensualist*
2. *Maharani*
3. *A Handful of Nuts*
4. *The Lamp Is lit*
5. *Rain in the Mountains*
6. *The Night Train at Deoli*

Ruskin Bond has recently penned several memoirs. I highly recommend *Lone Fox Dancing* and *The Beauty of All My Days.*

It's now evening as I type this essay. Ruskin Bond must be getting ready for tea and a bit of walking. I hope his gout is better, and I hope he isn't feeling too cold. And I hope he has many more years to write, to continue brightening the lives of solitary readers with new titles and adventures.

ESSAY 11

School Time and School Library 2

BY THE TIME I WAS IN THE SEVENTH GRADE, the BSS library had become the only reason I went to school.

I remember spending my birthdays there as well as entire weeks during the BSS concert practices, going through the shelves, picking up tomes to read.

It was a back-breaking task to keep that massive library clean, but it was always spotless thanks to the meticulousness of Aruna and the determination of a very strict Mrs. Ratnaswami. Sometimes I used to help out, but Mrs. Ratnaswami didn't like it.

"Child," she would say, taking the duster from my hand. "This is not your job. Go back and read comfortably before the bell rings."

I was spoiled silly by her, really I was!

I was growing up and having mood swings. I was heavily built and hated wearing a real bra. I was uncomfortable with everything involving menstruation. I did not have anyone to talk to about it. Mechu gave me talks about growing up, but not a hearing ear for what I was going through. Mama was too busy with teaching; she never spoke to me about the changes I was going through. I don't blame her. She was going through menopause and having a tough time at school; she wouldn't be able to handle a moody teenager as well.

Blaise says that I was very quiet during this period of my life. I never really spoke at all, so he never knew what was going on with me. He said I was busy reading all the time.

One day, at long last, a teacher pointed out to my mama that I walked with a hump, didn't look into the eyes when spoken to, and never uttered a word in class. Instead of speaking to me about it, Mama was so angry with me that she tore me to shreds verbally.

I didn't cry in front of her. But afterward, I ran to the library and put my head down on Aruna's working table and sobbed for three hours. No one came to look for me. It was like I was invisible. I dried my tears with my ironed purple handkerchief, wetting it to a pulp, and Aruna continued to watch me but pretended to be busy reading her Marathi novel.

I went back to class. No one had missed me. I took my seat and waited for the bell to ring to signal that it was time to go home.

Slowly Mama learned that I had a secret life in the library.

"Why do you go to the library so much?" she asked one day after I'd been in school for nine years.

"Because I love to read."

"Why do you love to read so much?"

"Because I have no friends. Books are my only friends," I said.

Mama was very angry. Teachers and her seniors at school had been filling her ears with nonsense about me being odd. They were nagging Mama, and it was all because of me.

"You will tell me why you go to the library, or I'll slap you." Mama raised her hand over my head. "What are you reading there? Porn? Adult books?"

"Leave her," said Rita, coming between us. "What's the harm if she reads? She hasn't murdered anyone."

I was sitting in a corner in Nana's house. I was short of breath and clutching a book from the BSS library to my chest. It was *Anne of Green Gables* by L. M. Montgomery. I was sobbing but no tears were coming out of my eyes.

Again, here comes a difficult part for me to write. If I tell, then I will yet again be subject to defamation. So, let's just say these canards about my so-called peculiar behavior were being spread by vested interests, and my mama unknowingly fell into the trap. I was a broken doll being pushed through the valley of emotional turmoil. It would take years to overcome my fears. Books helped the most.

It was 2002. My thirteenth birthday. I was at home opening gifts from Blaise, every single gift a book, when I heard screaming.

It was 4:00 p.m. sharp, and my mama was screaming, hollering, and banging our back door shut. Someone's arms were trying to push the door open on the other side.

"Mama..." I whispered. Were they robbers? We were the only two women in the house. Blaise had gone to collect the cake from Birdy's the confectionery.

"Mama!" I got up to help, until I recognized the voice on the other side of the door.

It was Papa. He was trying to break down the door. He was trying to come in, but Mama didn't want him in. She was not alone in this; I didn't want to see him either. But he was stubborn and violent. He was also yelling, "I have the right to wish my daughter a happy birthday. I have a right. I'm her father."

They were having a painful struggle, pushing the door between them. Neighbors were watching. And I was petrified. I thought Papa had come to take me away.

"Fiza *beta*," he cried as he pushed and banged himself against the back door. "Happy birthday, Fiza *beta*. Happy birthday to you Fiza *beta*, happy birthday to you!"

His voice was rasping though full of benevolence. Mama managed with her meager strength to shut and double lock the door. Papa, the madman, started banging on the glass windows and the front door, still singing the happy birthday song.

I couldn't take it. I ran with one of Blaise's books to the common bedroom. I shut the door and bolted it tight. Then I crouched in the corner and covered my head with my hands. My face was between my legs. I was shivering.

Papa continued to bang the windows and doors. Mama screamed abuse at him and the neighbors started ringing the landline.

"Happy birthday to you, Fiza *beta*, happy birthday to you!"

I remained in that position for half an hour. After an hour, by 5:00 p.m., he had gone. Mama made me open the common bedroom door. She told me all was safe and now I should get ready to go to church.

"I'm not going," I whimpered. "I want to sit at home and read."

Mama laughed and said I was not a true Christian to let a Muslim spoil my birthday.

"Why don't you divorce him?" I pleaded, but Mama ignored me and answered a call. I felt pain in my fingers. I was gripping the book Blaise had gifted me too tight. I lifted it to have a look.

A Little Princess by Frances Hodgson Burnett.

I went to church, shivering. Next day, I cried in the library near the classic books section. Aruna saw me weeping but allowed me my space. She went on cataloging the math books in the textbooks section.

❋

My silence deepened and my reading became even more serious.

I discovered Charles Dickens during this time. In the school library, his books required two shelves. I read all of the sad ones in the unabridged form. My favorite was *Bleak House*. I loved the 1950s paperback cover. That's how I felt: bleak, stuck in a school with no one to talk to. I read *David Copperfield*, *Hard Times*, *Our Mutual Friend*, *The Old Curiosity Shop*, *Oliver Twist*, *Little Dorrit*, and my Dickens all-time favorite, *Great Expectations*.

The library offered every kind of reading you could imagine: comics, magazines, newspapers dating from years ago, all preserved carefully if a student needed extra information for a school project. There were foreign encyclopedias, lots of them. There were thick, dusty tomes on the works of the ancients: Plato, Aristotle, Pythagoras, Julius Caesar, Cicero, Heraclitus, Hippocrates, St. Augustine, Galileo, Kepler, Erasmus, William Harvey, and so many others. I used to love Plato best, especially his analysis of Socrates's life and body of work.

There were bookcases for each subject: mathematics, craft, literature, sociology, ethics, post-modernist studies, biology, chemistry, philosophy, history, religion, art, economics, foreign languages, poetry, political science, social work, grammar, esoteric literature, and astronomy. I used to gorge on these books for hours and days on end, without speaking a word.

I started carrying a large paper bag to school for all the books I was taking home to study. I may have not been a brilliant pupil, but my reading tastes were eclectic even at that age, all thanks to the BSS library.

Mrs. Ratnaswami had her rules:

- No eating in the library
- No drinking water in the library
- No talking while reading
- Do not read books from the “teachers only” section
- Do not disrupt a library class
- Do not borrow more than two books

I was exempt from all these rules; I was the good child.

Once, Aruna was cleaning the glass windows of some of the iron shelves with Colin cleaner. As she was moving toward the classics section, she almost toppled over me. I was sitting in a Buddha pose with a shaft of sunlight falling on me, reading H. G. Wells’s *The Invisible Man.*

“Mad girl. Totally *pagali*!” declared Aruna, getting her bearings while Mrs. Ratnaswami and I laughed mischievously.

I was slowly coming to realize that I was becoming a sort of armchair scholar. I even fantasized about becoming a real scholar and writing books of my great theories, which would be shelved one day in my abode of abodes, the BSS library. I started doing queer things, harmless, but still queer. I filled my uniform pocket with large amounts of ballpoint pens, carried books under my arm or in my paper bag everywhere I went, and when I spoke, which was seldom, I did so in a Victorian English accent.

It was the books I was reading. They had made a home inside me. And one day, in 2003, out of the blue with another hardback copy of

Bram Stoker's *Dracula* on my lap in the BSS library, I said something. I petted the Stoker book lovingly and said, "Father ... Papa."

From then on, my fate was sealed. I had at last found a father, my real papa – books.

"Child," cried out Mrs. Ratnaswami from a distance. "The bell has rung. Go back to class and for heaven's sake eat something. Child, Pizza, CHILD!"

She called me Pizza instead of Fiza, and I loved it. I loved everything about her. From the way she drank her tea to the way she conducted her library period classes, to the way she gave me a star for my excellent book reviews.

"Don't you ever talk?" a classmate, a boy called Udit, asked me one day.

He was a new student at BSS, just inducted in our eighth-grade class E. So he really didn't know me and was finding me pretty odd, I guess, because I never opened my mouth in class and was always buried in books, even if it was just the Cambridge dictionary.

"Hey," he tried to catch my attention. "Hello! Well, you are a real specimen. Weirdo – weirdo – weirdo. You actually carry such a huge dictionary to school, why?"

I was terrified of him. I was terrified of everyone back then. I was only comfortable with papa – that is, my books.

But at least Udit spoke to me. He tried to break through the mesh, and I sort of appreciate that. But the mesh was made of paper, and I didn't want to come out anymore. I was happy with books.

Yes, I was happy. I had found a father.

And then one day, I would sell my soul to my new papa.

ESSAY 12

The Classics

I DISCOVERED A LOVE FOR the classics at the BSS library. As a writer, I have dedicated most of my educational books to the revival of the reading of these classics, the popular as well as the rare.

My love of the classics began with *Dracula* by Bram Stoker, of course, but then Mrs. Ratnaswami ordered new abridged classics and dedicated an entire section in the inner sanctum of the library to them.

"Today, you students have two options," she said in that distinctive nasal voice of hers that I so loved. "Either you can pick a regular fiction book placed on the table near the arts and crafts section, or you can pick a classic from the inner portion of the library. However," she cautioned us with a raised hand before we could make a racket, which we always did, "you will not be able to take the classics home to read. They are new and very costly, and I don't want anyone ruining or robbing them. You kids will have to read the classics only here IN THE LIBRARY and nowhere else. The books on the table can be taken home."

As my classmates of grade five E were making a beeline towards the classics section, I went up to Mrs. Ratnaswami. Before I could ask, she whispered into my ears, "You can take them home under mummy's name."

I dashed toward the classics section. I was last in the line. Aruna, who was monitoring the bookshelf raised her arms in resignation. "Only few left. Make your choice baby," she said and folded her arms.

The others opened their books to read.

There were only five books left, and I remember the one I picked: *Little Women* by Louisa May Alcott.

I took the book back to my place and started reading.

This new way of introducing classics to us did me a world of good. By the end of term one, I had finished most of the abridged classics and wanted to read the unabridged form. My mama's library card and clout came in handy, and I started reading unabridged classics; some first editions were more than a hundred years old and bound in calf leather.

Reading the classics improved my vocabulary, but then again, I never really spoke so I could only put that good vocabulary to use in my exam papers, especially in the essay and letter-writing section. My composition writing improved tremendously, and my skills in English were getting better with each passing day.

Besides, I lived and breathed in my imagination (which was wild and is still wild, I'll tell you that) the lives of all the amazing evergreen characters that I encountered: Anne Shirley from *Anne of Green Gables*, Van Helsing from *Dracula*, Uriah Heap from *David Copperfield*, the Monster from *Frankenstein*, Tom Brown from *Tom Brown's School Days*, Mr. Pooter from *The Diary of a Nobody,* and so much else.

My English language and literature teachers were very pleased with my performance. Mama was glad that I was at least excelling in something. By this time, I had already decided to become an English teacher.

"Are you taking after Mummy?" asked Mrs. Ratnaswami as she drank her cup of milky tea with biscuits.

"No," I said quite unsure. "I want to teach seniors English literature."

"Well, you'll have to speak louder, child, if you want to teach seniors these days," grumbled my dear Mrs. Ratnaswami. "I'm half dead conducting these library periods myself, then what of you and your little voice, eh?"

But the classics had engrained the love of literature in me. I wanted to teach and maybe write on the side.

Like the characters in the classics I was reading, I was very idealistic back then. Sometimes I wonder whatever happened to that idealistic little me over these many years that have passed? Where did I lose myself? In which chapter of the book of life? The answer is as mysterious to me as it is to you, dear reader.

I was idealistic and as naïve as they come. I wanted to be a teacher like Agnes Grey in Anne Brontë's book by the same name, and to write books or scholarly papers like David Copperfield in Charles Dicken's book did.

One of those books was *Emily of New Moon* by L. M. Montgomery, and to this day, I prefer Emily to Anne Shirley. Anne was a teacher and Emily a writer, and that's what I have become. So, who says classics don't influence the course of your life?! They influenced mine all right.

I think I have read most of the classic writers there are over the years, twenty-nine long years.

And I loved them all, each and every one of my classic papas.

I loved the pirate adventure of Robert Louis Stevenson's *Treasure Island*, the hilarity of Saki's collected short stories, the curiousness of Wonderland in Lewis Carroll's *Alice's Adventures In Wonderland*, the spirit of giving in Charles Dicken's *A Christmas Carol*, the eccentricity of Sherlock Holmes in Sir Arthur Conan Doyle's Sherlock Holmes books, the horror of being buried alive in Edgar Allan Poe's *Tales of the Unexpected*, the love of our canine friends in Jack London's *White Fang*, the true meaning of bravery in Stephen Crane's *The Red Badge of Courage*, the feeling of never growing up in James Barrie's *Peter Pan* and so much else that I can explode!

Blaise was thrilled with my fascination for the classics, for he had always been an ardent classics lover himself. He knew I was able to get most of my classics from school, but he wanted me to have a collection of my own as well. He therefore bought me a number of classics, which I cherish to this day. My favorite among all of them was *Daddy-Long-Legs* by Jean Webster. I still have all my classics and refer to them over and over again when I have the inclination to. Some classics have been a soothing balm to my aching soul over the years, especially *Dracula* by Bram Stoker. I've cried on its pages and I've made silent nocturnal prayers to the fiend in the coffin at the dead of night when I was afraid to go to school the next day.

The classics comfort and inspire us to greater perfection. I've always felt elated by the very look of a good classic in my pudgy hands.

I recommend the classics to all. I recommend abridged classics to young readers who want to improve their minds and enjoy a fantastic story. To adults, if you haven't read the classics yet, you should do so now and become enriched by the wealth of knowledge, language, and emotive elements in them. We live in an age where twentieth-century classics are available for us to read and love with all our hearts. There's Hemingway, Plath, Faulkner, Orwell, Salinger, Greene, Maugham, Joyce, Fitzgerald, and a whole lot of others to read and enjoy.

Blaise became closer to me during this time. He told me how one of his colleagues at the bank used to say that he never went to bed without reading at least one chapter of a classic. I multiplied that to one classic a week (I was reading two books a day, if you please!) and I stuck by my regimen. You should do so too. Go out there and buy that classic you were always meaning to buy. Then burrow into a world a bit different from your own. Soon it will feel like a part of you from some other time and from some other place.

ESSAY 13

Alice's Adventures in Wonderland and Through the Looking-Glass by Lewis Carroll

ONCE A TEACHER CAME HOME, when I had just turned thirteen. She was a Catholic like us, and a really dear friend of my mama. She basically was worried about me; about my silence. More than that, she was worried about my future, especially where my Muslim name was concerned.

"Change her name to a good Christian one," said the teacher, meaning all the good in the world, I'm sure. "It's not too late; the child is still in school – not even given her tenth-grade exams yet. Change her name to something more Christian and let her take your maiden surname." Mama's maiden name was Martis.

Mama nodded and looked at me. I think she was trying to picture me as Josephine Martis, Josephine being my middle name. But I had other ideas.

"I would love to be called Alice," I said enthusiastically. I had no qualms about changing my name back then, but everyone laughed.

"You mean the *Wonderland* Alice?" asked the teacher. "No, Josephine is much easier; it's already on your baptism certificate."

"But I don't like the name Josephine. I hate it!" I twisted the hem of my summer frock in my left hand. "I'll either be called Alice, or I'll stay Fiza."

And I stayed Fiza Pathan. I'm still Fiza Pathan, a Roman Catholic for these past twenty-seven years. I say twenty-seven, because I was only baptized when I was two years old, so the first two years of my life I was pagan Pathan!

Jokes apart, the reason for the choice of the name Alice was entirely because of Lewis Carroll's tales, which Blaise had bought for me with the original illustrations in a Dover thrift edition. I loved Alice. I loved everything about her. I wanted to change my Christian name to Alice. I abhorred that redundant Josephine name to the core; good heavens, I can never be a Josephine! I'm too full of myself to ever be a Josephine.

An Alice I am, very much so. To me, Alice was truly me, the girl who had curious adventures all alone in make-believe worlds filled with the most wondrous creatures and characters. I got a kick every time I read the Alice books.

Alice was alone. She had her cat, Diana; I had befriended a tomcat called Kevin. She liked books with pictures and conversations; I liked books period, and if there were pictures and conversations, that was an added bonus. Alice was always alone; I was always alone. But I was in love with Alice and wished to God I had a younger sister like her.

Papa had stopped calling on us. He and Mama had a really big fight – I still don't know for sure what it was about – and he turned his back on Mama as well. In a way, I was elated. I hated him. To be rid of such an odious man was reason enough to celebrate, maybe with a tea party, with a Mad Hatter, a March Hare, and a Dormouse for company.

"My Cookie is always in wonderland!" said Mechu whenever she saw me with the *Alice in Wonderland* book. I was always "Cookie" to Mechu back then. These days I'm "dolly girl", even now when she sees me stuck in a book, and sometimes in my office-cum-writing hut writing.

But back to Alice. Lewis Carroll has done a marvelous job of not only entertaining children through his Alice books but also entertaining adults and literary theorists through the satire and hidden symbolism, especially in *Through the Looking-Glass and What Alice Found There.* Normally kids come to know satire as adults, but since the BSS library was well stocked, I managed to get my hands on a guide to the Alice books printed before the 1940s and, while I can't remember the name of the leather-bound book, with analysis of the so-called elite society and their mannerisms and educational practices, I can tell you it was a feast for the literary mind.

I read it all by age fourteen. I used to regale Blaise with the satire at night after the evening rosary was over. We laughed so much! I loved the Queen of Hearts in the first Alice book, and Blaise loved the talking flowers in the second Alice book.

The Alice books are a feast for the imagination that allow one to dream, to think outside the boxes society has created. During this time, I created an imaginary world of my own, and I penned adventures into my diary. In my wonderland, I was part of a motorcycle and race car gang called "The Eagles," which used to compete with their nemesis from the other side of town, "The Scorpions." I was the ringleader of the Eagle gang, taking part in many races and solving many a problem.

Sadly, I burned most of those diaries. I was afraid Mechu or Mama would read them. I was afraid they would think I was mad, MAD AS A HATTER!

But, of course, the dear ones never read anything, and I really felt like boxing my own ears for having burned such a precious memory. I loved my Eagle gang members. Still do!

Lewis Carroll was a mathematics professor, and a bad one at that. To know that about him made me smile, as I wanted to be a teacher too, but not a math teacher, that's for sure, just an English teacher. I've almost come full circle because of my ten years as a teacher. I've taught *You Are Old Father William* and *The Walrus and the Carpenter* so many times that I've been able to nurture the love of the Alice books in my students as well.

I loved reading the Alice books before an exam; it always made me feel calm. That's the best part about the classics. They calm you down, taking away the tension of life, even if only for a little while.

If you have not yet read the Alice books, you should do so. I recommend them to children as well as adults. In fact, enough of making kids read the Alice books; it is time for college students and adults to pay attention to the great wealth of knowledge that Carroll offers us. Read *Alice's Adventures in Wonderland* first and then *Through the Looking-Glass and What Alice Found There*, and don't skip the Jabberwocky; read it all. Digest it and read them once again; these two books have changed the way we write and perceive literature.

But what about me selling my soul to books? When did that happen? Well, it happened during the last two years of my time at BSS. It happened because of love. Yes, I fell in love! And this time it was with a boy, not a book. Sort of!

ESSAY 14

School Time and School Library 3

I FELL IN LOVE. It was one-sided, sadly, and it's one of the best things that ever happened to me, apart from the books in my life.

I can't tell you his name because, it's ... no, it's not about defamation. It's just that I don't think he will like to see his name in my book. I don't even think he knows I exist! Oh, but he did exist for me, more than any man ever will.

We never spoke. We still don't speak, and we, I guess, will never speak. You see I was a confirmed weirdo by the time I met him; no one wanted to have anything to do with me. It was only me and my books – and him.

He liked reading; he used to read all the time. He read during free periods; thrillers like Arthur Hailey and Dan Brown were his favorites. He loved mathematics and science, so he even read a good number of books on those topics. He had a wonderful voice with superb diction. I loved to hear him speak.

"Child, you seem unwell today," said Mrs. Ratnaswami as she stamped my three Agatha Christie books. I just nodded and left.

He was smarter than me, and I was smitten, infatuated, in love as any teenager would be.

I read Richard Bach, Agatha Christie, Robin Cook, and the classics. He read Arthur Hailey, Lee Child, Dan Brown, and books on physics.

I was such an old silly. You see, I used to look for the books he had read in the BSS library. We had these old-fashioned library cards, which I still adore, which had three columns. First date, second name of student or teacher, and last the signature of the librarian with date returned. You see, I used to search for the books he had read in the library and when I found one that he had just read, like *Hotel* or *Strong Medicine* by Arthur Hailey, I used to take my Natraj pencil or black Uniball pen and write my name below his. It gave me a sort of thrill, you see, to see my name below his, near his.

I loved to watch him read. He was no daydreamer. He was very focused in his reading. He had a great sense of humor and was a gentleman in a modern and unorthodox way that I fancied, maybe a bit too much for my own good.

"Child, you seem unwell today," said Mrs. Ratnaswami again as I checked out a book he had just returned. Did she know? Did she guess? That her little, plump bookworm had fallen head over heels in love, not with a book this time, but with a boy, a real boy?

I used to think about him when I read Jane Austen's *Pride and Prejudice*. Like all girls, I searched in his eyes for my Mr. Darcy, and failed miserably. I read Emily Brontë's *Wuthering Heights* and tried to find Heathcliff lurking somewhere in this teenage boy's mannerisms. I read Anne Frank's *The Diary of a Young Girl* and delved to the surface of my infatuation to see if he was my Peter van Pels.

It ended as you might expect; he passed out of school unknowing of my tender feelings. I, as usual, had kept my words and feelings to myself. It was a one-sided, silent love, with only the sound of turning pages as background music.

There is a lot I learned from him that I will cherish all my life. His dedication to his work, his good manners, his sensitivity, his way of articulating words, his wealth of knowledge, his confidence in himself. I will cherish all of these things and try to work upon them and think upon them when I am not immersed in a good book.

They say that if a writer falls in love with you, you will live forever, immortalized in print. Today, I've tried to immortalize this teenage boy who was with me for only a short while, but who has found a niche in this bookcase heart of mine. Love you, dear boy of my silent youth, to the BSS library and back.

"Child, you seem unwell today," said Mrs. Ratnaswami.

I swallowed my tears and said, "Yeah! Yes, ma'am. I'm all right. I'm fine on my own."

Who was that boy who turned the ink in my veins to blood?
These arteries tell new stories and these veins empty their soul to you;
Reader beware, for my heart is a page to tear away from amour,
And yet the tearing heart whimpers silent sobs choked with
printer's new scarlet ink.

❋

I used to spend most of my last days in the BSS library reading and doing tuition homework. I penned a diary during that time in the school library, and that's how I remember many of the books I read during those last two years of high school.

I read indiscriminately – a bit of Thomas Hardy along with a W. Somerset Maugham short story, a lot of Charles Dickens and a heck of a lot of Wilkie Collins, a great amount of Rabindranath Tagore and snippets of Edgar Cayce, the sleeping prophet, a bit of this and a bit of that, and in no time at all, it was time to leave. It was time to leave my father, papa, BSS library.

"*Kya karege* Board exam *ke baad*?" Aruna asked me as I watched her glue book card envelopes at the back of some new plastic-covered hardbacks.

"I don't know," I said. "I guess I'll keep on coming here till college starts." I patted the pleats of my well-ironed skirt and gazed out of the library window overlooking the magnificent school garden. "Maybe I'll learn a new language, learn to play the guitar like Elvis Presley, join a book club or something."

Aruna clicked her tongue as she peeled the glue off her dainty fingers. "*Wo nahi re! Hamare bina tu kya karenge? Mujhe batao?*" (That's not what I meant! What will you do without us? Tell me?)

I had no answer to that. How could I have had an answer to that! This place had been my second home, my fortress, my father – my all! How could I leave this library, with its numerous books I had yet not read, with so many twentieth-century fictions from foreign countries still left to get through?

The answer came in the form of my principal, Dr. D. P. N Prasad, whom I even now respectfully address as Sir Prasad.

Well, Sir Prasad was my savior because after the tenth-grade exam he gave me the best coming-of-age gift even God could not give: he gave me permission to come to the BSS library for as long as I liked even after I joined college, and even after that, as long as I borrowed my books under my mama's name. And after my mama retired, I could take them out on any other teacher's name. However, I had to make sure I only stayed in the library and never entered the main school. I could dress in regular decent attire and enter and leave the school by the office connected to the library.

And all this because I was one of the most well-behaved students in the 2005 batch, the year I passed out from high school.

Mama was so proud of me, and I ... I was ecstatic, overjoyed, over the moon crazy with glee!

"Again, so much of love suddenly," Aruna said as I caught her in the middle of work and hugged her tightly.

Sir Prasad at last made me feel that I was wanted and that my love for the BSS library had not gone unnoticed. After the tenth-grade exam, the very next day I was back at the BSS library to do what I still do best – read as much as I like. Sir Prasad even graced me with a visit and was proud that I was still wearing my school uniform, from blue tie to well-polished, shiny black school shoes. He congratulated my mama on my good behavior throughout my school career; twelve long years.

During the summer vacation of 2005, I visited the BSS library every day. I read mostly nonfiction books, especially books about historical characters like Julius Caesar, William Shakespeare, Oscar Wilde, Michelangelo, Leonardo da Vinci, Martin Luther, Kabir, Rabindranath Tagore, Mahatma Gandhi, Dante, the patriarchs of the Bible. All of them were interests of study back then. I came in uniform, only abandoned the day I appeared on the first list of St. Andrew College (Bandra West). I had passed with distinction and was the second person on the list.

After that, I visited the BSS library whenever I had free time from college or during college holidays. Many teachers at BSS were made very erudite, judging by the books I borrowed in their names. And some new teachers were under the impression that my mama was a really well-read teacher because of the list of books "she" or rather "I" had read over the years!

"It's the daughter, not the mother!" Mrs. Ratnaswami would correct a new teacher with her cup of tea in hand. "The mother doesn't even step the place. It's the daughter who reads!"

When I passed out from school, I had grown thin due to a gastric disorder and looked kind of pretty in a plain way. I had fine features like mama, but with papa's forehead and mannerisms. I was thin as a rail and weighed only 45 kgs. All that would change in a strange and sudden way .... I was about to type the word *grotesque* but I shall avoid doing so and stick to *strange*, for although I am now 122 kgs and suffer from obesity, I'm not ashamed of my body. I'm a plus size and not ashamed of it.

But what happened in the middle? What books did I read and how did I land up as a writer? All that in due time. Do I still go to the BSS library? Is there a Bombay Scottish library anymore? I'll discuss all of that as we go on through these bookish scenes that have made up my life.

On the last day that I was allowed to wear a uniform to school, just before the school and of course the BSS library closed for the summer holidays of 2005, I sold my soul. I sold my soul to books, to the "Word."

That afternoon, before we could head for home, I did something that in all my twelve years of school life I had never done. I went to the BSS sports field. I went and stood in the middle of the field. I was alone and the hot wind of the Mumbai summer was burning my skin. I stood there, looking around the school. I could see the shortcut I used to take during PT classes to go and hide in the library. I saw the sweeper, silently sweeping the fallen leaves of the banyan tree. I saw the clear blue sky and dug my well-polished black school shoes into the sand of the field.

And that's when I made a vow. I vowed that as long as I exist, I will never stop reading. I, without any words, sold my soul, right in the middle of that sports field, to the "Word." This pact had nothing to do with the devil or anything else, just books. I would do everything for books. I thought about the eternal promise I was making and the words of Jesus rang in my ears:

> *"Man does not live on bread alone, but on every word that comes from the mouth of God." Matthew 4:4 (KJV)*

"Yes," I said aloud to myself, my hands stretched out as I twirled with happiness. "Yes, man does not live on bread alone – man does not live on bread alone – man does not live on bread alone!"

I kept on saying these words as I twirled round and round at the center of the sports field. And I swore that I would always be nourished by the words written in all books, every book.

Did I think that one day I would write? I sort of did and sort of did not. But I knew that a pact had been made; my fate was sealed, and even in my darkest moments since that day, I've never EVER stopped reading.

The pact was simple enough. As long as I existed as me, I would read on and on and on until someone, someone who realized I had fulfilled my eternal promise, a promise made at age sixteen, would tell me to stop!

My life at school proved that "man does not live on bread alone." I went back home in a car. The teacher in whose car we were traveling saw my dusty shoes.

"You actually went to the field, Fiza?" she asked chuckling. "With whom were you playing?"

There was a moment of silence in the car with the AC on full blast.

“I was alone.” That’s what I said. “I was alone.”

ESSAY 15

R. L. Stine's Goosebumps

I WAS ADDICTED TO THE GOOSEBUMPS series of horror tales by R. L. Stine. I even read them through my final year of college!

I came across R. L. Stine and his body of work first at BSS library. Mrs. Ratnaswami had ordered a whole stack of the books, and all the boys in my class were dying to read them. The girls were not that interested; they were into Judy Blume, Sweet Valley, and Meg Cabot's The Princess Diaries series, and of course, Harry Potter. But I secretly loved horror stories just like the boys.

So one library period I borrowed my first Goosebumps book, called *Werewolf Skin*. It was about two friends who felt the elders responsible for them were werewolves, but of a very unusual kind. I got so into the plot that I finished the book in one evening. It was scary for a thirteen-year-old, but I liked the thrill of it all.

I went back next day for another, but I came to a dead end this time at the BSS library. You see, there was a new junior librarian on duty and she categorically refused to give me another Goosebumps title.

"We must give other students a chance to read, *na*! And we have so few copies," she said and shooed me away in disgrace. The whole episode made me depressed the whole day.

When Blaise came back home, he saw that I was a bit low. He asked, "Baby, what's wrong?"

I told him that the junior librarian hadn't allowed me to borrow another Goosebumps and that I wouldn't get one until next month, that it was a first come, first served basis.

Blaise heard me out, nodded, and went out. He came back later with three omnibuses of R. L. Stine's Goosebumps. There were three books in each volume – nine books in all!

I was so overjoyed that I hugged Blaise tight – an endearing action in which our family rarely partakes; hugging just doesn't come naturally to us. I immediately started reading the very first book, *Dead House*, and was happy as a pig in sludge.

I loved (and still love) R. L. Stine's writing style. I loved the way he built up the suspense and created lovable characters. He also kept descriptions to a minimum. As a young teenager, I felt really hip, reading American Goosebumps.

Some of my favorite Goosebumps books were *It Came from the Basement*, *Bad Hare Day*, *Vampire Breath*, *Night of the Living Dummy*, *How I Got My Shrunken Head*, and *Calling All Creeps*.

Goosebumps are evergreen horror books that can entertain a preteen or teenager to glory. That kids are more intelligent than adults is a common factor in his stories, along with the fact that the ending is always gruesome, in true R. L. Stine fashion.

"Reader Beware – You're in for a Scare!" is the tag line for all Goosebumps books, and I lapped them up like vanilla ice cream (my favorite). Unfortunately, I had no one to talk to about the Goosebumps books. I talked about the Goosebumps I was reading with my imaginary friends, or I wrote about the book in my diary.

I was addicted to Goosebumps and, even when I entered high school, I was still reading R. L. Stine.

I learned Stine's writing style and adopted it in my own compositions. I still write somewhat like him, according to Blaise. Of course, nowadays, my writing style is a mix of R. K. Narayan, Ruskin Bond, and R. L. Stine, three *R*'s with which I've managed to concoct a writing salad of my own. But Stine is the main foundation; yes, he is there!

R. L. Stine's pen never ceases to create wonders in horror fiction for preteens and teenagers. Before I knew it, I was even reading his Fear Street series. I lived on the Fear Street series in the eighth grade, one of the loneliest school years of my life. I survived thanks to the writing of R. L. Stine.

Blaise was my main supplier of Goosebumps and Fear Street books. Mama was not pleased that I was so much into horror, so I played it safe by always reading a classic along with a Goosebumps to keep the disagreements at bay.

Mechu was horrified that I read Goosebumps. "Dolly girl," she would say, "you will become a ghost if you read so much about ghosts."

But in a way, I was already a ghost. I wasn't really me; I'm still not. I'm still the ghost of myself. The real me is stuck in a coffin somewhere deep inside my being, and she doesn't want to come out.

I still love the horror genre; I'm a sucker for it! I've grown out of Goosebumps, but I provide all my students access to my private collection. Some of them really get spooked, and I wonder how come. But then, it's a Tower of Babel trying to understand Gen Z kids anyway.

Bob is R. L. Stine's real name. He was a great companion of my childhood. I owe him more than these words ever can or ever will express.

Reading about protagonists in the Goosebumps who had siblings, younger or older, made me yearn for a sibling of my own. But I was old enough to realize that wish of mine would never be fulfilled. Papa had washed his hands of us for good. Not a penny did he send for my upkeep, nor Mama's.

He really didn't want me. And, to be frank, I didn't want him.

But it was reading R. L. Stine's Goosebumps, which features families in the United States who don't discriminate between girls or boys, that made me realize I had been abandoned. It was a double whammy for me when my peers shrugged me off as well. I'm no badass feminist, not all of us can be that way. I can't fight, but I can write. Twenty-six letters of the alphabet are the only things I have, and they have seen me through this life. With these twenty-six letters, I can go the distance and write away the resignation, pain, and bitterness that slowly melts as I do the things I love to do: reading, writing, and teaching.

I recommend Goosebumps to all children because these books are awesome. But if you frighten easily, stay away. Because a scare is guaranteed with these books. For those kids who love *Dracula* and *Frankenstein*, Goosebumps are the next best thing for you. Plus, R. L. Stine wrote more Goosebumps after the year 2000 to suit the temperament of kids today, and they are as good as the earlier ones, if not better. Try *Brain Juice* – you will love it! It's a favorite at my private library.

When I finished my tenth grade and spent the summer of 2005 at home, I gave away some of my Goosebumps collections to Step-In. Prakash uncle was very grateful and made a whole lot of cash on them. He recently gave me some as keepsakes to remember those books I had read and touched as a kid. Sweet of him to have done so. Sweet of Blaise to have fed my addiction. Sweet of R. L. Stine to have scared me many a day and night. Sweet thrills of the dark night! "Reader Beware – You're in for a scare!" – live on!

CHAPTER 16

Robin Cook's Medical Thrillers

I NEVER KNEW ANYTHING about the actual sexual act until I read Robin Cook's *Brain*, a medical thriller par excellence.

That was when I had just started ninth grade. I had now access by the permission of Mrs. Ratnaswami to the teacher's bookshelves and believe me they were packed with thrillers, cheap paperback copies from the 1970s and 1980s, well-worn and thumbed.

I liked the synopsis of *Brain* and borrowed it. When I read my very first sex scene in the book, I was aghast for a few minutes then just took it in my stride and went on reading. It took me a week to finish the book.

"Oh, you are reading Robin Cook!" exclaimed Blaise when I came back from my math tuition class with the library-borrowed Robin Cook still in my hand. He sounded shaky and a bit uncomfortable. I knew what was going on in his head: "THERE ARE SEX SCENES IN THE BOOK!"

The boy I liked at school was also reading medical thrillers, though he preferred Arthur Hailey to Robin Cook. But I loved Robin Cook. Reading his books made me a mature girl and introduced me to the word *sex*.

Mama was not pleased that I was reading thrillers from the teachers' bookshelves.

"Why are you reading porn?" Mama growled as I read Robin Cook's *Coma* on the common bed on a rainy July afternoon. For Mama, adult books meant porn. She has changed her opinion and has become more broad-minded since I've become a writer.

But back then, she was always on my case. Still, I was hooked on Robin Cook, not because of the sex but because of the mystery, the workings of a hospital, biology, biochemistry, and so many science-related things that I was interested in reading.

Robin Cook's style is character-centered; his books always have strong protagonists. The suspense in his books kept me on the edge, and I started to love biology after reading his books. In fact, even though I am an arts student, I have taught biology at my tutorial for the past seven years because I learned a lot about the subject, thanks to the medical thrillers of Robin Cook.

I've practically read all of Robin Cook's books; I read them in ninth and tenth grade. I read *Brain*, then *Coma, Harmful Intent, Godplayer, Mutation, Vital Signs, Mortal Fear, Terminal, Fever,* in that order, then ...

"She is reading porn," my poor, deluded mama went on as she saw me reading more and more of Robin Cook's books. Mechu stepped in and tried to make peace. She had to, because there were a lot of fights and disagreements about the type of books I was reading.

Mechu tried her very best to calm mama down. "Fiza is growing up. She is a reader; it's natural for her to read these books."

But Mama wouldn't listen. I felt so mortified, but I continued to read.

Then surprise, surprise, during the second term of ninth grade, something awkward happened. As I've mentioned before, each term we chose from three books to read for compulsory reading, and then we were tested on them. Well, this time a forward-thinking teacher suggested the following three books for our reviews:

1. *Hotel* by Arthur Hailey
2. *Strong Medicine* by Arthur Hailey

3. *Coma* by Robin Cook

The parents at BSS were in a rage. All the books had sex scenes and one had a rape or two.

Mama was furious. A parent called and informed her about the contents of each book, and I was given the lecture of my life. I was angry, and when I was angry back then, I stayed quiet in one place and continued reading.

Everyone was sexed up. And I found the whole thing such a drag.

In 2017, I was binge-reading Robin Cook books borrowed from a local library. I was twenty-seven and Mama saw me sitting there with my book. She looked at it, smiled at me, and said, "He's a really good writer, isn't he?"

I nodded and Mama went back to the tuition house to teach her next class. As I watched her receding figure, I remembered the days when she was so overprotective that she couldn't even bear to see me read books that contained sex scenes. Mama is old-fashioned and a true Roman Catholic. I am just an avid reader.

Eventually the biology teacher in the tenth grade taught us about sex. In my case, no one at home wanted to broach the subject, so I'd been on my own on the subject. I grew up with the help of books, and I loved my Robin Cook thrillers.

My favorite Robin Cook is *Harmful Intent*. I just love the flow of that book. It taught me the ways of the world of medicine. I loved the anaesthetist protagonist and, since his love interest was a cat lover, she made a place for herself in my bookcase heart – the one with the hairballs! – as well.

Robin Cook's books are well researched, interesting, and easy to follow. He keeps you guessing through to the end. I encourage all adults and young adults to read his books.

If I grew interested in the subject of biology in high school, it was only because of the writings of Robin Cook. I always read every book he releases, and I am waiting to get his latest sometime in 2019.

I presume parents have become broader minded over the years and have realized that it's all right to allow your young adult or teenager to read a sex scene in a book. I've always believed that books introduce this delicate topic much better than anything else can.

If you are looking for a medical thriller, Robin Cook is your man. Other writers in this genre are Michael Crichton, Tess Gerritsen, Michael Palmer to name a few. Looking for a medical thriller as your first, but don't know whom to pick, Robin Cook is the best bet. If you are reading Robin Cook for the first time, I suggest *Coma* or *The Life of An Intern.* His books are page-turners so, you will need to have two to three Cooks with you if you are traveling long distances by plane or train or ship. Doctors who want to read something about medical life must read Robin Cook's books – a vast repertoire of thirty-seven books and counting.

ESSAY 17

St. Andrew's College Library

AFTER THE BOMBAY SCOTTISH SCHOOL closed for the summer in 2005, I spent the long two-and-a-half-month summer vacation in a way most students in Mumbai do – I started working on my CV.

I had practically nothing to put on it; I had to start from scratch. First of all, I was not a good public speaker. In fact, I couldn't speak at all, couldn't converse properly, couldn't make conversation. I couldn't open my mouth in front of an audience. I used to freeze. And how, pray tell, can a teacher afford not to speak? I had to do something quickly.

So, I started out by joining the public speaking course conducted by the Redemptorists, whose main task is preaching the Word of God. The class was given under public speaking expert Father Frankie. It was a two-week course that taught adults public speaking.

After two sessions, Fr. Frankie called Blaise for a private meeting, without me.

"The girl doesn't speak," he said bluntly. "She doesn't speak at all. She needs to read less and speak more. Otherwise she can forget becoming a teacher; the girl will not be able to converse with anyone in society."

When Blaise tried to explain my quiet ways, Father Frankie was adamant: "She must concentrate on speaking. She is living in a society. The girl will have to speak."

The girl will have to speak.

I didn't stop carrying novels to the workshop, but Father Frankie pushed all of us to speak, especially me. He dubbed me an intellectual, but one without a voice. I am grateful to him and the Redemptorists for giving me a voice, a powerful loud voice and good public speaking skills. Without their help, I wouldn't be the Shakespearean expert I am today. I passed and got my very first certificate, my first ever certificate for my CV.

Then I took to playing the guitar and piano. I learned French for a month, I did a yoga course, and read and read and read all through the day. The books I read during this period were Agatha Christie's, thrillers, and the complete set of Sherlock Holmes mysteries.

I was a new person when I joined St. Andrew's College. I was still a solitary soul, but I had made some friends and had a lot of conversations. In the eyes of others, I was a bit pretty, too. So it was easy to make friends. (If only I knew then how easy it is to lose friends when one gains weight, but I'll talk more about that later.) Back then life was good. I studied, I passed every year either with a first class or a distinction. I took part in extracurricular and co-curricular activities. I joined many college clubs and organizations. Yes, St. Andrew's was good to and for me.

Along with St. Andrew's College, I owe gratitude to its vast library that educated me and changed the way I looked at myself and the world.

In fact, I chose St. Andrew's because I got a peek into the library before the admission lists were out. You can trust me to choose a college because of the library.

Besides, I didn't want to go to a college in town, because that's where my schoolmates were going, and I didn't want to see their faces again, not for another three centuries! So I chose a college they would never think of applying to, and that's how I became the only

Bombay Scottish student in the Arts batch of 2005 First Year Junior College (FYJC).

Before I got my identity card ready, I had already checked myself into the library. Whenever my friends couldn't find me in class, they knew where to check; the college library.

I took part in college discussions and activities. But everyone knew that I was a bit different. They knew I liked my own space, had quirks, and was highly eccentric. Basically, I was a reclusive introvert just trying to fit in with the crowd. I won my way through sometimes, and sometimes I didn't. I was different; I was always introspective, not to mention always reading!

I read a vast number of books in college, including those written on the subjects of psychology, sociology, logic, philosophy, literature, history, ethics, political science, case studies, biographies – you name it and I was there reading it!

The college librarian was not a Mrs. Ratnaswami, so there were no special privileges for me. Either we followed the rules or we were banned from using the college library.

"Tea-chai?" The librarian once held out a cup to me. I had started staying long hours in the library, and she'd noticed.

"Thank you, ma'am!" I accepted the milky hot tea and took a sip.

"You're the one from Bombay Scottish, yes?" she asked in a whisper as if we were discussing a touchy topic.

"Yeah!" I answered. "I'm in the Arts section."

"So, I've heard," she muttered and then walked away.

That's the only real conversation we ever had. Oh, how I missed Mrs. Ratnaswami and Aruna, my library buddies.

I joined college wanting to graduate with honors in English Literature. Everyone in my family thought I would do just that.

"Then I'll do my MA," I told Mama one day, when I had returned from college full of pluck and with a Simone de Beauvoir book in my sling bag.

Mama was to the point. "None of that," she said. "After majoring in English, you will go straight to teachers training college and get your license to teach."

"But Mama," I whined.

"No." She was firm. "This MA can be done any time. But the government's rules keep on changing day by day. There is no telling what they will do next. The country's educational universities are in turmoil. If you don't have that teacher's degree, you will not get your proper salary. The master's degree can wait. The teachers' college cannot."

Seeing the reason behind her words, I listened to her.

Yes, the country of India and the city of Mumbai were not at their best. Goof-ups were happening in the University of Mumbai: papers were being leaked, results were not declared on time, the mismatching of names and marks often occurred, and the university lacked qualified staff to teach particular subjects. In general, there was a faulty examination system, so the whole business of getting a degree was a nightmare!

Terrible tension existed in the city of Mumbai as well, what with the 7/11 train bomb blasts in 2006 and the 9/11 terrorist attack in 2008. It was a time of uncertainty, corruption, insurgency, and confusion.

I spent hours in the library or in the history room, alone, studying for my exams or reading books. I first read books based on literature, but soon became drawn toward history and sociology.

I read books about the National Movement in India, the Cold War, feminism, the LGBTQIA community, the Green revolution in Punjab, the Civil War of America, the history of the USSR, the Kashmir issue, the LOC border, sexual crimes against minorities, the battle of Waterloo, the Constitution of India, the Dalit movement, the legacy of Subhas Chandra Bose, communalism, the Chinese Civil War, the Naxalite movement, communism, the rights of minorities, regionalism, racism, Black history, and so on and so forth.

The St. Andrew's College library was brimming to overflow with all the books I needed to feed myself upon. I was studious and idealistic, good at desk jobs and meticulous in my studies. I realized there was a whole world doing queer things out there, and here I was, a solitary soul not making even a dent in the annals of this vast expanse of current contemporary living.

I read and reread. I was the first to enter the library and the last to leave. I read newspapers: the *Mumbai Mirror* and the *Mid-Day*. However, I was so involved in my books that I didn't have time to read other papers unless something really urgent had happened.

Then one day, I veered toward religion. I wanted to join the convent.

"It's a phase," Mechu told Mama, who was wary and heartbroken. "She'll move on. The convent is not a joke these days."

But everyone else was not so sure. I was really into not only my religion but *all* religions. I was seventeen years old, and I wanted to know the truth!

"The truth is you are mad," said good old Ratan uncle on one of his monthly visits to our home. "Those nuns are lesbians, aren't they? Nah – nah," he clicked his tongue in disapproval. "Not the convent for heaven's sake! Don't get married if you want, but don't join the convent, Fiza."

"That's what we've been trying to tell her," said my exasperated mama. "She has such a bright future. She is doing so well in college, standing first in Hindi and history and what-not. Why the convent?"

"By the way," asked Ratan uncle in between slurps of tea. "Which convent are you planning on joining?"

Mama looked the other way. Blaise narrowed his eyes. Both knew what I would say but were praying I wouldn't say it to Ratan uncle. But I did. I couldn't hold myself in.

"The cloistered convent," I murmured.

Ratan uncle thought for a minute. The smile drained from his face. He sipped his tea with a disturbed mind.

Cloistered convent, the one where once you get in, you never come out again. Ever.

ESSAY 18

Crossword Bookstore, Bandra

THE COLLEGE WAS A TEN-MINUTE DRIVE away from my home and I used to either take a rickshaw or walk, if I couldn't get one.

Near St. Andrew's College on Turner Road, in 2005, the new branch of the Crossword Bookstore arrived. I was there with Blaise and Mama the first day it opened. I bought omnibuses of Wilbur Smith's books, a medical thriller by Robin Cook, and some classics I had not yet read.

"Well," Mama said happily. "I am sure you will be spending a lot of time here."

"It even has a café attached to it," said Blaise pointing to the first floor where the teenage and children's books were displayed. Yes, there was a corner café, so there would be plenty to eat.

We were not that well off, and yet I was so obsessed with books (still am) that I did not feel bad spending any amount of Mama's, Blaise's, and Mechu's hard-earned money on brand-new books, and hardbacks at that! That was perhaps not so nice of me, but my family was so supportive of my reading obsession that they gladly went along.

"It's not drugs, at least," reasoned Mechu as she shelled out money at the cash counter.

I should have known better, but I was sixteen and I had sold my soul to books so, for me, there was no argument where that was concerned. When I was not browsing and buying books, I used to sit in the café, eat a sandwich or two, and people-watch. I loved people-watching. I still love it. Little did I know that the people-watching I was doing would one day provide characters for my stories.

I brought my college friends to the bookstore a few times, but everyone found that a drag. So I was usually alone while visiting Crossword. Those were the days of great reads. I usually bought the latest fiction and nonfiction from Crossword because neither BSS library nor the college library kept the latest copies of paperbacks penned by Jeffery Archer, Lee Child, David Baldacci, Jo Nesbo, Robin Cook, Dean Koontz, Mary Higgins Clarke, Håkan Nesser, Jack Higgins, et al. (As you can see, I'm a sucker for thrillers!) And I used to buy them in hardback at astronomical prices.

As the years went by, I graduated to reading better literature, known as literary fiction. I read a lot of V. S. Naipaul, starting with *A House for Mr. Biswas*, and went on to read Orhan Pamuk, Alice Munro's short stories, Salman Rushdie's *Midnight's Children*, and others.

But the best part about Crossword was its classic section. There were so many different classics arranged according to different publishers. The classics were cheap then, some retailing at ₹125 or ₹150, about $2 in American money.

"What do you like so much about a bookshop?" my collegemate Lata once asked me. Lata loved Bollywood gossip and watching Hindi soap operas and listening to Bollywood and Hindi pop on the radio.

"I asked you a question," she went on when I didn't answer, pulling at my white sweatshirt. "What do you like so much about a bookshop?"

I got out of her grip and smirked.

"Books are my father; I was abandoned as a child by my biological father because I was a girl."

"Do things like that happen these days?" asked Richard, my desk partner.

I bit my lip.

"Well, it happened in 1989 on the nineteenth of March," I said and went back to the Jeffery Archer book I was reading.

I was conversing with friends and acquaintances during this period in my life, but I still preferred being on my own. To be frank, I hated talking; conversations bored me. They drained me as well. And Lata used to talk so much! Back in the FYJC and SYJC, she used to fry my brains with all her nonsense about this and that and the other.

I often hid out at Crossword when I wanted to get away from Lata and the others. It was my fortress, my haven. It had a wonderful smell, which I loved inhaling as I entered the premises. Yes, I hated talking, but I had to in order to conduct projects, do assignments, and win debating prizes. But all that meant very little to me. All I wanted was to be by myself, and to read and write stories.

Mama retired as a teacher from Bombay Scottish School in 2009, during my final year of degree college. She broached the money angle to me very gently. "Look, Fiza," she said, "I'm not working anymore, so I can't pay for your new books anymore. I need to build up on my tuitions. I suggest you start working to earn your keep."

I looked at her and then to the floor. She nodded encouragingly. "When I was at your age, I was already teaching and earning for the family."

I was twenty when she said these words. That made me an adult overnight, and I started tutoring schoolchildren.

I started out earning ₹2,000 a month (about $30 in American money), teaching history and geography to an eighth-grade student. I saved ₹1,000 monthly in a new savings account I opened with Corporation Bank and kept the other ₹1,000 as money for books. When I went to Crossword after that, I started buying only one or a maximum of two books. I selected my purchase, took it to a corner, and calculated what I could afford on my cell phone calculator. The old watchman at Crosswords used to see me do this and nod in approval. Today, he is still there at Bandra Crossword, and when he sees me stepping out of Crossword's carrying bags of newly purchased books, he salutes me.

He remembers when I had to count my pennies. And I'll remember him too.

News spread that I was a good teacher. By the end of 2009, I had four more tuitions to teach history, geography, English language, and literature. I was now earning a whopping ₹12,000 a month, about $120, all in less than a year's time. I banked ₹6,000 and used the other half to buy books at Crossword.

I've come a long way since then. It's hard to believe fourteen years have passed since the first time I walked into Crossword. I still have much to do, more books to write, more children to teach, and a masters' degree in history to complete.

Mama is proud of me. She always boasts about me to the kids we teach. Mama has been my idol as a teacher and an organizer. She taught me to break the mold. She taught me to be independent. She taught me that I did not need a man in my life to get the things I want. I'm grateful to her in so many ways.

"You have his mannerisms," said Mama one hot afternoon as I was cooling under the fan.

"What mannerisms? Whose? Papa's?"

Mama nodded. "Your smile and face come from me, but your mannerisms, certain things are all his. And it's so strange that you have them," she mused as she drank her cup of tea. "Because you've never really known him or lived with him. I guess it's genes?"

"Yes," I said in a faraway voice full of bitterness and resignation. "Genes!"

I now rarely go to Crossword. It still has its smell and the coffee there is good. The watchman is the one who misses me the most.

"*Bahut dino baad aye hai beti* (You have come here after many days, baby)," he'll say as I enter the store, and I get all choked up. My elderly friend, the Crossword Bandra watchman.

But what about the convent? Yes, I thought about it and was dead serious, even while I was going to Crossword. But a storm was brewing that would shake my life apart, and that's why I once again with-drew into myself.

ESSAY 19

St. Andrew's College Library 2

I WANTED TO JOIN the convent; the cloistered convent.

It was a craving I couldn't let go of. Everyone at home was at a loss when it came to what to say or how to go about discussing it.

"She doesn't belong in a convent," Blaise would tell my mama. "What put that in her head?"

I was brought up as a staunch Catholic with liberal views thanks to all the reading I did, and also the talks I had with Blaise. I was fascinated by convent life and thought that a cloistered order, away from everyone, was the solution to all of my problems.

I worked hard in college. I was getting excellent grades. I spent hours writing and reading in the history common room and the college library. It was during this time that I started writing parables and articles for various Catholic magazines.

I was featured in *The Examiner* in their youth pages, in my college magazine, and "The Vision and Venture" magazine many times. I joined the church youth group. I managed to become the deanery youth head in 2008 and the female youth representative of Archdiocese of Mumbai erstwhile Bombay. I became a lector for every Wednesday-evening mass. I taught Sunday school. I was the youth representative of my parish for *The Examiner*, I attended SCC meetings, attended Bible classes, did desk jobs for the youth events of the Diocese Youth Committee (DYC), and studied religious works like a professional.

Against my better judgment, I had told everyone in college that I wanted to become a nun, and that was a mistake. Everyone thought I was joking. When they realized I wasn't, it made them really uncomfortable.

"You are Muslim, aren't you?" one of my college classmates said. "Your name is Fiza Pathan."

"I am a baptized Roman Catholic and follow my mother's religion," I answered.

"But then why keep that horrible name?" he said.

I smirked and continued reading a book about the lives of the doctors of the Catholic church.

In school I didn't face any kind of communalism or racism because no one ever spoke to me. So, I was quite stunned with the way some of the people I knew in youth group needled me about my Muslim origins. It was becoming seriously annoying. I believed and still believe in pluralism. I couldn't understand why some people, especially people from the church, questioned and made jokes about me and my Muslim name.

To make matters worse, I was proving to be difficult to deal with. I had a mind of my own and, for me, my first responsibility was to my tuitions and studies. The church couldn't or maybe didn't want to understand that; they wanted me to be totally dedicated to church work. They also wanted me to do something else:

"Fiza, why can't you mingle with the youth and be like everybody else?" asked one of the priests in charge of my area of work. "Act like a *normal* youth and be fun loving, chill, and ready for adventure. Stop acting like an old scholar bathed in the dust of books, and live!"

I never understood why being a reclusive introvert was such a crime. This was the same priest who, when traveling in a group on church work, said to the others, "Look there. It's Fiza's church!" when we passed a masjid or mosque.

I faced this kind of opposition everywhere I went. Everyone wanted me to be what I was not. Sure, I'm a good worker, but I'm a loner. Is that a crime?

Things got nasty at one youth event in Mulund, when one of the nun's called me a terrorist in public. That was a very awkward moment; I was frozen in place.

I told this story to Blaise, Mama, Mechu, and the rest.

"And this is the mentality of the people you want to join?" asked Blaise in anger. "How dare she say something like this. A terrorist has no religion. She should do a brain scan!"

I felt odd, cheated, and worthless. The feelings I experienced at BSS came rushing back like vomit. I started withdrawing. I began to spend all of my time in the college library and history lecture room, studying my course material.

There was another bombshell I dropped on Mama. I refused to major in English Literature. I decided, instead, to do a double major in history and sociology, my two favorite subjects, which I'd come to love during my years of study in college.

"If that's what you want it's fine with me," said Mama as she corrected tuition books on her lap dressed in her floral nightdress. "But you know you are a natural in English. You are so good that tuition kids are pouring in just for your expertise in teaching English."

But I was adamant, just like I was adamant about the convent. And so, in 2010, I graduated in Arts in my chosen subjects. I secured a first-class degree, majoring in history and sociology. I joined teacher's college, run by the Carmelite nuns. The experience was so horrible that my "vocation" disappeared, or rather I threw it out of the window.

I spent the last year of college at St. Andrew's reading books about history and sociology.

I was fascinated by the Indian National Movement and read everything about it that I could get my hands on. I was also studying, rather ironically, terrorism and about al-Qaeda along with their impact in all institutions of life. I also studied library sciences with Lata, who was doing a project on it.

Both Lata and I had decided to become teachers and join the same teachers training college. Unfortunately, Lata's orthodox Hindu father refused to allow Lata to study further than her basic BA.

"In our community, girls don't study, much less work," he said in a matter-of-fact tone when Mama and I went to his house to change his mind. He stood firm as a rock.

"Girls in our community don't spoil the family name by working. My daughter has to get a husband and for that she must stop studying."

When we continued to argue with him, he turned on us and aimed his poisoned barbs. "You both are without male figures in your lives, so it doesn't matter what you do. You both are free to do as you please. But not my daughter. She has a future, madam."

Lata's dreams of a further education were dashed to the ground. I was put in my place and stayed there, sort of.

❋

In my last year of college, I did a sociology project on the Muslim woman's hijab and its history. I got nineteen out of twenty for it. I was called to give a talk about it as chief guest at St. Andrew's while I was studying at my teachers' training college. It was that good. I researched it in the college library. Father Frankie's training made me a good public speaker. I held the audience's attention.

I also did projects on topics like the history of East Indian cuisine, the Discovery of India Museum, and a study of my alma mater's heritage.

I passed out of St. Andrew's College in 2010. I had changed in many ways, some of them mental, some of them physical. When I entered, I was 45 kgs on the weighing scale. When I left, I was 100 kgs.

I had become obese.

And no one let me forget that.

❋

I had made friends in college easily when I was 45 kgs. But the moment my belly fat started showing, I had girls and boys saying the rudest things to me. In BSS, my trauma was that no one spoke to me, and now here it was that everyone spoke to me, but only because I'd become an object of ridicule. The people I had considered my best friends were even worse than monsters.

"Hey, check her tummy tum," said one of my closest friends as she lifted up my T-shirt in front of everyone in a girl's common room. She was even wanting to lift it higher, almost undressing me. I pushed her away, pulled my shirt down, and ran for my life back into the college library.

The snide remarks, nicknames like fatty, fatso, gummy fatty Fiza, *moti*, fat cunt, etc., showed up more and more often, along with so many hopelessly embarrassing moments, that it felt like all these so-called friends of mine had only liked me because of my waistline.

It was like I *lost* every single friend when I *gained* weight.

I was back to square one. Back to being alone in a library. No Mrs. Ratnaswami or Aruna here to help me out. I was shaken. I was broken. And who stood by me? Only books.

I wrote my first book, *S.O.S. Animals And Other Stories,* when I was twenty years old, sitting in the history lecture room. It took me two months, and then I submitted it for serialization in a Catholic magazine.

They accepted one of my stories but then backed out of their promise to me. I knocked on the door of another Catholic publication house but they turned me down as well.

After securing my BEd degree in 2011, I taught for a year in a prestigious ICSE school. Then, in 2012, after a brief stint at teaching, Blaise and I published *S.O.S. Animals And Other Stories* on Amazon through CreateSpace. I was by then working at home, giving tuitions, and writing full-time. I was twenty-two years old when I became a published writer.

I have spent years teaching, writing, and looking for a peaceful place to write.

I would eventually become a publisher by age twenty-seven and would rent my own office-cum-writing hut.

But before that I was struggling. Blaise and Mama helped out with time but not money. The money was all my own. I had earned quite a sum. Some of the amount I banked every month. Some I spent on my publishing needs and, of course, books to read.

My weight was increasing year after year. I was a joke in the eyes of everyone. I was obese. I was fat. I was ugly. I didn't deserve respect. I was all alone once again.

ESSAY 20

Agatha Christie's Detective Books

I DISCOVERED AGATHA CHRISTIE in the BSS school library. The queen of detective fiction became the queen of my heart. I so loved her books.

"Child," Mrs. Ratnaswami said shrilly, as I piled up nine Agatha Christie books to be checked out of the library before I went on mid-term break. Aruna laughed as she dusted the preschool section of books.

The first book I read of Agatha Christie's was *After the Funeral,* a Hercule Poirot mystery. It was a perfect work of suspense and detection on the Belgian detective's part and I was hooked.

Hercule Poirot became a greater detective to me than even Sherlock Holmes (blasphemy – blasphemy – blasphemy); his detection skills are legendary. The mind of Agatha Christie, his creator, is out of this world.

My first Miss Marple book was *4.50 From Paddington.* I liked Miss Marple but I *loved* the dandy, moustachioed Hercule Poirot even more.

I discovered these pearls in a bookcase dedicated to the queen of detectives and whodunits. BSS library actually had two copies of *And*

Then There Were None, though they were rare editions from the 1930s with the original racist title, *Ten Little Niggers*.

It was the winter of 2003 and I was in the ninth grade when I started reading Agatha Christie books. After reading *After the Funeral* I went on a binge diet of Christies and read:

- *After the Flood*
- *4.50 from Paddington*
- *They Came to Baghdad*
- *The Big Four*
- *And Then There Were None*
- *Three Little Pigs*
- *The Mirror Crack'd from Side to Side*
- *They Do It with Mirrors*
- *Cat Among the Pigeons*
- *Hercule Poirot's Christmas* and
- *Evil Under the Sun*

Blaise was also an Agatha Christie fan and gifted me her books during Christmas. I read *Murder on the Orient Express* in less than ten hours' time and immediately took up *Murder Is Easy*. I could spend hours without moving, totally engrossed in an Agatha Christie mystery. Blaise liked Poirot but had a soft corner for Miss Marple because of all her chattering and digressing.

"If you read her digressions, Fiza, you'll become a master in writing," Blaise always swore.

Agatha Christie books of detection were entertainment unlimited, with a lot of suspense, no sex, and with such sinister plots that it could give you the creeps if you read them at night. I made a big mistake by beginning a new Agatha Christie, *And Then There Were None,* at 1:00 a.m.! I was so freaked out that I had to hug my mama in order to go to sleep.

Most of the kids at BSS had already read Agatha Christie, but I've always been a late bloomer. Even the boy I had a crush on had already read Agatha Christie books way back in the sixth and seventh grade. He found my fascination amusing. I was happy that he took any interest at all in me, even if it was not exactly in the way that I wanted.

Agatha Christie's plots are intricate, which makes it very difficult to close in on the murderer or homicidal maniac. I never guessed correctly; Christie always managed to stump me. *And Then There Were None* really stumped me. I was wondering if there was a supernatural element to the plot.

"Are you planning a murder, child?" Mrs. Ratnaswami asked me with an air of mirth. "Thinking of poisoning a teacher?"

"Oh, I wish!" I said as dear Mrs. Ratnaswami stamped the book and I headed to my corner to read.

When I joined St. Andrew's College, Blaise had provided me with omnibuses of Agatha Christie books. They came according to the detective or according to the decade when the collection was penned and published. I used to read these gigantic omnibuses in college, mostly the Marple books that were easily available in Mumbai. This was way before Amazon hit Mumbai.

It was 2005.

"Hey, want to come?" asked one of my new acquaintances at college.

"Come where?" I asked my eyes never leaving the book.

She came close to my right ear. She whispered, "Rave party, in Navi Mumbai. An all-weekend party."

I almost dropped the book.

"Er, no thank you, I don't do drugs."

"Who's telling you to become a druggie?" this acquaintance asked, "Just hang around and try some of the stuff once in a while. And it's not just me who wants you to be there," she looked furtively around as she spoke. "The host, a college senior and a really handsome guy has taken a shine to you. He asked me to invite you."

"No, thank you," I said, not the least bit flattered. "I'm busy reading now, please excuse me."

She left thinking I would end up changing my mind. I never did. I don't like parties, drinks, drugs, or smoking. I was reading *Murder at the Vicarage* by Agatha Christie and wanted to continue doing so.

Throughout my first two years of college, I received several invites to parties that I refused. It was always the same: a senior had a certain something for me, and I was supposed to accept. Most of these parties happened either at Lonavala, Khandala, Thane, Navi Mumbai, Pune – basically outside of Mumbai. And, yes, most of them were raves. I was too busy with my books to go.

I quickly gained the reputation of a bookworm. I was left alone with my select group of friends, mostly girls. I introduced Agatha Christie to these friends of mine, and they really liked her books. They especially loved *And Then There Were None*, the story of ten people ferried to a deserted island and one by one dying according to a nursery rhyme jingle. Spooky, but it won me a few friends.

Lata never read, as I've mentioned before, but she was fascinated by the omnibuses and loved to smell their vanilla-fresh print pages. That's one of the reasons I liked her, and ultimately she became my best friend in college.

I've read almost all of the Agatha Christie detective novels and short story collections. All except one. I have never read *Curtains*, Poirot's final case, and I'll never read it because I don't want to see my hero detective die. Not now, not ever. I read Miss Marple's final cases while at college, but no, I could not read *Curtains*.

Blaise is always teasing me about it. He read *Curtains* ages ago and said it was a masterpiece. He doesn't read the Agatha Christie fandom fiction because he prefers the original. I read the fandom books and really love them, too, but please don't ask me to read *Curtains*.

I continue to read Agatha Christie to this day. I highly recommend her detective stories to all.

If you haven't read a detective book yet and you are in middle or high school, then look no further than Agatha Christie. If you are an adult and haven't read her books yet, what are you waiting for? Start with *And Then There Were None*, but don't read it at night or you will be spooked. If you prefer detective books set in the early part of the twentieth century, then her books are your best bet.

If you want to sample a good Poirot book, try *Murder on the Orient Express*. If you want to start with little old Miss Marple, *4.50 from Paddington* won't disappoint.

Agatha Christie created immortal detectives that will never fade from our minds. She is the originator of whodunit books of detection. I've read many detective stories in the twenty-nine years of my life, but Agatha Christie still holds a prime place in my life as a writer who is par excellence. She deserves all the accolades I and the whole writers' fraternity shower upon her. May her legacy always live in the minds of future readers.

"This is a detective book, nah?" asked Aruna when I was reading, during one of the free days of college, at the BSS library. "What's the name?"

"*Murder on the Links*," I answered.

"*Yeh murder* Link Road *pe hua hai kya*? Bandra *mein*?" asked a naïve but adorable Aruna. "*Nonfiction hai kya*?"

No, I told her, *Murder on the Links* isn't about a murder in Linking Road in Bandra, and it's not a true story. And that is one thing I'm glad of. Agatha Christie's stories are fictional. I would have freaked out if murderers were as evil as she makes them out to be.

ESSAY 21

The Hurting Years

MY YEARS OF PAIN CONTINUED when Mama retired from BSS after a long and dutiful service of thirty-five years. Can you imagine? Mama spent thirty-five years of her life teaching in one school! She was more than willing to continue, but the rule was clear: a teacher retires at the age of 58. The law of the land, the law of BSS.

Mama informed me that money would not be plentiful anymore. I would have to work, and since I was going to be a teacher myself, I'd might as well take tuitions to provide for myself. Back then Mama made it clear that I didn't have to pay for the family's upkeep; that was her department. I just had to earn and provide for my own needs, which was books mainly, and that too only a few – it was a fair bargain.

I started giving tuitions. The tuitions multiplied, like the four loaves and two fish that Jesus multiplied. I went to teachers training college and after a grueling day's work of teaching I ran back home to teach my new students, most of whom studied English with me. I didn't have the best time of my life at teachers training college. I came home crying practically every day. The same went for my first job as a ninth- and tenth-grade teacher at an ICSE school in Mumbai. Somehow or the other, I was always doing something wrong. People hated me. They thought my behavior queer, but it was only my reclusive and introverted personality trying to fit in with the rest of society.

I was hurting. Seriously hurting. Everyone wanted me to be something I was not. I was twenty-one years old and I was teaching sixteen-year-olds at the ICSE school. I was feeling trapped, ostracized, and depressed. My idealism died a cruel death. I don't want to go more into this because of, you've guessed it, defamation. What I have to say is that 2010 to 2012 was a hell for me. I was hurting, but I couldn't confide in anyone. Dr. D. P.N Prasad retired with Mama. The new rules of the new BSS principal stated that former students would not be allowed into the school unless they were invited for a special function. The door to the BSS library had been slammed in my face.

Mrs. Ratnaswami retired, and I never had a chance to say goodbye. I was not allowed in the school without prior permission. Many other things happened that I cannot afford to write about.

But the worst cut of all was the way my father, the BSS library, was taken from me. Little did anyone know what I lost when I lost my true papa. Little did anyone know of my agony and tears.

By 2012, I left my day job as a teacher. I was broken, but I was on fire. I knew what I wanted. I immediately started work again from scratch. I built up the tuitions into a tutorial. Blaise and I finally published *S.O.S. Animals And Other Stories* on Amazon through CreateSpace. It was a gamble that made way for my life afterwards. I became a writer overnight. God or providence closed many doors in my face, but He did something even better. He opened the windows, so many windows, and all of them reeked of printer's ink.

I apologize if I've let you down by not divulging the truth of these "hurting years."

It's not that I can't bear to talk about it. I'm a reclusive introvert, but I am very open in my writings. Yet, I cannot talk about the pain and suffering I went through during the hurting years. They happened ten years ago, and I've come a long way since. I have my own tutorial, I am a multiple-award-winning author and poet, I am the director of my own publishing firm, and I publish books under the imprint *Freedom With Pluralism*, a registered trademark. I'm a distributor of my own books in Mumbai. I write and teach full-time, and I've written twelve books so far, not counting the abridged classics I'm working on with my author-colleague, Michaelangelo Zane. I read at least one hundred books in a year, I blog on the website insaneowl, I review books, and do so many things bookish and in keeping with who I am. To me, all of this seems miraculous and would have been impossible, if not for certain choices made and by dint of hard work, persistence, and ambition.

These days I teach, write, read, and publish my own books. To make Hilaire Belloc's words my own, "When I am dead, I hope it may be said: Her sins were scarlet, but her books were read."

I work and live in my office-cum-writing hut. That's where I am right now, typing these words on my Dell Inspiron 11. My office is just two steps away from my ground-floor apartment. This is where I write and do the business work of the publishing firm. I have rented another flat next to mine for tuitions. These are the two places where I spend most of my time. Everyone here knows me and doesn't know me. I'm an enigma; rarely seen outside and once seen it's hard to believe that I was holed up either in my home, writing hut, or tuition room for such a long span of time.

But that's me, the recluse, the introvert, the book phoenix. For me, the following saying works both ways: "I live to read and I read to live."

How did all of this happen? Let's just say that everything fell into place once I knew what I wanted from life and myself, and after meeting the right people at the right time. I'm twenty-nine years old, I've got miles to go. With books by my side and books as my target, I've managed to live the life I've dreamed of: the life of a reclusive writer and reader of Mumbai.

I have no social life. I have no friends other than my colleague and co-author Michaelangelo Zane. People in my neighborhood know me as the silent but mad book lady who reads, writes, and teaches away from the crowd.

I'm alone, but I'm not lonely. I'm a solitary soul, but I also seem to be everywhere on the internet.

What's my story? Yet again, it's the story of all the bookstores and libraries in Mumbai that helped me on my way to where I am today. The story of the book phoenix of Mumbai is yet to be told, and I hope you as my reader will like to take this trip down memory lane, to all the book haunts that made me the silly old bookish fanatic I am.

❋

As for papa (BSS papa), when I managed to get a substituting job there in 2015, I went first thing to the library. But alas, all was over. The old heritage books had gone. The BSS library had rid itself of all of them.

"Baby?" came a familiar voice. I smiled, tears in my eyes.

It was my dear Aruna. Aruna the ever efficient and the ever dutiful.

"Baby – *tum ho na*?" she asked tentatively.

I rushed into her arms. We both were pale with fond memories.

"The books?" I asked in between sobs. Aruna turned her face away to hide her emotions. "Nothing is left, baby," she said with a steely voice. "Nothing of your time is left."

I silently passed through the shelves. Aruna went back into the inner sanctum of the library.

She was right; all the nineteenth century and early twentieth century books were gone. In fact, all the rare books and classics of the BSS library had been taken away and replaced with trash. This was the junior library. The senior one was in the new building, run by the then junior librarian of my R. L. Stine past who was now the senior librarian there.

I ran. I ran, hoping against hope.

The senior library was a disappointment. It was so small and with very few books worth mentioning at all. The librarian of my past recognized me as I came off the lift.

"You are Fiza Pathan, right? Mrs. Pathan's daughter? I'm sorry, child, but they got rid of it all."

"They were heritage books," I choked on my words unable to hide my resentment and my pain. "They were worth more together than the school's heritage structure. How could you?"

She lowered her gaze.

"I'm sorry for your loss," she said gently. She meant it. She was a good person. She understood.

"Why don't you come in here?" she asked in a friendly tone. "Let's have tea? Or would you prefer coffee?"

I never went in. I was too broken. BSS papa – gone forever.

Whatever you tore from me made my paper heart bleed,
I cried but there were no pages to stain with salty drops;
No message and no telegram to say you were gone,
No more paper cuts but emptiness still as a vein inking the song –
A song of rustling paper and once-black blood, printers' ink!

I have never gone back. I still mourn my loss every day and every hour. This was the deepest cut of all, and I have not yet gotten over it. It still makes me cry to think I'll never see BSS library papa again.

Meanwhile my biological papa had found religion.

He started begging me to forgive him for the pain he had brought upon me. He asked me to accept the money he had saved all these years for me, apparently so that he could go without a guilty conscience for the Haj.

Can you believe this man!? He wanted me to accept his money so that he could go on a religious pilgrimage! Where was he when my mama needed him the most? Where was he when I was born? Where was all this money when my maternal family looked after me using their hard-earned cash? Where was he, and why the sudden mock show of religion?! What kind of religion allows you to go on Haj even if you have neglected your duties as a husband and father?

"Fiza *beta*," Papa crooned through my smartphone. "Please accept this money and let your old Papa go on pilgrimage, *beta*. *Beta*, please. Then my responsibilities will be complete. *Beta*, please, I am your papa *beta* – Fiza *beta*, please."

I told him I didn't want his money. If he is so insistent about going on his Haj then he can take all that he has saved in my name and donate it to an orphanage – where girl children are abandoned at birth because they were born girls.

He still is adamant about the money. He hasn't seen the light yet.

"She has hit upon the right solution," Ratan uncle said on one of my birthdays as he drank a glass of Pepsi. "Let him donate it to an orphanage. Mother Teresa's ashram is there in Byculla. Why does he have to annoy this little one? I can't understand his logic."

"What logic?" Blaise groaned in frustration as he sat folded armed next to me. "He doesn't even know a thing about her. How she has managed it all on her own, her books, her international success – he doesn't know anything. He was always unreasonable and a leech. First it was the way he behaved with my sister; now it's her daughter."

I've had to change my phone numbers so many times. The loathsome man still talks down to me, as if I'm a child of five. Technically, I'm his legal heir. But I reject him and everything he has – just the way he rejected me twenty-nine years ago all because I was a girl.

"Forgive him and forget it all," my confessor and our family priest Fr. Bento Cardozo tells me when I make my confession to him. "He is to blame, certainly. But more than him it is you who will be healed by forgiveness. Because forgiveness works both ways: on the one who accepts and the one who gives."

I try to make sense of what Fr. Bento says. He holds my hand and absolves me for the sin of resentment. Then he says, "You are a son to this family. A son, born as a daughter, whom we all love and call Fiza Pathan."

I have always listened to the kind and compassionate words of our Fr. Bento. He has been a rock of strength for my family and me. He has stood by Mama, as well as her decision to separate from her husband. He has counseled me on the ways I lead my life. He has always tried to make a good Christian of me. More than that, Fr. Bento has worked very hard along with other male figures from my maternal family's side to tell me that a daughter is as precious as a son, if not more.

"Be healed by forgiveness, Fiza," Fr. Bento says as he reads a passage from the Bible during my confession. "Forgive us our debts as we forgive those who are indebted to us."

My biological papa believes he owes a debt to me. I can't change him.

But I can make him a chapter and turn the page over to start afresh. My bookish journey is yet to be told.

ESSAY 22

R. K. Narayan's Books

I HAD ALREADY READ *Swami and Friends* by R. K. Narayan from the BSS library. However, at that time I was more into international literature, not Indian fiction.

This would change in 2011.

It was the hot summer of 2011. I had just finished my teachers' training. I was spending my hot days taking long walks and reading books that I wasn't able to make time for when I was at the training college.

As I was going through my TBR (to be read) book pile, out popped *The English Teacher* by R. K. Narayan. I checked the publisher: it was by the Indian Thought Publication, on the occasion of the centenary of the writer, who happened to be the first Indian writer to have written books in English in pre-Independence India.

I was attracted by the title and the cover design of the book. I was going to be an English teacher in the coming school year, so I sat on the mat on the ground, pulled the table fan right next to me, turned the knob to full blast, and started reading.

I would never be the same person again. I was enthralled. I was overcome by R. K. Narayan's blunt prose.

This was it. This was literature. This was a master.

All these thoughts went on in my head as I read the story of an English professor who loses his wife to an illness and struggles to continue his life without her. R. K. Narayan's prose, his descriptions, his humor all captivated me.

I finished *The English Teacher* in two days' time. I then went to the Crossword Bandra bookstore to see if they had any more books by R. K. Narayan.

They did. I bought a bagful. I was addicted.

Known as the creator and Grand Old Man of Malgudi (i.e., the fictional South Indian town), R. K. Narayan has written numerous novels and short stories that mostly take place in the town of Malgudi. Malgudi is to me like Hogwarts is to some kids. I loved Narayan's fictional town and how his stories resemble the foibles of real people. Realism is what Narayan stands for in his art, and I love him for that. His humor is contagious, his characters intriguing, and his town of Malgudi eternal.

I read *The Bachelor of Arts* after *The English Teacher*. I loved the novel and the inanity of Indian customs and traditions left me in splits. I also read *The Bachelor of Arts* because that was what I was in the summer of 2011, a BA first-class graduate with a double major in history and sociology. If I passed my teachers' training board exams, I would become a BEd graduate.

I used to walk in my light blue jeans and black Elvis Presley T-shirts in and around Bandra West, my neighborhood. I carried a small sling bag in which I kept my water bottle and the latest Narayan novel or short story collection I was reading. I would sweat away, pass by familiar Bandra churches like St. Andrew's, St. Peter's, St. Anne's, St. Theresa's, etc. as I made my way to a new bookish haunt called the Sangita Library, near the St. Paul's Bookshop. I would return the *Archie* comic or the R. L. Stine Fear Street book I was binge reading, and pick something new for the day. I loved the smell of the Sangita Library, especially at dusk when the jasmine sticks were lit to ward off the mosquitoes.

I would then walk to the Guru Nanak park, which was near the library, sit on a park seat and read a Narayan book. I remember reading *The Vendor of Sweets* there as children played in the sand. I remember reading *The Painter of Signs* there as the elderly took their constitutional strolls. I was dripping wet with sweat, just like the characters in the fictional town of Malgudi.

"I've never read Malgudi books," said Blaise when I came home one evening after one of my long walks. It was dusk and the gulmohar tree's red-orange blossoms had carpeted the ground outside.

"Is he good?" asked Blaise as he thumbed through *The Vendor of Sweets*. "Seems very plain."

"You couldn't be more wrong," I snapped, defending Narayan, whom then I took to calling "my Narayan." I would narrate funny incidents from the books I was reading. Blaise laughed at most of my jokes. And then he experienced a brainwave.

"You know," he said, "when you were not born yet, in the 1980s, a chap called Nag made a Hindi-cum-English serial, *Malgudi Days*. Crosswords is selling the DVD collections of most of the old shows, like *Nukkad*, *Zabaan Sambhalke*, *Dekh Bhai Dekh*, etc. They may be having *Malgudi Days* as well."

I never had gone to the DVD section of Crossword. Never liked watching anything on TV, such a waste of precious literary time! But the next evening, Blaise and I made it to Crossword and there it was: a whole DVD collection of *Malgudi Days*.

Ta-na-na-na-na-na-na-NA!

"Oh, you two have brought home *Malgudi Days*?" said Rita as she recognized the jingle. "Fiza do you know, Nana loved to watch *Malgudi Days* on Doordarshan TV, and she loved the jingle tune. She would always sing it while working in the kitchen or grinding the masala with the grinding stone."

"Ta-na-na-na-na-na-na-NA!" came David uncle's voice, my elder saintly uncle as he sat down to watch a series he had first seen a very long time ago.

Blaise, Rita, Mama, and David uncle watched the series and I, more than watching, was trying to see if Nag had stuck to the original story or not.

"Fiza," David uncle, the patriarch of our family said. "Nana, before she became sick, would always sing this tune to you: Ta-na-na-na-na-na-na-NA! Ta-na-na-na-na-na-na-NA!"

I mulled over that memory. So that's why the tune sounded so familiar.

❋

As the years went by, my addiction to Malgudi stories increased with a passion unlike any other. I read all of R. K. Narayan's works by the time I was twenty-four years old. Narayan's prose and style of writing had been absorbed by me to such an extent that I have adopted his writing style as my own, with some of my own improvisation. The Narayan in me was evident in my novella *Nirmala: The Mud Blossom,* and it became a fixture in *Amina: The Silent One.*

My favorite Narayan books, which I am especially partial to are as follows:

1. *The Vendor of Sweets*
2. *The Talkative Man*
3. *Malgudi Days – Short Stories*
4. *The World of Nagaraj*
5. *Salt and Sawdust* and
6. *Mr. Sampath: The Printer of Malgudi*

I return to these R. K. Narayan classics whenever I need fuel in a literary sense.

To me R. K. Narayan is badass. He is the best writer I have ever read, and I don't care what anyone else thinks. The funny South Indian people of Malgudi may be fictional but they're so utterly real (you can find people like this in every part of the Indian subcontinent past, present and, I'm sure, future. Yes, we'll be dragging our eccentricities to the future as well, I'm quite sure about that.) And the future is when we'll realize that R. K. Narayan's books were not made for a particular age, but for everlasting time.

R. K. Narayan is my favorite writer. I owe most of my success in fiction writing to him.

His picture is framed upon a shelf that showcases some of my awards. He is in the center of my display, his face grim as he reads

Grahame Greene's *Reflections*. It is a black-and-white photo, and I love it. To his left are Munshi Premchand and William Shakespeare, and to his right are Dr. B. R. Ambedkar and Ruskin Bond. These are my literary masters, Narayan being the best of all.

Seems like a coincidence that the jingle from the television serial *Malgudi Days* that my nana loved in her old age would become my favorite jingle and would inspire the literary talent within me. Such are the circumstances that prompt me to think that somewhere out there, there is something or someone who has the answers to it all, even something as simple as the legendary South Indian town of Malgudi.

I recommend you read Narayan's work. Young readers should be cautious when making a selection because not all the Malgudi books are meant for younger readers. For students studying Indian literature, the Malgudi books are something you should be reading to see what the middle-class English-speaking professionals were thinking in the early years of our independence. Those of you who love books that make you laugh can choose any Narayan books that you wish. My favorite writer cannot hide his humor just the way I cannot hide my sadness.

Enter Malgudi and do not come back. I haven't come back yet, and it's done me a lot of good.

ESSAY 23

The Sangita Library

I JOINED THE SANGITA LIBRARY because it was close to home, had many of my favorite books from my teenage years, and was a good place to walk to and from during the college holidays.

The Sangita Library is situated in one of the inner roads of Turner Road, Bandra West. I don't know much about the owners of the place because, being the reclusive person I am, I never talked much with the two women who ran the library.

I loved my long walks in the Bandra West neighborhood, though. I loved visiting the numerous Bandra churches, the Guru Nanak park and the places thereabouts.

I used to go to the Sangita Library because it was reasonably priced and within my budget. I borrowed Archie double digests, R. L. Stine's Fear Street books, old paperbacks by Sidney Sheldon, Mary Higgins Clark, James Rollins, and Stephen King.

Whenever I went in there, I just picked my books and left. I always felt happy after coming out of the library. And I loved my old-time favorites.

I spent my time at the Sangita Library from 2009 to 2012. After that, I stopped going and quite forgot about the place. Many things were happening in my life at the time: My books were just published, I was gaining a presence of sorts on social media, I was in the process of writing more books, and I was tutoring students at my tutorial. My life's pace had speeded up. To date, I'm still juggling my time and the many professional caps that I wear.

Life is hectic now, but it wasn't back then.

The time between 2009 and 2012 were days of teaching, reading, and finding a publisher for my first book *S.O.S. Animals And Other Stories.*

Memories of the Sangita Library were about jasmine-scented prayer sticks, long walks, people-watching, and reading for leisure.

The place was small, only big enough for a few shelves and the librarian's desk. Can you believe that I was thinking of getting a summer job there? I used to think I'd help out at the library and earn some cash to save. I was a great saver when I was younger; it is the trait I miss most about me.

One day as I was having lunch before I left on my journey to the Sangita Library, I heard my name being called. There was a tussle at the doorway. I was half raising myself up from the dining table when in burst Papa, my old and gray-toothed father.

"I've come to say sorry for all I have done," he cried. "I'm sorry, Fiza *beta*. I'm your papa, *beta*, but I failed you. Sorry, *beta*!"

Then he made a great show of touching my mama's feet in remorse. I found the whole thing so disgusting.

"Get out," I growled like a tigress whose lair had been encroached.

"Forgive me, Fiza *beta* – I am your papa, Fiza *beta*, don't you recognize me?"

Who could forget a loathsome man like him!? I was in a rage. I was twenty-three years old and I was in a rage.

"Get him out of here," I said through clenched teeth.

Mama looked beseechingly at me. "He's come to say sorry, Fiza. Forgive him."

"Get him out of here," I roared. "Because I know why he is here today!"

You see, a new serial called *Satyamev Jayate* had started on the TV and was hosted by the intellectual actor Aamir Khan. His shows always aired in the morning before lunch and always featured a specific social topic. The topic would be analyzed, discussed, and put into focus: rape, child marriage, agrarian crisis, minority issues, et al. Aamir Khan always did a good job, and that made his show the talk of the town.

That Sunday, the day papa came "to beg forgiveness" was the same day Aamir Khan had analyzed the social issue of "the girl child unacceptance." He'd made mention of how unwanted baby girls were killed in the name of "accidents," by their paternal families mostly. Aamir Khan had even discussed one case where a baby infant girl's head was crushed by the foot of a paternal relative.

That was it. Papa had been hit with remorse. Aamir Khan, the Bollywood actor who could move the hearts of millions, had managed to move the stone heart of my father, Papa!

That's why he was here. He had watched the show. It had brought back horrible real-life memories.

"Fiza *beta*, forgive me – Fiza *beta*, I'm your papa *na*? Fiza *beta*, I'm your papa."

"Either you get your husband out of the house," I said menacingly, "or today I'll break all the bones in his body and reduce them to a pulp."

Mama and Rita tried to push Papa out, but the man was too heavy and adamant.

"Good-bye, Fiza *beta* – we'll meet in Jannat, Fiza *beta* – I'm your papa, Fiza *beta* – I'm sick and dying, Fiza *beta*...."

With all the energy Mama and Rita could muster, senior citizens though they both were, they chucked the madman out of the house and slammed the door in his face.

Satyamev Jayate.

But this time, I didn't crawl into a corner and weep. I sat back and ate my lunch heartily. Then I put on my favorite light blue denim jeans and Elvis Presley T-shirt (Aloha from Hawaii) and sling bag on my right shoulder, and I got ready to leave the house to head toward the Sangita Library.

"What if he is still out there somewhere?" asked Aunt Rita. "Don't go out today."

I folded my arms across my chest. "Who's afraid of one's own father? *Mein to Pathan ki aulad hu.* Pathans don't get scared of anything."

Rita smiled. Mama massaged her aching arms, which had helped push him out.

I left. I didn't meet the brute anywhere.

ESSAY 24

St. Paul's Bookshop and Media Center

I EARLIER MENTIONED A PHASE in my life from around 2006 to 2011, when I had a craving to join a cloistered convent. For Mama, it was her worst nightmare.

"She can't do without her books. What books will she get in the convent?" Mama asked, rubbing her aching forehead.

"A Bible?" ventured Mechu, thinking it over seriously.

"If she's lucky," added Blaise with a twitch of his gray-black whiskers.

Blaise was against the whole idea, but Mechu and Mama could be swayed because they felt that what is God's is not ours. Mechu, who was my godmother, visited us from Malad once every week. I always looked forward to her visits as a child, and I continue to look forward to them to this day.

In 2007, Mechu started tutoring me for Confirmation. I was supposed to receive the Holy Sacrament in January 2006, but due to a recurring stomach illness I couldn't attend the classes at church and was denied a completion certificate due to poor attendance. By the end March 2007, I had enrolled myself again for Confirmation classes. I was determined to finish this time, come what may, and then I would begin serving the church to the best of my ability.

So it was from March 2007 that Mechu started tutoring me for Confirmation. I was going to receive the sacrament at my parish church St. Francis of Assisi.

Because of my vocation, Mechu started taking me on little adventures and expeditions to various churches, convents, etc. to meet different religious individuals to counsel me. One of those many adventures landed me at the St. Paul's Bookshop and Media Center on Waterfield road in Bandra West.

It was heaven on earth, literally.

The place was filled with everything Catholic. They had books on the faith, imported Catholic bestseller books from TAN, religious statues, vestments, crosses galore, holy relics from Jerusalem, rosaries of every type, religious cards for every occasion, holy oil bottles, holy water bottles, chalices, tabernacles, holy pictures, holy bookmarks; you name it, they had it. And yes, loads of Bibles and Bible commentaries.

I was shocked by the amount of religious reading material I had at my disposal. I selected book after book to purchase, and poor Mechu was left with very little money in her purse. I was such a naïve old silly that I didn't realize that all these books, especially the foreign ones, didn't really fit her budget. Yet we visited the shop, again and again. It was an infatuation with religion and all things Catholic. I was grooming myself to enter convent life.

"Sometimes you used to buy so many books, dolly girl," says Mechu with a laugh these days, "that I used to wonder whether I would have any money to travel back home to Malad!"

Yes, when we visited St. Paul's, I really emptied Mechu's pockets. I just couldn't help myself; I was religion crazy, and there was so much to learn and so much to read about.

Today, St. Paul's has grown bigger and has become a huge name in the market as a media-training institute. The bookstore is vast. I still go there once in a while to update my religious reading. I have always read, and still read, books about the works and lives of the saints. Biographies published by TAN Books were my favorites. Some of my favorite saints, whose works I've read and studied and whose lives I enjoy reading about over and over again, follow:

St. Francis of Assisi

St. Catherine of Siena

St. Theresa of the Child Jesus

St. John of the Cross

St. Augustine

St. Vincent de Paul

St. Don Bosco

St. Dominic Savio

St. Paul

St. Faustina

I love many more, but St. Francis of Assisi is my favorite.

St. Paul's also had a lot of religious literature penned by theologians and highbrow professors that I gorged on. The works of Fulton Sheen have been a favorite, as well as the Man of God series, which I didn't complete reading but I hope to do so very soon.

I learned a lot about my religion from St. Paul's and was ready to work for the glory of the church.

By March 2008, I received the Sacrament of Confirmation. I came back home and posed for photographs with my whole family. I especially posed a lot with Ratan and Minoo uncles, my Parsi uncles. They were not of my religion, but they were and are still always by my side.

"Congratulations on your ... big day," said Minoo uncle, a bit clueless about the Sacrament of Confirmation but glad all the same that I received it. We celebrated the day with the family along with Fr. Bento and Fr. Willie, my childhood rectors and mentors.

After that, I enrolled as a lector and became a Sunday school teacher. I also became a participant of the youth group of St. Francis of Assisi Church, as well as the neighboring parish, Mt. Carmel's Church, Bandra. I became the deanery head of Bandra and I was the female representative of the Diocesan Youth of Mumbai.

All this sounds like I was a bigwig in the church, but not really. I was as much a recluse then as I was before my so-called vocation. I did mostly desk jobs.

I represented the youth of St. Francis of Assisi mostly, if not only, in *The Examiner*, a weekly newspaper that ran articles related to the church. I wrote short stories, articles of the faith, and movie reviews for the youth pages. I met a very good friend who was then a brother studying at the seminary. He was in fact in charge of *The Examiner* youth pages. His name was Br. Joshan and is now Fr. Joshan. He gave me a lot of exposure as a writer and Catholic youth journalist, and his faith in me and my work cultivated the idea that I could write well, that I could become a "real" writer.

"You are not like the other youth," he once told me over the phone. "You write differently, you seem like a new age C. S. Lewis."

That was a big compliment – A REALLY BIG COMPLIMENT THAT I DO NOT DESERVE!

Because I'm not an MFA. I, just as Ruskin Bond says, am using the small craft that I have been born with.

I'm only human. A reclusive introvert, and no one has been able to change that.

"Congratulations on the article in *The Examiner*," my dear Fr. Bento told me on the phone. He always received *The Examiner* before we did because he was then ministering at the Holy Name Cathedral, at Colaba, which was close to the Examiner Bookshop. He would scan the publication to see if my article was there and, once he saw it, immediately call me to congratulate me and give me his opinion and blessings.

"May you always serve God through the power of your pen, Fiza," Fr. Bento would say. "Remember what the Lord said. 'Don't hide the fire under the bushel, take it out and let it shine out.' God bless you always."

I am the kind to keep my existence under the bushel, if possible, but the dedicated priests and nuns in my life have managed to make me stand out.

"Hey, Fiza," said the DYC youth director way back in 2008. "Don't look so sad *yaar*! Smile, *na*."

We DYC youth members had just attended a talk on Bible Sunday. This was the pre-selfie days and we, about one hundred of us, were posing together, pointing toward the Bible held aloft in the center by the tallest member of the group.

Apparently, everyone was looking and posing right. Except me.

"Come on, Fiza!" whined the director. "It's the Bible, your favorite book. Raise your hand and pose. Now say 'Jesus' everyone."

"Jesus!" everyone cried as the snap was taken.

"Jesus," said I, but I still stuck out like a sore thumb in the picture. I always stick out.

❋

It was in the name of Christ that I read a lot of religious literature.

It was in the name of Christ that I made a sort of Mumbai Darshan of all the Catholic Churches in Mumbai.

I often took desk jobs at Catholic youth events for the following reasons:

- I could avoid taking part in the actual event and have time to read my book.
- I had a bird's-eye view of things going on and then could report my observations in the Catholic Youth magazines.

So, I hired cabs and made my way to different churches. I've been to Mulund, Thane, Andheri, Malad East, Malad West, Matunga, Dadar, and Colaba. I met a lot of people, especially youth but I was put off by the gregariousness and all that chatter. More and more, I was envisioning myself a cloistered nun in a far-off convent dedicated to small works of charity and prayer. Yes, I prayed a lot. Still do in a sort of different way.

Those were the days I asked for favors in my conversations with God. I was delving into scripture and theological works. St. Paul's Bookshop kept me occupied and I always found a new book that I wanted to purchase and devour in the market. The more I read, the more I wanted to follow the dictates of my vocation.

"How about a talk with Mother Bernarda?" asked Mechu as we set out on one of our merry adventures.

"You mean Mother Bernarda of the Carmelite order in Byculla?" I asked excitedly as I put down a commentary I was studying of the Gospel of Mark. "The same nun who looked after you all when you were at school?"

"And when we were very poor," added Mechu, hailing a cab. "Maybe she will give you some much needed advice about your vocation. Dolly girl, you are so precious to us, but whatever the Lord wills I support."

We met Mother Bernarda in the small old library of the convent school Mama, Mechu, and Rita studied at way back in the fifties and sixties. Mother Bernarda was affectionate and warm, but she was not very convinced that I had a vocation.

"You are still young, child," she counseled me gently. "Only eighteen or nineteen. You are idealistic, ambitious, and too quiet for someone your age. You must live in the world for some time. And even if you must join, don't join a cloistered order, my dear." Her old wrinkled hands were petting mine; her eyes spoke of a sadness that showed in her demeanour. "What are you reading right now?"

"Everything I can get my hands on about religion and the Christian life," I said, meekly.

Mother Bernarda turned to Mechu, who was also a part of the conversation. She spoke like an old aunt to Mechu, with much compassion. "Does the child know who also lives down our road?"

Mechu nodded. I knew who she was referring to. The Current Bookstall down the lane, next to the Gloria School and convent, opposite Our Lady of Glory Church, Byculla. It was my papa's shop.

"Have you forgiven him?" Mother Bernarda asked me. My jaw clenched tight along my then-still-prominent jawline.

"Hmmm ..." she murmured. "Then that is what the Lord has called you to do today."

"What – huh?" I stuttered.

"Forgiveness and mercy," intoned Mother Bernarda. Teatime was approaching, and she placed a slice of marble cake and a glass of mango juice in front of me. "Forgive him after you go out from here, and then will you be able to forgive others who are worse than he."

Forgive my father? For ditching Mama? For abandoning me because I was born a girl?

Mother Bernarda sipped her mango juice. Mechu nodded and looked my way. I gazed up at the photographs of the stalwart principal nuns and mother superiors on the walls where we sat and ate.

Forgive Papa?

We left just before it turned dark. I told Mechu, "I'll go first, then you come later."

She nodded, and we moved ahead. I shoved my hands into my black denim jeans pocket. I was wearing one of my school pullovers. I turned the corner. Mechu remained behind. I came face to face with Papa, standing among his stationery wares. He looked older and very haggard.

He did not recognize me.

"*Kya chahiye beti*?" he asked with a Muslim salaam. I kept silent but hot tears started falling from my eyes. It was then he looked more carefully at me. He saw my mama's face.

"*Tu Fiza hai na*?" he asked me, half stunned and half afraid. "Everything is all okay at home? Has something happened to Phila?" Phila was the name he called my mama, whose actual Christian name was Philomena or Philo, for short. He didn't like both names because they didn't sound Islamic enough, but he loved my mama.

Mechu came up and stood behind me. The young boy working with Papa stared at us, mesmerized. I think he too saw my father's reflection in my face. The young boy asked Papa whether he should take his leave till our meeting ended and my papa said a curt yes.

I clutched my Bible in my sling bag in my hand tightly as I went up to Papa.

It's now or never, I thought to myself.

"Papa," I mumbled looking straight into his eyes. "I've come here to forgive you."

"Forgive me?" My papa threw back the words with scorn. "What have I done to you?"

I clenched my teeth. The grip on my Bible tightened and later when I picked it up to read, the cardboard cover hand holes in it.

Mother Bernarda was right. She knew my father better than I did. She knew his mentality, living just a few steps away from him for more than forty years. She knew that if I could forgive him, then I could tackle anything after that.

"Papa, I forgive you for abandoning me as a child because I was a girl."

Papa's moustache twitched. He smirked.

"Why have you come here to dig up the past? Are you perhaps a history student at college?" he asked, mocking me.

"Father," I called him father for the first time. "I forgive you for everything. I forgive you for the past."

Papa flinched. He offered me his seat, and I took it.

"Iqbal's daughter has come to see him," came a voice from one of the neighboring shop vendors.

"I never knew he had a daughter," another neighbor said before he stood behind Mechu to have a good look at me. He saw me on my papa's seat, the seat of the master of the shop. Then he went away, dazzled.

"Which class are you in now, Fiza *beta*?" asked Papa as a crowd of people who were coming back from the factories after a long hard day of work gathered.

"FYBA, the thirteenth grade," I answered tartly. "I study history."

"That's why you are here eh? To uncover the past?" he asked with a chuckle and the pull of his beard. "Fiza *beta*, life is like a river you know, it has its ups and downs but empties at the same source. Just take me as one of those 'downs' in your life and forget it all." He offered me tea or coffee, but I was still crying hot tears.

"How is my Phila?" he asked in a tender voice I've never heard from him in my life. "Is she well? Does she still have diabetes? Does she take her medicine? Does she know you've come here this evening?"

Papa still loved Mama. And I know for a fact that she also still loves papa. I knew it then; I know it now.

My grip on the Bible eased. We hailed a taxi home.

I had forgiven my papa, as the Gospel asked me to. But I'll never be able to forgive myself for coming in between these two lovers, who after almost twenty-nine years of separation have still been faithful to each other.

It was I who came in the way. Me, miserable little bookish me!

❋

I continued with my yearning for a Catholic vocation. I studied the Bible to the hilt, until one day the carpet was pulled from under my feet. That happened at teachers training college. It was run by the Carmelite nuns. I had to mingle with a lot of nuns from different orders and with different temperaments. I don't want to go into great detail, but it was a horrible experience. I observed nuns acting with bitterness, treacherousness, and fickle mindedness, and those who were prone to currying favor and given to shows of dross. I lost my vocation in less than three months' time while attending the institute.

But I'm still very attached to my faith, and St. Paul's Bookshop is still a place where I go to buy books of religious and theological nature. I am greeted as an old friend by Mehmood, the teller at the counter. He remembers me from the time I first entered the bookshop with Mechu. The day my books were displayed at St. Paul's, he was teary eyed. God bless him for the memories gone by.

Mother Bernarda, the only true nun I have ever known, passed away during the middling years of my twenties. I couldn't visit her when she was sick because of my writing and hectic teaching schedule post-2012. But the fact remains that she wanted to desperately tell me something, something that she wanted to convey to me alone and in front of no one else. I never went, and she passed away with her secret buried in her pure heart. God rest her soul! God rest the souls of the departed!

God rest the remembered departed and the forgotten living!

❋

ESSAY 25

The Diary of St. Faustina

I BOUGHT ST. FAUSTINA'S DIARY during the time I became aware of my vocation. I bought the book from St. Paul's Bookshop on Bible Sunday. One of the priests in our church recommended the diary, and I was dying to read it. It was the first time I would be reading into the life of a real nun.

Little did I know how impactful St. Faustina's diary would be in my life as a practicing Catholic and as a youth. I was around eighteen years old when I read her diary.

The diary is the collection of the blessings and visions of St. Faustina, who is the saint who was given a sublime vision of Jesus's Divine Mercy and the portrait of the Divine Mercy picture of Jesus Christ for the new age. The diary describes every personal detail of St. Faustina, her little joys, her silent stigmata, and the pain she had to endure for being different from the rest. I read the book in less than three days' time.

I started to keep a spiritual diary after that, which I was to burn the moment I gave up the life of a wannabe religious. I carefully made mention of my sins of the day and the good deeds I had done, along with my feelings for the religion and, more specifically, my belief in the Divine Mercy of Jesus Christ.

"What in the world are you doing?" Mama asked sternly. She did not like what she was seeing. I was kneeling on the hall sofa and reciting the Divine Mercy chaplet I had discovered in St. Faustina's Diary, with closed eyes. I was reciting it as if I were in a trance. Mama was not pleased at all.

"I don't like this," Mama declared. "Please stop this at once. Concentrate on your studies and don't, for heaven's sake, act like a mystic."

But I persisted. When no one would tolerate my prayers at home, I went to the St. Francis of Assisi or Mt. Carmel's churches and sat in the chapel before the Blessed Sacrament and prayed there. I used to read and reread the Diary of St. Faustina. Everybody at home thought I had gone barking mad.

"Do you think it's drugs?" Mama asked Mechu one day.

Mechu, caught unawares, spilled her tea, making a mess of the table. "Dolly girl on drugs! No way. It's just love."

"What love?" Mama asked, quite upset. "She is still a kid, immature to the limit. She doesn't know anything about what it is to be a nun. Why me, Lord?" Mama moaned.

I heard the whole thing because they were talking right in front of me while I read the diary.

If you look at the diary from a nonbeliever's point of view, then certainly one would think that St. Faustina was a psychiatric patient and needed counseling along with a few meds. But for believers of the Catholic faith and those who have been blessed by the Divine Mercy symbol and rosary, this book is the genesis of it all.

The book instilled in me a great love of my faith, but unfortunately it couldn't save my vocation. But maybe you, dear reader, may like to dip into this book of spiritualism to guide you on your path toward a better life. In short, if you believe in a God, then read the book. If you want to believe, then read the book. If you want to just have a look because you are curious, go ahead and read this book. It is meditative in nature, packed with spiritual fruits, and it tells the story of a wholesome life spent in the belief of a Savior who showered Divine Mercy upon his people, especially in the new millennium.

I have since read more books on the subject and now have a greater understanding of the Divine Mercy. This is something about my religion that I like and, although I'm more of an existentialist these days, if given a chance to worship the Lord, I would definitely choose the way of Divine Mercy.

I need Divine Mercy in my life. Especially now that I have no friends other than books and lead a reclusive life far away from the hassles of the world, locked up and typing away my days.

I need Divine Mercy because I'm a plus-size woman. I'm 122 kgs, and when, if I ever, I walk down the road, the Mumbai public jeer at me. I am massive but I have a certain grace. That grace, if it has sprung from anywhere, must have been from those days in 2007 when I was reading the *Diary of St. Faustina.*

It is hard being plus-size. No one takes you seriously.

It's hard being a winner of more than seventy international book awards. You get to stand alone with the certificates.

It's hard being in the world and not totally being a part of it. But I've managed to do it well so far. St. Faustina laid the groundwork for that. I am very contented with my modest means. I don't have to go far to travel the cosmos – just leave me in my office-cum-writing hut with a book or two, and I'll be fine.

So, my dear St. Faustina of the Divine Mercy Chaplet, if you are out there reading this, know that I am a great fan of yours, what you stood for, and the way you came to be a saint in the Catholic church. We human beings need mercy. A lot of it. I forgave my papa a long time ago. Now the man is asking for mercy – so is mercy even greater than forgiveness?

"Fiza *beta,*" cries my half-crazed papa on the phone. "Fiza *beta*, have mercy on an old man and let me go on Haj. You mustn't deny an old man his Haj, his religion, his belief. Have mercy, take away my load and let me go on holy pilgrimage. Do you hear me, Fiza *beta*? FIZA *BETA*, HAVE MERCY!"

The sound of his crying is nauseating, but his plea is odd. Money for mercy – money for a girl who grew up without a father. Lord, I do not understand your ways.

❋

ESSAY 26

I Am Malala by Malala Yousafzai with Christina Lamb

I WAS DONE WITH TEACHING in a school. I had published my first book on Amazon and was teaching at home every afternoon and evening.

I was twenty-three, reclusive, patient, and older than my years. I wanted to be both a teacher and writer, and I was going to make that happen whatever the result. In came news of a girl from Pakistan called Malala who was shot in the head by the Taliban.

"What was she shot for?" I asked one of students who had just seen the news on TV.

"She stood for education of girl children," said my little sixth-grade preteen.

The autobiography came out in 2013. I picked it up from Crossword, Bandra. I read the book and it changed my life.

Malala Yousafzai survived the Taliban point-blank gunshot, but that didn't stop her from fighting for the rights of children to be educated irrespective of whether they were girls or boys. She spoke at the UN and at age sixteen became a global symbol of peace, the youngest ever nominee for the Nobel Peace Prize. She lived to tell her story to the world. She became a heroine for me. She still is.

I was instantly caught up with the autobiography. Mama asked for her own copy of the book, and we bought one from Kitab Khana, the best bookstore in Mumbai, which I will talk more about a bit later. Mama finished the book in one night's time; she just couldn't put it down. It's one of the few books I've seen her read with so much enthusiasm. But that is not shocking because Malala's tale is something that is as close to us as it is to all the children in the world out there who are not getting their deserved or entitled rights.

In Papa's family, girls were not educated. If they tried to go to college, they were beaten. Papa used to beat his younger sister who wanted to work in a bank after her B.Com degree. My paternal grandmother was not educated at all. Mama was sure that if I had lived with Papa, he would not have allowed me to study if he had the chance to. The horror of that thought sends chills up my spine. Whatever would I have done without my education?

Nana was only educated in English till the third grade, but she made sure she educated all five of her children: David uncle, Mechu, Mama, Rita, and Blaise, to the best of her efforts.

"Don't do the housework," she used to order her children. "Concentrate on your studies. Otherwise you will all be servants, you hear!" Everyone studied, everyone got decent jobs and became part of the middle-class society which we belong to even today by the sheer dint of hard work and most importantly, AN EDUCATION!

Malala's story hit me hard. I've read the book twice and always recommend the autobiography to my students, especially my girl students. Most of my students are from elite backgrounds. They will never to be able to understand the struggle Malala had to face, her dedication to her cause, and the bravery she has shown at such a tender age. But I have taken my education seriously, especially after reading *I Am Malala*.

I Am Malala is one of the best biographies I've ever read. I was proud of Malala's father for his pride in his daughter, in his fight against oppressors and his passion for education, especially the education of girls. Now, here is a father any daughter would be proud of. He didn't see any difference between his two sons and his daughter; they were all equal in his eyes. Give them a book, a pen, and a teacher – they will soar to the greatest heights.

I identified very strongly with Malala. I would go on, as the years progressed, to follow her speeches, her movements, the additional books about her life and work, but I would never forget the impact *I Am Malala* had on me when I was twenty-three years old, a rookie writer and teacher waiting for her big break.

After *I Am Malala*, I went on to read more biographies about women in oppressive and difficult situations and how they managed to rise out of those situations and go the distance. I have a fascination for Dalit women and Dalit feminist educators, but the contribution of women and girls fighting for their rights all across the globe stimulated me to write about their conditions. Their stories and hardships led me to write social issue fiction like *Nirmala: The Mud Blossom* and *Amina: The Silent One,* both of which won numerous accolades.

Nirmala and Amina are my babies: unwanted girls who fought patriarchy and dire circumstances. Malala was always on my mind as I penned their stories.

The dedication in the book, which is actually a clarion call, stirs me even today at the age of twenty-nine:

"To the girl-child who suffers abuse from the cradle to the grave."

Whenever I conducted my book club sessions in the tuition house I rent next to my own apartment, Malala's story was always the first book I would discuss with my students, who were eager to listen to everything that came out of my mouth; for a recluse, I have a sort of unusual charisma when I am with children.

I was and still am passionate about the book, and if you've not read it yet, you must do so before you leave this world. *I Am Malala* is a must for anyone who is dealing in academics and education. It is meant for anyone who has stood up for their right to be educated. It is meant for young and old. *I Am Malala* is a clean book, which can and should be read by any child who needs to learn the value of an education.

How blessed I've been that I was returned to my maternal family! How blessed I've been to have received a good education, especially through the books I have read and enjoyed over the years. These books have fueled my passion for becoming a writer, to write books about topics I would like to see on bookshelves.

I love the way Malala narrates her achievements in her school in Pakistan, about how grateful she is to be alive and to educate herself and others further. But Malala Yousafzai is in the public eye. She is brave enough, even after having been shot at by a ruthless force, to remain in the public light. My hat is off to her and many others like her. I, on the other hand, protest from a corner of Mumbai which is like a fortress against the world surrounded by towers of books.

I can't be what I'm not. I shiver when I think of what Malala must have felt when the alleged terrorist halted her school bus and called out: "Who is Malala?" I would have crumbled there and then, fear killing me more than the gunshot wound he inflicted. Yes, I am a fearful person. I'm afraid, but I will in my own way continue to write and read and teach about the diversity of life; diversity that needs to be celebrated, not to be shot down at gunpoint.

As long as I have my pen and a bit of paper, I wage war on fundamentalists in all forms and guises. Some of them use guns on children; some teach children to play with guns.

ESSAY 27

I, Phoolan Devi by Phoolan Devi

I PICKED UP *I, Phoolan Devi* from the Maharashtra Mitra Mandal Library, also known as the MCubed Library, which was near my college, St. Andrew's. It came into being much after I graduated from college and I got to hear of it from a friend of mine.

I was around twenty-four when I read *I, Phoolan Devi*. When I first read it, I was absolutely in a rage that such atrocities were committed on a girl child only because she was from the "lower caste," a girl without a father with clout in this derelict world we have created here in casteist India. Devi's tale of sexual and physical abuse made me feel like I was being assaulted instead of her. There were some parts of the biography that made my hair stand on end. I couldn't digest it as easily as I do now, at age twenty-nine.

I, Phoolan Devi is the autobiography of the first real "Bandit Queen" of India, who was sexually assaulted, physically abused, and gang raped several times before she turned on the heels of her evil doers, took the place of her bandit lover, and became a bandit leader herself. She filled the hearts of men with fear during her career as a bandit; journalists named her the Bandit Queen of India.

I chose to read the book because I was reading a lot of feminist biographies and autobiographies at the time. What shocked me most about the story was the apathy displayed by the police and government officials of the 1980s when Phoolan Devi lived a piteous life under the thumb of the upper castes.

I think I grew up after reading *I, Phoolan Devi.* While reading it, I even fainted at a certain point right in the middle of the American Library, now known as the Dosti Library. I had to be revived and had to splash water on my face – the book was that shocking. But the worst part is that it was true, every gory detail of it all absolutely true.

"Are you okay?" Blaise asked as I revived from my fainting spell. "Can you sit?"

"Yeah, I hope so," I said, but I was cold, numb, and petrified. Were such things happening practically everywhere in the country? The Phoolan Devi reign continued through the early 1990s when I was a babe in arms; what was the situation now?

I went then on a mad search for articles about Phoolan Devi. I was sad to learn that she had been killed in 2003 by her enemies as she campaigned to be elected to our Parliament. I tried to read more about the case of OBC/SC/ST castes in India. This would ultimately result in buying a lot of such books in two major bookstores in Mumbai: Kitab Khana (Fort) and Trilogy: The Eternal Library (Lower Parel). More on them as the book progresses.

After Phoolan Devi's book, I felt as if I'd been scandalized and brutally shaken from a deep slumber. How could I have not known about the situation of women in so-called twenty-first-century India? Devi's story still stands out for me as one of the major feminists' biographies of my life. It woke me up to the madness of the boxes we, as Indians, have divided ourselves into and placed ourselves in with quick cement, never to move from that position. This further led me to Dr. B. R. Ambedkar's (Babasaheb's) works, the Dalit movement, Dalit biographies, the Dalit Panther movement studies, the Naxalbari movement, etc., which I had not gone so deep into when I was studying at St. Andrew's because I was focused on history more than social issues, and the theories of political theorists like Durkheim, Giddens, Karve, Marx, etc.

I recently read a book penned by Sohaila Abdulali, *What Do We Talk About When We Talk About Rape*, and in it, the writer mentions that a certain fascination occurs in reading gruesome accounts of other people's sexual assaults or molestations and rape, where the reader thinks, "It won't happen to me," or "I'll protect myself better," or "Her rape was worse than what I'm going through right now." Maybe consciously or unconsciously as a girl who has been rejected at birth, I was wanting to read more about Devi's life because I was feeling that some things in my life were far better than hers.

If you want to get rid of such a train of thought and if you want to see the grim reality of the situation of lower caste women in India, read *I, Phoolan Devi*. But I caution you, the biography is not for the faint of heart and certainly not meant for anyone below age sixteen. It is a defining moment to read something that, however gruesome it be, you'll be coming back to again and again, to get energized to battle yet another day as a person the world doesn't want you to be.

I returned to the book when I was twenty-eight years old, in 2018. I was less traumatized this time because I've read even worse, but the tale of India's Bandit Queen makes me laugh to myself when I think of tiny Phoolan Devi fighting bandits with her comrade-in-arms, Man Singh, at her side. I loved returning to the parts of the story in which Mastana was still alive. Mastana, I wish there were more of you around; India is becoming a terrible place for women, girls, toddlers ...

Read this book when you are seeking courage. Read this book and salute the Bandit Queen. She had no one but herself and her anger and her comrade-in-arms, Man Singh; sometimes you need that anger to teach the perpetrators of heinous crimes a lesson. But try not to use violence like Phoolan Devi did, for violence only begets more violence. We have a Constitution, right? Let's make use of it.

"What is a bandit queen?" asked one of my senior students who had noticed the book I was reading while he wrote a composition.

"I'll become one if you don't finish your work," I snapped, lowering the book.

The student chuckled, "I'll google it."

I rolled my eyes. So much for modesty. I continue to read. And he googled it, I know, because when he came back for the next class, he said: "Those perverted sick men deserved it."

I pretended not to hear and went on teaching the literature lesson.

ESSAY 28

MCubed Library (aka Maharashtra Mitra Mandal Library)

I USED TO TEACH EVERY afternoon and evening at the tuition house I was renting next to my own flat. I was on the lookout for a place to write my books.

It was somewhere around 2012 to 2013. I had resigned from my teaching job at the ICSE school at Santacruz, had published two books on Amazon via CreateSpace, and had started writing as a profession full-time. My life as a reclusive reader and writer of Mumbai was beginning to take shape. But I was totally out of shape myself.

I weighed 100 kgs at the start of the year 2012. By 2013, I was 120 kgs and I was becoming bloated in the face, especially the cheeks. People had started making rude comments about my physique as soon as I'd graduated college. I cried myself to sleep at night or live in the college library to get away from my so-called concerned friends. Their jibes and daily insults were getting to be too much for me. Besides, I was growing a business and I didn't need that kind of negativity in my life. I don't think anyone who is plus-size needs that kind of attention. So, I broke off from everyone. I retreated into myself, keeping contact with people as minimal as possible.

I'm no badass feminist, don't get me wrong; I'm not saying that if one is plus-size one has to seclude oneself from the world. I'm just saying that's what I did, and you are entitled to your own opinion just like I am entitled to mine, and my own analysis of what my home situation is and how I can be as little of a hindrance to productivity as possible. (Besides, I have a book to write, so get off my case all you body-shaming people out there who I once called friends – I am quite all right without you.)

So, here I was, looking for a place to write and read in the mornings without the students of the morning classes or Mama disturbing my peace. It was then that a counselor friend, an acquaintance of mine, recommended a government-run library very near St. Andrew's.

She was incredulous. "You stay right there in Bandra West and you don't know about MCubed yet!" She lifted up her hands in a dramatic way and then dropped them onto her skinny tights. "Seriously, Fiza, if you miss the tall shelves of BSS, then this is a place you should check out."

She also told me that they served tea at "chai time" and had super-clean toilets. By the next day, I was at MCubed Library, or more formally, The Maharashtra Mitra Mandal Library. It was on the ground floor of an apartment complex in a super-posh Catholic neighborhood. I was greeted warmly by the librarian in charge of evening duty and was given a tour. The large room next to the librarian's desk was the children's library. The one a few steps from it was for adults. I fell in love with the ambience of the place at once. It was homey, had a lot of chairs, sofas, and tables to sit on and plenty to read. I checked the lady's toilet; it was perfect.

I took a galaxy membership which allowed me to borrow four books for two weeks. Blaise later on would take another galaxy membership for four books and two weeks as well. Not for himself, but for me.

"You won't be satisfied with just four books," he said as he handed me his library card.

After that, every free time I could get away from teaching, I could be found at MCubed. I've managed to write so much there, including two whole poetry collections titled *So This Is Love* and *The Flame Will Always Burn,* along with sections of my first two non-fiction books: *Classics: Why We Should We Encourage Children to Read Them* and *Classics: How We Should Encourage Children to Read Them.*

Back then I used to follow the old Ruskin Bond method and write all my work by hand and then have Rita type it later. All that stopped after 2018, when I started typing my books myself, to the detriment of my eyes and sanity. But my blue Dell Inspiron 11 is a good companion.

Back then I wrote and read a lot; there was a lot to choose from at MCubed. I especially started reading a lot of biographies and autobiographies of various personalities. I discovered Maya Angelou, Malcolm X, Phoolan Devi, Kamala Das, Nelson Mandela, and many other rare but insightful biographies and nonfiction books.

I used to drop by early. Most of the time I was the very first person at the library. The cleaning woman at MCubed was very fond of me; she used to fuss over me.

"*Laadli ladki hai,*" she would say as I wrote in my books in longhand. "Read and write and become a big person. Doctor *banogi kya,* English *ya* history *mein*?"

"Just a writer, *dost,*" I used to say. But yes, I had dreams of pursuing a further education.

"When are you going to do your masters'?" Mama asked one day. "And at least this time don't make the mistake you made last time. Take English this time."

But I was adamant. I took sociology. When that did not work out, I tried an MA in history from the Open University of Mumbai. But that didn't work out either; the students at the tutorial were increasing in number and I was getting no time between corrections, making worksheets and PowerPoint presentations to bother about my studies.

"Take a break from writing full-time," said Mechu, and Mama backed her up. But Blaise knew better. He saw the glint in my eyes when I wrote and knew I would die if I was not allowed to write.

"Leave her alone," he said. "You get MA students cheaper by the dozen in Mumbai who can't even frame a single sentence in correct English." Then, looking at Mama, he continued, "An MA can be done at any time. Let her follow her ambition and make her money."

Blaise convinced Mama and the rest of the household that I was heading in the right direction. If not for his support and love, I wouldn't be the writer I am today. Blaise has been the rock behind me as I face the literary world with no godfather and no MFA or other degrees next to my name. Blaise believed in me; he still does. He and I are the greatest team in the world of books.

But back to MCubed. I wrote and read my days away. I studied there, too, for my IAP Career exam, which I took online and graduated with a 100 percent. My subject was publishing.

I used to study there and people-watch as well. I loved to watch the various characters in search of books to read wander by the shelves of MCubed. I loved to see where their hands reached toward. At this time, Jeffery Archer and James Patterson were favorites of mine, but so were Ali Smith, Elif Shafak and P. G. Wodehouse.

The library was swept and swabbed every morning by the aforementioned cleaning maid. She used to save my place so that I could sit on the best sofa opposite the fiction section. Students would crawl in after me, wonderful characters worthy of becoming characters in a book.

They would sit in their preferred places. Well-bred young adults studying accounts, economics, mathematics, psychology, history, for the IAS, etc. I wrote, watching them as I did so. Some of them appeared in my stories later on. Some of them are still on my waiting list of characters. We all worked silently, taking hot, cutting chai at tea break.

"Madam, chai?" the tea man personally came to me and asked gently, not wanting to disturb my writing. It seemed that I was the most serious-looking worker there.

"Two minutes," I requested, and the dear man moved on to the next student. Normally, after tea, I would stop writing and read. As mentioned earlier, I read a lot of biographies. Some that made me grow up and some that fueled me with a passion to write on sociological and social issue topics.

The adult library also had a ladder leading to a sort of platform bed near the ceiling where one could read in peace, without the disturbance of those coming in and going out. I have never been bold enough to go up there; I am afraid of heights. But many readers loved to relax and read in that little nook.

The children's section of the library is huge with all sorts of books, comics, encyclopedias, and kids' magazines. In addition, there are always events taking place, such as movies for both children and adults on Sundays.

"Why don't you come for one of our movie sessions?" asked the librarian Mr. Oliver Noronha, whom I call Oliver sir. "You will like it very much. We choose the best."

"I can't. I don't have a fixed schedule," I said, which was true, as back then I was teaching every day of the week and was certainly not following the Sabbath law. I had to make do with any free time that came my way. It was taxing, but I pulled on. As Elvis Presley said, my ambition was like "a V8 engine." I wanted to make this work, and I wanted to save enough money to use for my future.

"And marriage?" Mechu asked over her horned-rimmed glasses. "Any prince charming in your life, dolly girl?"

I remembered the boy I loved in school. The only boy I have ever truly loved. He never spoke to me, never showed any interest in me, and flew away from my life, leaving me with an aching heart that sometimes rents its paper fabric. Even the paper hearts of bookworms can beat in the name of love.

"I've no one," I said, opening a new book borrowed from MCubed. "I'm not going to get married ever. It's not for me."

The book I was reading was Ann Patchett's *This Is the Story of a Happy Marriage.*

By 2015, going to MCubed was my regular practice. I would come in and sign the register, exchange some pleasantries with Philo ma'am, the day librarian, and head to the bookshelves to pick a book to read. I used to carry them back home in an old jute carrier bag that I got free from the Mumbai University. I still borrow books from MCubed and I place my books in the same bag even today.

These days I don't sit around libraries much, especially because I've got my own office-cum-writing hut.

In 2015, I appeared in a documentary called *Black Sheep*, directed and conceptualized by Reshel Shah Kapoor about the Kinnar community or Hijra/eunuch community of Mumbai. I had written a short story on the community called "Flesh of Flesh," which I was planning on developing into a full-length novel. In lieu of that, I was contacted by the *Black Sheep* team to do an interview with them about my work. I gave an interview and interacted with many kinnars at a workshop. After the workshop, I went straight to MCubed to chill out. The adult library was packed because of an event so I had to sit in the children's library. I read some short stories by Rabindranath Tagore as well as a short book of stories by Sudha Murthy called *How I Taught My Grandmother to Read and Other Stories.*

It was so peaceful that day. I felt like I was in heaven.

MCubed also has new books coming in every month, and I try as much as possible to attend the day when the new books are put on display for borrowing and reading pleasure; it's so exciting.

MCubed also has a special table where donated books are put out for sale for a small sum. I discovered the Adrian Mole series from that table as well as Marian Keyes, both of which are rip-roaring funny.

"Do you have Ruskin Bond books?" I asked Oliver sir one day in 2016. "I didn't find them in the adult's library."

"His books are in the children's library. Just a moment," the ever-efficient, ready-to-help Mr. Oliver typed into his computer. "There, I've got it; it's in the nonfiction section of the children's library. There're plenty of his books there."

I ran inside and found the shelf. There, standing side by side were my old Ruskin Bond favorites: old copies of *Rain in the Mountains, The Night Train At Deoli, Landour Bazaar,* and *Scenes from a Writer's Life.*

I took them all, sat in the inner sanctum of the library where private tuitions used to be held for needy students in the evening, and began reading *Rain in the Mountains.* The sun was setting but a large ray of sunlight fell over me as I read at the table. I read there for over three hours, interrupted only when a yellow butterfly entered the library and settled on my book. That's when I coined a phrase I like to use – "Ruskin Bondish" – it was a very Ruskin Bondish day.

Whenever I spend some time with nature in my modest garden and spend time reading as well, I tell Blaise that "I had a very Ruskin Bondish day."

MCubed is still the place I go to feel Ruskin Bondish. Its homey feel, its active life as a library, and its books always bring a smile to my face. I have spent much time there, doing the things I love doing best.

"Shall we start displaying the new books?" one of the supervisors asks.

"Wait, Fiza is not here yet," Oliver sir says.

"Let's wait for her," Philo ma'am agrees.

The others are skeptical about whether I will arrive. But in the end, I always do. Then the displaying of the books begins, and I take some of the best ones home to read at my leisure.

ESSAY 29

Title Waves: The Boutique Bookstore

I DISCOVERED TITLE WAVES when I was passing by Waterfield Road in Bandra, as I was coming back from buying new textbooks to make notes for the children I was tutoring for the coming year. When I spotted the books through the glass windows of the bookshop, I almost jumped out of the moving rickshaw.

"Fiza, be careful," Mama cautioned. The rickshaw man pulled up to our destination, and Mama paid him. I didn't wait for her and ran like a bull into the shop. Title Waves coincidently occupied the space below the new St. Paul's Bookshop.

I looked around. The place was a boutique store, spacious, with a wide variety of books of all genres. I looked to my right and saw that a coffee shop was attached to the place.

"Perfect!" I said while my mama hit her forehead with the palm of her hand.

I started going every morning to sit in the café and write. MCubed was my original spot, but the number of students had increased and, most of the time, I couldn't find a place to sit. So, when I discovered Title Waves, I was happy enough. I started writing there in 2015 just after I'd finished my final revision with my ninth- and tenth-grade students.

I was always the first one at the coffee shop attached to Title Waves. I always took the same seat, the single one near the heater, the one I was sure no one would ever want. I lived on English Breakfast tea with milk, Earl Gray Tea without milk, or a good old cappuccino with lots of milk and cream. There I wrote short stories and the first draft of *Nirmala: The Mud Blossom* in longhand.

I used to write there from 10:00 a.m. till 8:00 p.m. without food, living on the beverages I have mentioned. After 8:00 p.m., I would pack up my things and roam the boutique bookstore. The books there were fabulous, fresh copies, and there were many different varieties. I read a lot of modern twentieth-century literature there, like Camus, Hemingway, Faulkner, Amis, and Foster. Classics were there in abundance as well as many of the latest books, which I bought whenever I had enough cash in my purse.

By this time, we had engaged our trusty taxi driver-cum-bodyguard-cum-family member, Narayan, to drop me and pick me up from Title Waves. I did my job and, without looking left or right, made my way out.

Because of all the meals I was skipping and the large quantities of caffeine I was drinking, I grew terribly ill. I suffered from severe acidity and, to date, it's a problem for me at every step of the way.

I had by this time, become a complete introvert. One day, something terrible happened that could have landed me in trouble, if my influential friends of the family had not stepped in.

It was about my weight. I was by then very crabby, eccentric, and touchy about my plus-size figure.

One fine afternoon, when Narayan, our taxi driver, was not around, I was making my way from MCubed to Title Waves to write at the café. I had my pink ladies' umbrella with me, a backpack, and a jute bag full of books from MCubed. The sun was beating on the tarmac. I unfurled my umbrella over my head and walked on, in search of a rickshaw.

Suddenly, ahead of me came a man in his late thirties. He was unkempt and had a lecherous look about him. I kept my poise and tried to ignore him as I continued to hail a rickshaw without success. As he neared, the creature smirked and stopped me in my path.

"Madamji, madamji," he crooned. "You are fat, way too fat. You should do some jogging and shake all your fat parts."

I was frozen in place. "What? Huh?" I stammered.

The man elaborated, "You are too fat. You are a fatso and have fat parts. Shake them hard and lose weight."

He was standing there, quite proud of his performance and even clapped a bit at his own cleverness before continuing on his way.

Meanwhile, I was in a rage. Boiling mad.

"Hey, you!" I called out to him, running to catch up. "Stop."

He turned and smiled. Then he got a hard whack on his face with my closed umbrella.

He was stunned. He had not expected retaliation.

"What happened, sister? What happened?" came the voices of concerned passers-by.

"This man eve-teased me just now," I screamed with a trembling hand. "Hit him – *MARO*!"

Mumbai is the city of frustrated tempers. When people get an opportunity to let it out, they do. Men, boys, and women beat up this lecherous guy, some with slippers, some with their hands, and some with their own umbrellas. He did not expect any of this.

After they left, the man got up. He looked me squarely in the eye and raised his hand.

"I won't forget this, *moti saali*," he sneered. "I will teach you a lesson another day."

He thought I would cower and go on my way. But I was on fire.

I beat him up with my umbrella and slapped him with my *ulta hath*. He kept on saying the same thing.

"I'll teach you a lesson, *moti* fatso. Remember you are a girl. Remember you are a girl."

I halted. Remember you are a girl – a girl!

He ran ahead thinking he had frightened me at last. He walked fast, taking a different route from the way he had come.

REMEMBER THAT YOU ARE A GIRL!

A GIRL!

I howled, which made the pedestrians shiver. And then I did something that I had never done in my life before nor since. I ran after the man.

He was walking faster and faster. An empty rickshaw at last pulled past me, and I hailed it.

"Follow that man," I shouted. "And then take me to the Bandra police station. I'll reward you with a ₹100 note."

"I don't want to get involved with the police, sister," said the rickshaw driver with a tremor in his voice.

I clenched my teeth, "If you don't follow that man, I'LL TAKE *YOU* TO THE POLICE STATION, YOU HEAR? Now, go on, step on it!"

"Yes, yes madamji," stammered the driver, and he zoomed his rickshaw ahead. My prey saw us coming. He cursed himself and began to run, but we were much faster. I held out the crook of my pink ladies' umbrella and as we passed him, his neck got caught in my crook and I hauled him in.

The rickshaw driver headed to the police station. I was beating the shit out of my prey. I beat him with my umbrella and my "ulta hath."

"So, I'm a fat girl, am I?" I said. "But tell me, how fat am I really now?"

And then I pressed my left foot upon his right toes. I pressed all of my 120 kgs on him.

"Mercy madam, please mercy," he squealed like a schoolboy with tears running into his eyes. "I never knew you would take my remarks so seriously, madam. Please have mercy – OUCH MY TOES!"

They bled. I roared. I was a girl.

We came to the station. I caught my prey by the scruff of his shirt full of grease and dragged him crying and wetting himself like a baby into the station. It was a sight to behold.

A policeman came up to me. “Well, madamji, what have you got here?”

“He eve-teased me on the street as I was walking to get a rickshaw,” I spat. “So I caught him and brought him here.”

“You did this alone?” asked the policeman with surprise. Civilians inside the station along with some few criminals clapped their hands.

“That’s the spirit!” someone cried. “What a girl!”

Girl. Just a girl.

I did it alone. Just a girl.

“Mercy, police sir, please. I’ll never eve-tease or threaten a woman for the rest of my days. Tell her to let me go. Please, let me go!”

❋

Mama was appalled and in tears. Blaise couldn’t speak for a whole week. Everyone was clear now on one account. I was not to go out alone. If no one else was going with me, I would have to go out with Narayan.

“Why did you have to take him to the police station?” Mama exclaimed in frustration. “He only said empty words. You should not have lost your cool.”

“Just like the empty words of your husband?” I shot back as I arranged the MCubed books on my library book rack.

“Don’t bring your father into it,” Mama cautioned me. “Don’t change the topic.”

I sighed as I put *Outcaste* by Narendra Jadhav on top of the other MCubed Library books. “We are still on the same topic. We always will be.”

Since the dawn of the second decade of the millennium, crimes against women and girl children in India have increased to disturbing proportions. Be it eve-teasing, molestation, or rape, sexual assaults on women have become the norm. They have increased to such gruesome proportions that a toddler girl child was gang-raped in a temple, a place of worship, sending the nation into a fit. In 2012, a young girl, Nirbhaya (not her real name), was gang-raped in a bus and a rod was pushed through her vagina, destroying her innards.

She ultimately succumbed to her injuries a few weeks later in hospital.

From then on, after the police station incident, I was placed in the charge of our trusty taxi driver Man Friday, Narayan. He would go with me wherever I had to go out, even to a place as close as MCubed Library or Title Waves. Going anywhere by myself was strictly prohibited. I felt trapped, but not too much. I was already a recluse and loner, and I had thrown all of my college friends out the window. Only books were my friends, and Title Waves became a place where I would spend my time.

Title Waves truly is a marvelous boutique bookstore. Along with a vast collection of fiction and nonfiction books, it sells fancy stationery, curios, cloth bags, scented candles, designer pens, Kindles, record players, do-it-yourself grow-a-plant kits, DVDs, and more. When I started doing well financially, I started doing a lot of my shopping at Title Waves.

Rita has suddenly taken to books. I buy all her books from Title Waves. Her favorites are Chetan Bhagat, Kiran Nagarkar, and Sudha Murthy. But however much I try, she never volunteers to come along with me to shop.

"You go, *baba*," she'll say gratefully. "And choose for me. I love your choice. And besides, whatever will I do in a boutique bookshop?"

She is my sweet aunt. And she cooks the best butter chicken ever.

These days, when I see my own books being sold at this boutique bookstore, I think to myself: how far I have come from that body-shaming-cum-eve-teasing incident to now!

"*Par manna padega beti*," said the police officer who saw me out after my assaulter was jailed. "I've never seen a girl coming here who has been eve-teased with her abuser in tow at the scruff of his neck. You looked like Goddess Durga. *Manna padega – manna padega*, you have created history here at the Bandra West police station."

"You have too much of anger in you," Blaise told me later that day as I was reading *His Majesty's Opponent* by Sugata Bose. "You must control your temper. You are overweight. That is a fact. There will be many men who will make remarks on your weight everywhere you go. You must just ignore them and go about your own business."

I couldn't digest anything that Blaise was saying. I'm a plus-size. Does that mean I am obliged to accept the lewd remarks hurtling my way? What's my crime? Why this paradox? Why should the abused be punished instead of the abuser? What is this rubbish!

But when I looked into Blaise's eyes, I gleaned what he was trying to say. He just wanted to protect me in a Mumbai, in an India, that has suddenly gone mad, where the rowdy "*goonda*" *raj* or reign, has taken over common sense, security, and respect for all.

"I don't want to lose you," Blaise said, pleading with his eyes. And I promised him I would control my temper and hands henceforth.

Mama was so shocked by the incident that she couldn't speak for a whole day. But I was fine. I went about my business, maybe with a bit of nervous energy, but I was all right.

The loner in me was taking hold. I had no social life other than my visits to libraries and bookstores.

ESSAY 30

The End of Mr. Y by Scarlett Thomas

I READ THOMAS'S BOOK IN 2015. I had borrowed it from MCubed and read the whole thing in a week's time because I was busy with tuitions and studying for one of those MA exams which, finally, I would abandon.

The book made an existentialist of me. It changed the way I look at the world and the way I analyse the things that happen in my world.

The book speaks of a wayward woman's journey through strange paths in search of a Mr. Y. It has everything that I like in literary fiction: university life, professors, intellectual dialogues – the works.

I can still remember the day I finished reading the erudite book. It was raining outside, accompanied by crackling thunder and lightning. There were only two of us there in the MCubed Library: just me and an elderly woman, Neelam who, like me, kept to herself and studied.

Philo ma'am, the librarian, wondered aloud when the rain would stop. The cleaning woman fussed over me as usual.

"*Laadli* is studying a lot today." For her, reading meant studying.

"Just reading a book, *dost*," I clarified, and then shuddered as another clap of thunder sounded; the sky was looking ominous with dark rain clouds.

"Oh-ho," complained the cleaning maid. "And I don't even have an umbrella today! *Laadli* girl, do you have a spare umbrella?" she asked me beseechingly. "You come in a taxi. Think of me. I have to visit all the houses in this and the next two lanes before I'm done for the day. I'll give it back to you tomorrow."

I cleared my throat. Neelam looked at me for a spell and then back at her work. I got up from my sofa seat after placing a bookmark in *The End of Mr. Y* and went to get her my notorious pink ladies' umbrella, which these days acted as if it didn't know what its actual use was – an umbrella or a cudgel. I fumbled with it as I gave it to the cleaning woman.

"Blessings on my *laadli* girl who studies so much," she said and left the library. She would return the next day with the pink umbrella and deliver it to me before she swabbed the adult's library. But I would be a different person the next day, and all because of *The End of Mr. Y*.

Thomas's prose is simple, but her story is captivating and mesmerizing. I am not that much of a fan of fantasy and dystopian literature, but this book is a cut above the rest, teaching us how we should look at the world and realize that there is more to it than what we have clubbed into patriarchal boxes.

This book was my walking ticket into the subject of philosophy and everything deviant to regular, everyday thought and action. If you are keen on existentialism, then this is the book for you. If you like dystopian fantasy that will make you see the world through different eyes, you should be reading this book. It is amazing and impossible to put down!

That was in 2015. It is 2019 as I write this essay. It is springtime and my birthday is close.

Neelam stayed till lunch and then went on her way. Others took her place, but the rain did not abate. Philo ma'am, the morning librarian, was busy on the phone when I returned the book to the desk. When she saw me, she pointed toward the return basket and there I placed *The End of Mr. Y*. It was the end of the book for me, but it was the beginning of a life dedicated to new knowledge and wisdom.

In search for what I read in *The End of Mr. Y* I would, in the span on two years, join the United Lodge of Theosophists and attend their sessions and meetings. I would agree and disagree with them. I was twenty-five and still trying to get a grip on who I was and the meaning behind all that we did.

I read their books, studied their tenets with the mind of a skeptic, like one of the characters in *The End of Mr. Y*. Back then I was stoicism personified. I had a question for every answer and for every question. The guides at the lodge were patient with me.

I ultimately stopped attending their sessions because of my increased workload. I was mostly teaching ninth- and tenth-grade children English language and literature. I became well-known for my proficiency in English, to my sort of disdain for I preferred teaching history.

I am technically still a member at the lodge and can go back anytime. Maybe I will, maybe I won't. Maybe when I am a bit less mercenary, I will return and fulfill my duty to the wonderful people there who imparted their knowledge and showed me the unity behind the various philosophies and religions of the world.

"*Laadli* girl, you look worried today," said my *dost*, the cleaning maid back at MCubed, one morning as I was reading a biography of Rabindranath Tagore. "Everything is fine, right?"

I sighed and smiled sadly.

"Everything has changed, *dost*, and yet nothing has changed."

All this emotional turmoil at the hands of a lightweight paperback.

ESSAY 31

Outcaste: A Memoir by Narendra Jadhav

FOR EVERY INTELLECTUAL INDIAN, there is that moment in life when you read your first Dalit biography or autobiography and come face to face with the awful caste system, that hydra-headed monster that we have fattened over the years, and which only now seems, at least a bit, to be dying a slow death. But with anti-social and anti-constitutional elements everywhere, and people in the name of Hindutva killing in the name of religion, the very religion which according to revered Dr. B. R. Ambedkar is the reason this caste system exists, one wonders what mess we are getting into now, when everyone in the world is on tenterhooks.

Basically, my first Dalit memoir was *Outcaste: A Memoir* by Dr. Narendra Jadhav. *Outcaste* is the tale of his father, born in the lowest caste, who became a Dalit, and what Ambedkar and being a Dalit meant to him.

I found the memoir in MCubed and immediately got down to reading it. I read it in a very odd place – at BSS when I was substituting for one of my teachers, back in 2015. It was a two-month substitution period after which I was back to tuitions.

The book touched me, the humbleness of Jadhav's father made me cry and made me wonder about the plight of Dalit women. I wondered what it meant to not only be born of the lower caste, the untouchables, but also to be a woman.

For those who don't know what I am talking about, here is a brief: It is said in Hindu philosophy that the four castes of humans emerged from the four different parts of the Creator. From the head of the Creator came the priestly caste, or as it is called in Hinduism, the Brahmin. He is the giver of knowledge and is next to the Divine, for he emerged from the Creator's head. The Brahmins are the highest caste group in Hinduism. Next, from the shoulders of the Creator came the warrior caste or the Kshatriyas. They are the rulers, the kings, the emperors, and soldier caste. They are a high caste but not higher than the Brahmin. They protect the people of the tribe. It is then said that from the stomach of the Creator emerged the working caste, or the Vaishyas. They are subordinate to the Brahmins and Kshatriyas. The Vaishyas serve the upper two castes where food and other essential necessities are concerned. They are the farmers, blacksmiths, iron mongers, barbers, et al. And finally, from the feet of the Creator, it seems, came the lowest caste of all, the Shudras. They were the untouchables and allowed only to scavenge and perform other jobs of low estate like cleaning latrines, septic tanks, and clogged sewage drains, carrying dead cattle out of the village, etc. They would never be educated and never rise from their lowly position of life. They were born to serve the upper three castes.

These are the four castes of the land. One was born into a caste or Varna and died in that same caste. Birth was the deciding factor, not the merit of the person.

The caste system originated in the Vedic Age of India, when the early civilizations of Harappa had been destroyed. The sad part is they continue to exist to this day.

Many who preached against the caste system have come and gone, but the terrible curse of caste hierarchy has remained with us. Worse yet, its poison has seeped into other cultures and customs of religious communities in India: Muslims, Christians, Roman Catholics, Sindhi, Jains, Buddhist etc.

It was in this light, with this background knowledge, that I read *Outcaste* and was edified. I make it a point to read all biographies and memoirs of the so-called lower castes, untouchables, or Dalits to give me strength, knowledge, and understanding of the poison of the caste system.

I don't believe in the caste system. I abhor it, and I hope I've made myself clear. Through the writings of Narendra Jadhav, I was educated and became a Dalit by adoption. I was introduced to Dr. Babasaheb Ambedkar, who I look up to with reverence. Dr. Ambedkar, a Mahar untouchable by caste, not only educated himself, but also fought the caste system, leading a mass conversion of untouchable Shudras whom he named Dalits, to Buddhism. He was the architect of the Constitution of India, the largest Constitution in the world.

In spite of all my sociological training in St. Andrew's College, I had never gotten down to analyzing the caste system. Now, after *Outcaste,* I suddenly was a changed person. I became an armchair Ambedkarite. Dr. Ambedkar is one of the writers I have a framed photo of in my office-cum-writing hut. He sits between the photographs of R. K. Narayan and Ruskin Bond. He is an inspiration to many, and God incarnate to the people he served. Never have I met a man in Indian National Movement History that I have loved so much.

If you, dear reader, find my nonfiction writing more pleasing to the eye and the mind than my fiction, then that is so because I try to emulate the nonfiction writing of the late Son of the Soil, Dr. Ambedkar. He is my inspiration in nonfiction writing – blunt, to the point, no beating around the bush.

But I was introduced to him by *Outcaste,* and I hope you too read *Outcaste* so that you may realize the struggle that a huge number of lower caste Dalits and other OBC/ST/SC castes are going through. I hope that one day they may be treated as equals in society. Do read this memoir and be enlightened. Support the Dalit movement and the teachings and writings of Dr. B.R. Ambedkar.

When I was reading this book in BSS, my mind was troubled. The old library was a shadow of its former self and all the books that I had read and loved had gone. They had taken away a part of my soul, and to this day I feel like I'll need some more grace from God or fate or Providence if I am to be able to forgive those who did this to my BSS papa.

"Why do you want to come back here, little one?" said one of my teachers as I was heading to the canteen on our floor for snacks. "You don't have to be here. This place is not meant for you. Go out, live your life. Forget BSS."

She knew about my love for the BSS library. She used to see me when she corrected papers there. She knew my pain.

After school that day I headed to the MCubed Library to return *Outcaste.*

"You always read unusual books," said Philo ma'am, the day librarian. "You are the only one who has ever taken this book. See, look here," she pointed to the book's library sheet. "Yours is the first stamp."

I looked. I smiled. Yes, I am different. Yes, I am different, and I don't know what to do about it. Except maybe write another book or read another.

ESSAY 32

Ambedkar - Awakening India's Social Conscience by Narendra Jadhav

AFTER READING *Outcaste,* I was dying to read a biography of Dr. B. R. Ambedkar. I was lucky, for at MCubed Library there was another book, a tome by the author of *Outcaste,* Narendra Jadhav, who had written this book which I am going to recommend now: *Ambedkar – Awakening India's Social Conscience.* After this book, I would go on to read most of the books pertaining to or penned by Dr. Ambedkar himself. This book was that good an introduction to the life of a God among men.

I came to love the book so much that I would buy a copy of my own from Mumbai's best bookstore, Kitab Khana, but more about Kitab Khana later.

I read Narendra Jadhav's book when I was studying for one of those MA exams which I would finally never pursue. Unlike other books I read, this book questioned my dedication to my job and not to my studies. Dr. Ambedkar was dedicated to his studies while in America as well as in England. He was around my age at the time when he was studying and gaining double MAs, PhDs, and a law degree, and here I was grappling with earning a living, writing, and trying to study.

"Ambedkar's time was different," Mama said as she and I were retiring after a long day of teaching. "His was a different time. Believe me, you can't do what he did. You are a single girl. You need to make your career."

After that, she went to sleep, and I read Ambedkar beside her, wondering who was I to listen to, my mama or my heart.

I long to finish an MA either in history or sociology. I tried, but it was impossible to attend lectures due to all of the teaching and writing that I do.

As I read Narendra Jadhav's book, I was amazed and astounded by Dr. Ambedkar's rationalism, devotion to realism, and his call to all Dalits to "wake up." Going on as I read the book, I realized Ambedkar's hunger for reading, studies, and books. This was someone I liked. I kept on reading.

Blaise always says that the greatest story ever told is the tale of Jesus. I tend to disagree with him. To me, Dr. Ambedkar's fight against a caste hierarchical structure that had lasted for millennia is the greatest story ever told. It's about one man, one word (*education*) and one goal – awakening the social conscience of a country steeped in social rigidity.

This book by Narendra Jadhav hit me so hard in the pit of my stomach that I declared myself to be a Dalit by adoption. So easy for me to say, for I can take the name without the shackles of the term *Dalit* in all my papers. How difficult for one who has been born a Dalit. But India must not sleep; she must get up from her slumber, and books like these will do the trick.

"Fiza miss, what a big book you are reading," one of my fifth-grade students says. "Who is this Ambedkar?"

"He is my hero."

"Is he like Gandhi?" asks the child. "They place his pictures next to Gandhi and Nehru in Government buildings."

I sigh and shake my head.

"They are different but they both had good hearts."

Through this book I learned more about the freedom struggle in India, the side of the story away from Gandhi and the rest. I learned about the Chal Mahad tank episode and felt a choking in my throat. I realized that Dr. Ambedkar's struggle and the Dalit struggle were more difficult than simply obtaining freedom from the British. Making the British leave India would have resulted in independence, but what about the social issues like casteism that plagued the country? Who was going to rid India of that? Alas, years have passed and yet there it exists, this degrading caste system.

I have overheard my own students from posh and well-educated homes telling one another the name of the caste their family belongs to. It makes me shudder. Well-educated people retaining caste fidelities!

I remember, while reading about Ambedkar, my days at St. Andrew's. I remember Lata, the ever talkative and unstoppable Lata, going on about her marriage proposals pouring in every second day.

We were only sixteen. The marriageable age for a woman in India according to the Constitution is eighteen years.

"I can't marry just anybody," went on Lata. "I can't just marry any Hindu. He has to be of my Varna."

"Varna?" I asked hesitantly, wondering what the hell that meant. Lata belittled my ignorance.

"Caste, of course, you silly Fizzy." She loved playing around with my name. "My groom has to be of my caste."

I knew caste system basics. So, I casually asked, "What's your caste, Lata?" expecting her to answer with Vaishya, for she wasn't that well-to-do. I was not prepared for the answer I got.

"I am a Kshatriya Marwari Rajasthani Vaishnavite Rajput," she said in one breath.

"Come again!"

"Kshatriya Marwari Rajasthani Vaishnavite Rajput caste."

I remembered this conversation with Lata and that googly of an answer as I read about Dr. Ambedkar and had a moment of silence. It was then I realized that if the youth in this country are still steeped in this nonsense, India has a long way to go.

"Mama," I asked casually one day. "Did Nana or Nanaji (my grandfather) believe or practice caste?"

"Not practiced, certainly not," Mama said as she corrected someone's test paper. "But your nanaji always claimed he was a Brahmin and Nana was a Shudra, or that other one, the one a little bit better than a Shudra. ..."

"Vaishya?" I suggested.

"Yes, that one," Mama said as her red pen corrected one math sum after another, staining her right index finger with red gel ink. "He used to be mighty proud of the fact that he was a Brahmin Mangalorean Roman Catholic."

I changed the topic.

We've got a seriously long way to go.

Until that time, we must educate ourselves. Reading about Dr. Ambedkar's life is the best place to start. I recommend Narendra Jadhav's *Ambedkar – Awakening India's Social Conscience* to anyone, no matter what your country, who would like to research the caste system of India as well as the accomplishments of Dr. Babasaheb Ambedkar in fighting against this hydra-headed social evil in Indian society. If you like reading about the Indian National Movement the way I do, then you will be enriched by the story of the Dalits and how they were a very important part of the National Movement, especially under the leadership of Dr. B. R. Ambedkar. If you are already an Ambedkarite thinker and reader, then this is a good book to add to your collection of Ambedkar biographies. It is detailed, well-paced, and good for academic research as well as reference work. It is a tome, but it's also a page-turner.

Dr. Ambedkar dedicated his life to awakening our minds to facts, and not decadent thoughts. He had the guts and the grit to take the bull by the horns. I've yet to see a leader like him in this, my one and only life. Do yourself a favor and read this biography; if you do, you will be a changed person – a better man or woman, better able to help society.

Maybe you will want to start a movement of your own. I wanted to do so after I read the book. But I wanted to do it in my own way.

Today my publishing firm stands up for freedom with pluralism (the phrase "Freedom With Pluralism" is printed upon each of my published books). As a publisher, I am dedicated to books that expose reality and speak the truth about social issues that affect all of us. I am an armchair social activist, using my pen and solitude to change the world, one typed word at a time.

ESSAY 33

Trilogy: The Eternal Library

IT WAS 2015. I had just finished substitution work at BSS and was also done with daily tuitions.

Now I only had to teach the ninth and tenth graders their English language and literature in preparation for the new term in June. I would teach from 2:00 p.m. to 7:30 p.m. Before that, I needed a place to write in yet again. The café at Title Waves had shut down. MCubed Library was like a houseful of students who had learned my trick and were arriving early, taking up all of the table space.

It was then that Blaise read in the newspapers an article about a curated library-cum-bookshop in Lower Parel at the Raghuvanshi Mills. In fact, a couple who were dedicated to books and reading had opened it in 2014. They offered space for writers to come and write their works there. I was intrigued, and so Mama, Blaise, and I got in our trusty taxi, with driver Narayan at the helm, and we searched out the place.

It was next to the Phoenix Mall in Lower Parel. It was surrounded by tall peepal trees and overlooked the Jewish graveyard. The place was serene, clean, posh, well-kept and had plenty of room to write. The toilet was clean. I took out a library membership for one book for two weeks to begin with. It was a private library and bookstore, and only library members could sit and read in the premises. I still remember the first book I borrowed from Trilogy. It was *The Little Friend* by Donna Tartt. I came in the next day to write.

It was bliss! As a member once said, the only sound one could hear in that peaceful library-cum-bookstore was the turning of pages.

The couple whose venture this was are Meethil Momaya, a professional wildlife photographer, and Ahalya Naidu Momaya, a professional editor. They cutely mentioned in their brochure that the day they truly got married was the day when they started sharing the same bookshelf space. He loved David Attenborough and thrillers. She liked Terry Pratchett and literary fiction. I softly entered their lives, and they gave me a little space in their vast kingdom of books. I'm grateful.

Narayan would drop me off at Trilogy every morning at 10:00 a.m. sharp and wait for me there in the parking lot. I would sit in my favorite chair, which looked onto a large peepal tree whose leaves shimmered in the sunlight. I was spoiled silly by Meethil sir and Ahalya ma'am. Whenever I was writing there, I was given hot ginger tea with sugar biscuits of various kinds. By 1:30 p.m., I would head back to class.

I wrote *Amina: The Silent One* there. It was written on an impulse. I was testing the genre. It turned out to be one of my best works and fetched me a lot of awards. That's amazing, when you think that I was just going along with the story wherever it led me. It was the only book of mine picked up at a foreign book fair by Saikatham Publishers and was translated into Malayalam. Now whenever Blaise hears that I'm writing a book "on an impulse" or just to "pass time," he gets terrified.

I spent the whole summer of 2015 at Trilogy. I first completed *Amina: The Silent One* and then started on my LGBTQIA book, which is a collection of short stories based on LGBTQIA situations in different parts of the world. That one was also a "pass time" book. It is called *The Love That Dare Not Speak Its Name: Short Stories*. It won me sixteen international awards, including the prestigious 2018 Digital World Book Award for short stories. My fellow finalist in this category was a PEN America Book Award finalist, and when I was declared a winner in that category, I felt truly humbled. My "pass time" books are dangerous!

Trilogy became a second home to me, the place where I wrote my books. I still wrote in longhand. When Blaise retired from the bank, he started to accompany me to Trilogy. I would write while he would read their excellently curated collection.

Ahalya and Meethil's book collection, both in the store section as well as the library, is awe inspiring. I have read and bought some of my best books there.

The place is quiet and classy. It has cushioned chairs, well-maintained wooden furniture, strong and well-dusted stylish bookshelves (some with beautiful bookends), coffee-table books, photographs on the walls taken by Meethil sir on his expeditions into the wild. And books, books, and more, you guessed it, BOOKS!

By the time 2017 rolled in, I had changed my library membership from one book to eight books a fortnight. I was writing and reading there practically all the time. When the situations were such that I couldn't go there, I used to go either to MCubed or to Starbucks at Khar West. I used to spend weekends at Trilogy whenever I was free and not taking class. I used to sit there, drink ginger tea, eat sweet sugar biscuits, write in my diaries, and then read to my heart's content.

Trilogy also allows post-it notes of recommendations to be stuck on the bookshelves or on a book where it could be seen but did not spoil the book in any way. I love Ahalya's little notes tucked in all different colors all over the bookstore and library. Here's a sampling of notes I've seen:

- Our favorite bookshelf
- Books we love shelf
- Don't like short stories? Give Alice Munro a chance
- Books about food
- Books written by woman

- Over
- Why is the book over!
- Don't pull the book from the pile, call us and we'll help you

I have had wonderful experiences at Trilogy. Some of my most important business decisions have been made there as well.

I wrote in Trilogy till the day I rented my own office-cum-writing hut. That was in 2016. That's when I went into publishing and incorporated my own publishing company, run by Blaise and me.

These days we don't spend hours or weekends at Trilogy because we have so much to do with my writing and publishing firm. We are a busy bunch here, my maternal family and me. If we don't manage to get things done during the week, we put in extra hours during the weekend. I miss going to Trilogy. I miss spending the weekends there writing in my diary or reading a Trilogy library book.

I am still a member at the library and continue to buy books in the shop. Mama loves to accompany us sometimes and to sit in the place where I have written some of my best work.

I bought two boxes of books from them recently, in March. They are all books by the pioneering feminist publisher Zubaan Publishing. Trilogy offers a large number of specially curated and rare books in their bookstore and library, allowing me to read so many awesome and very different books that I otherwise might not have had the chance to read. Zubaan, Left Word, Women Unlimited, Yoda Press, Navayana Books, etc., are some of the publishers I've been able to read and study at Trilogy.

Trilogy is warm, peaceful, chic, and very comfortable. Once you get in, you really don't feel like leaving.

It's March 2019 as I write these words. Trilogy has grown to be five years old and I've spent the whole latter half of my precious twenties here, among its many bookshelves, looking for another good book to read.

"What do you like best about Trilogy?" Mama asked me one day.

I mused over it for a while and then say, "Roaming around and taking a look at the books on their shelves."

"You find that interesting!" Mechu says, then sips the tea Rita made for her. "You can do that here too. I bet you've got a bigger collection than them."

I sigh, "It's not the same thing."

Sometimes my own family members fail to understand what I'm hinting at. I've never known a person who has invited me over to see his or her bookshelves. No one spoke to me at school, not even the bookworm boy I loved and still love. In college my classmates hardly read at all. They also never invited me home or to go to their favorite cafés to chill out. They felt I stuck out like a sore thumb.

"Why don't you call my daughter over to your parties?" Mama once asked a friend of mine. This was just after I had graduated from college.

"Aunty," the so-called friend said. "Fiza doesn't fit in with our crowd. She is too intelligent. And she is very bookish. Besides, we all drink, smoke, or do drugs once in a while. She doesn't, and so what's the point?"

"Well," my poor scandalized mama stammered, "she can sit and keep you all company, can't she?"

"Don't be ridiculous aunty," my friend said. "She'll never fit in with us."

I've never met anyone like me. Never met another solitary soul who loves reading books and writing on the side. No one.

The only bookshelves I've perused are the shelves of the bookstores and public libraries that, without discrimination, have allowed me to go through their shelves, pick a book, and be myself. One of these benevolent places has been Trilogy, and I'm highly in their debt.

More than any regular library or bookstore, Trilogy is a place of certain tastes. There are plenty of books on wildlife and photography which point to Meethil sir, while the literary fiction and feminist books point to Ahalya ma'am. I am nowadays also displayed on their shelves – my books are, that is.

It's been a blissful journey from book to book all around the Trilogy library-cum-bookstore. I still think of my Amina and my

LGBTQIA book when I drink ginger tea these days. I hope I will one day get to spend at least one day in my usual seat overlooking the large peepal tree, writing a piece in my diary. Maybe I'll write something about a book I recently read and liked. Or about the parrots that visit the birdfeeders hanging from the windows of Trilogy. Or about that boy I loved at BSS and still cling to. Or of how a day full of books, nature, and bliss seems very much like a Ruskin Bondish day indeed.

ESSAY 34

The Hidden Life of Trees by Peter Wohlleben

ONE CANNOT BE AT TRILOGY and not manage to fall in love with nature and its denizens. This is also true where Trilogy's choice of good books about nature are concerned. One of the best books on nature I have read from Trilogy Bookstore is *The Hidden Life of Trees* by Peter Wohlleben. It's a charming and dainty, but scientifically sound, book on trees – how they feel, communicate, grow, live as a community, etc.

The book title and cover were so eye-catching that I just had to buy it. Also, I had by now started growing and maintaining a modest garden of my own which I tended to with a lot of love and care. And just like R. K. Narayan's maternal grandmother, mentioned in his autobiography *My Days*, I too am quite fond of growing trees in large pots. I'm a crazy tree woman. I feel elated when I see my trees, my little babies, growing so tall. I especially have a fascination for neem, magnolia, and drumstick trees. I have a colony of baby neem trees; three are only one to two years old, yet they are far taller than me.

In this book, I read about how trees communicate, have a sort of "world wide web" under the soil and like to grow among trees of the same type. I read about how important it is to grow new trees (chin up for me), and also how equally important it is to maintain the forest soil – which must be rich in humus and so much else – that we as global citizens are not paying attention to. Peter Wohlleben mentions so many scientific facts about trees – their long lives, how to keep them "happy," how they feel pain, the importance of forest cover – that his book blew my mind.

Practically everyone who lives in my neighborhood knows that I love plants and animals. As I've mentioned in an earlier essay, I have a tendency to go pale if confronted by a snake or a scorpion, but otherwise I'm quite compatible with nature. Especially with trees.

I love neem trees. I love growing and tending them, and Peter Wohlleben's book provides good advice on how to do so.

If I'm not spending money on books, I'm spending it on plants and trees. I have a modest garden, which my gardener and I tend to from time to time. The gardener's name is Anil. He used to be a gardener at the DYC where I was a female representative for the Catholic youth for Mumbai.

"You recognize me?" I asked Anil one day.

"Not at all," he replied.

"Good," I answered happily. "We will get on well together."

"As you say," he said, wondering whether I was nutty. But we get along well. Together we have grown the following:

- Green indoor money plants.
- White and green money plants.
- Yellow and green money plants.
- Two white scented champas/magnolias.
- A bonsai plant.
- A large philodendron (Anil calls it a "*bada jaad*").
- Ginger plant.
- Yellow ixoras.
- White ixoras.
- Pink pentas.
- White pentas.
- Yellow and green schefflera.
- Green schefflera.

- White bougainvillea.
- Two aurelias.
- Five China grass plants.
- Many jasmine plants/Moghra.
- A dozen cacti.
- White euphorbia, also called spurge.
- Peach and yellow euphorbia.
- Neem trees (cheaper by the dozen).
- A drumstick tree.
- Pink syngoniums.
- White and green syngoniums.
- Dark green syngoniums.
- Yellow cosmos plant, and
- Japanese gardens with small decorative plants that were small when we started out but have grown mighty big.

Interested in anything? No, don't come and meet me. I hate visitors, but I won't send you away if you do come to have a look at the garden. You can watch the garden while I'll have a close look at you, and maybe later put you in one of my books.

Peter Wohlleben is a master at bringing out the significance of trees without going into the metaphysics. That suits me very well. He, of course, speaks mainly about the trees of Europe. It would be a wonderful reading experience if he managed to do a book on our Indian plants and trees – in the hills, we've got quite a variety.

"I loved the book," I told Ahalya ma'am, the next time I went to Trilogy. "I so love trees."

I felt so ecstatic after reading the book. Maybe that's the Ruskin Bondish part of me, or maybe that's just me.

I read most of this book during the spring, so my garden was looking really beautiful at that time. The building people are having a problem with my "large" garden. Do you call this large, I ask you? It's a tiny little baby nursery!

But, yes, this is another non-bookish side to me that people don't know about. I feel blessed to have planted so many beautiful flowers, plants, and trees, and I look forward to increasing the variety in my garden. When the neem trees are too big for their pots, I'll transfer them to the soil either in the main building garden or in the woodland behind my apartment complex, just like Peter Wohlleben advises his readers to do. Why does he say so? I'm not going to tell you why. Read the book and find out for yourselves.

It doesn't require much from you to care for ecology. It's something as simple as looking after the trees that already grow in your garden or neighborhood, as well as the trees you grow from seed to trunk with your own hands. If you love trees and want to know more about how they feel about certain things we humans do, read this book. If you want to know about how we can do a better job of looking after our trees, or if you want to grow a tree, then this is the book for you. If you are new or old to this thing called "conservation, ecology, forest heritage" and want to be further educated, this is the book for you.

I would also like to add here that if you are a skeptic and think that trees are not living beings – that they don't get hurt, depressed, or agitated – then please challenge yourself to read this book by Peter Wohlleben. Everything he mentions is a scientific fact, take it or leave it, and you will love the way he has presented his material in such a clean-easy read.

Try this book, and, yes, plant a tree, at least one tree in your life. Then look after it, send it "good feeling" telepathic messages. Trees have been here longer than we have. Let's keep them happy. Maybe someday they'll let us in on their longevity secret. Then I'll get to read books until eternity. And maybe after that too!

ESSAY 35

Our Lives, Our Words: Telling Aravani Lifestories by A. Revathi

As I have mentioned, I managed to read a lot of diverse works written by previously unknown authors and published by new independent publishers which were stocked and sold by Trilogy. One of the very first books I read back in 2015 was *Our Lives, Our Words: Telling Aravani Lifestories* by A. Revathi. It's a Yoda Press book. It was Meethil sir who introduced me to these books, especially when he heard I was turning my short story, *Flesh of Flesh,* into a novel, and that I was researching material for a LGBTQIA short story volume that ultimately became my most celebrated book.

"Try Yoda," Meethil sir said, showing me some of their titles. "They print books on LGBTQ topics that might interest you."

The books did interest me, and I bought a few of them along with A. Revathi's book. I learned the most from her book.

A. Revathi is an Aravani (in Tamil Nadu) or a Kinnar (in Mumbai) part of the transsexual or eunuch community of India, whom we in India derogatively address as Hijras. A. Revathi, in her book, shows us the human side of transsexuals and the Aravanis. She writes about their customs and traditions, about how they undergo Nirvana, a castration process that all Aravanis aspire to, the human side of this community, and how Aravanis (or Kinnars) are someone's son, brother, cousin, uncle, friend, lover – and yet they have made a controversial and somewhat negative impression in society.

I was really impressed by the book. It's thin, but it is very beautifully penned, proving that a good writer does not necessarily have to be a Penguin, HarperCollins, or Bloomsbury writer. Yoda Press and others are doing a great job bringing important books and their issues to light. They are publishing books that inspire and are thought-provoking, thus engendering a discussion on topics like the Aravani community that normally wouldn't happen in households, let alone in public.

The book is simple to read but very emotional. And since I'm so connected with this community of people, I really felt it when the girls in this book spoke about their activism, their pain, their anguish, and their gender identification and sexual orientation issues.

I guess I feel very strongly for this community because I have been a sort of victim of society regarding my gender. To tell you the truth, after all is said and done about me and how I was abandoned because I was a girl – the fact is that I've never in my life acted like a girl. I'm not a boy, and I'm not personally part of the LGBTQIA community (which is one of the most beautiful communities I've had the privilege to research, write on, and interact with in my early twenties); instead, I've been brought up as an independent being. A person who should strive for good grades at school, attain a career, stand on their own two feet, and be someone who can be of use to society. You see, gender training had nothing to do with it. "Be a decent person" was what Nana drilled into my family member's (and my own) heads, then be whatever else you want to be, as long as you are not harming anyone.

As I've mentioned before, Nana never discriminated between her two boys and three girls. They all were the same in her eyes. She never forced anyone to get married, but she forced everyone to study, get good grades, get a job, and refrain from becoming anyone's slave. Nothing about her parenting had to do with bringing Rita up as a girl or David uncle as a boy. Instead, it was about BRINGING UP DECENT, INDEPENDENT HUMAN BEINGS. So, really, I don't know what it means to be a girl or a boy. Maybe I'm only human, and that's good enough, right? I'm doing my own thing back here, right? I'm doing a good job, right? Girl, boy, black, while, weak, strong, rich, poor, tall, short – who cares?

But we DO care. We have not learned how to be good human beings first, so how the hell are we going to figure out how to be a good boy or girl? And then, what about those who stand out as the third gender, the Aravani – what about them?

We don't respect girl children. We abort them illegally; kill them by cracking their necks during childbirth; get them married when they are only children; burn them to death if their families don't meet dowry demands. Aravanis most of the time wish they could be a "normal" girl! My Kinnar friends, girls are not exactly experiencing a heyday here in Mumbai, or anywhere in India for that matter. WHY WOULD YOU WANT TO BE US? Look at me, I was dumped for no other reason than being XX!

Aravanis, too, are not having a heyday. That is the truth, verified by the testimonials of transsexuals in A. Revathi's book. Read it and be educated. I read it because gender and sexual identity played a part in the reasons my mother lost the love of her life, and I, a daughter, lost the entire paternal side of her family.

Do read this book and realize that everyone is human first. None of the other stuff matters once that fact is established – we are human.

The Aravani community is a beautiful community of people who celebrate their lives every day in their own way. Why should they or anyone from the LGBTQIA community be thought of as being deviant? Mother nature is all about deviants and doing things differently in every age, every millennium, every era – every time known to man. Let's read books like these so we can stop this discrimination. Let's be human first.

I loved this book and the testimonials found within; I'm sure you will too. It's time we took the scales off our eyes and looked at the world the way Adam did on that first day (in Genesis). He was naked and he didn't know it, and with a friend like his God to walk in the Garden with him, he couldn't care less. Let's do the same. Let's get back to basics.

Decent humans first – we can get to the rest whenever we get to it!

ESSAY 36

The Vegetarian by Han Kang

I PICKED HAN KANG'S *The Vegetarian* from Trilogy because Ahalya ma'am recommended it to me.

"Everyone is saying it's really good and one of the best International Man Booker Prize books ever chosen," she said as she handed me the book. I read the synopsis and was hooked.

"Okay, I really want to read this one," I said. I bought the book in 2017, but I only managed to read it in 2018.

I read it during the first winter days of 2018. I was spread out on my office recliner, and I finished it with my heart thumping and my eyes red. I was numb. I had never read anything like this before!

I read the book again this year, and once again I felt numb at the end. The book truly records the life of a woman in a society created by man; the symbolism and plot were perfect and the translation from Korean to English excellent.

Whenever I think of *The Vegetarian,* I thank my lucky stars, or fate, or whatever it was that has allowed me to grow up to be independent and unlike the sorrowful protagonists in the book.

Han Kang is a genius. She has shown us through her literary mastery that we live in a world that is the very "thought," "word," and "deed" of the male gender – Man! I have read so much in my life, a modest number of books that have taught me that everything that we have ever thought was our reality is but a male reality. The way we look at the world, the way we think EVERYTHING is governed by patriarchy, whose shackles we have only just begun to break, and I too hope to break free from. You might be thinking I'm a nut, but like *The Vegetarian*, there are hundreds of books out there to educate you and to tell you that this wonderful world of opposites, is a very, very male way of thinking, working and living.

Now, the protagonist in Han Kang's book was once a hardcore meat-eating human. She faithfully follows the patriarchal rules, until one day she decides to look at life from a different perspective. It's not a female perspective, but it's a really different perspective all the same.

She becomes a vegetarian in a world (Korea) that only looks up to people who are non-vegetarians. And thus, the story goes on. And thus, you are hooked to the plot.

The book was a breath of fresh air in the cloud of literature I'd been reading at the time. I love books that challenge the established norm. I am not exactly a conformist, as you know by now, dear reader.

I've been told throughout my entire life that I'm not your normal type of girl. Even diehard bookworms can't really stick with me for too long. Maybe that's why this book resonated with me so completely.

I personally find the symbolism hard to miss. It's all there: the gender stereotyping; the projection of women in arts as sexual objects; marital rape; objectification of women in society; woman's inferior status to man. It's all there, right in front of your eyes in plain printers' ink through the art of Han Kang.

"How did you like the book?" Blaise asked me, but before he could say anything else in 2018, I thrust the book into his hands.

"Read this!" was my order. That's it.

Blaise doesn't usually follow orders, but he always does my bidding, so he dutifully read it.

When he was done, I asked him, "Well, didn't you love it?"

"What's with all that sexual stuff in it?"

I face-palmed myself. Even he didn't get it.

Basically, some people get it and some don't. I am one of those who got the message loud and clear, and what a deep and powerful message it is indeed.

Han Kang's book has had an enormous impact on me during the last two years of my twenties. Her haunting prose is a cut above the rest. I am glad that I read this book. I consider it one of the best books I've ever read.

"Got more Han Kang?" I asked Ahalya ma'am, the next time I went to Trilogy. She went to one of the shelves and picked up a book. It was *Human Acts.*

"Want some tea?" asks Meethil sir, as I inhale the scent of the book. I say yes, even though I've just had a mug of milky BRU Gold coffee. We sit along with Blaise and talk about books. I sip my ginger tea and "taste" my Amina in the tea. Ahalya ma'am brings in refreshments (*farsan*), which she loves to munch on during the day. Their Man Friday, Anil, brings me sugar biscuits.

"How are you, brother?" I ask Anil, as I dip my sugar biscuit into the ginger tea. He smiles and holds a hand to his heart. He's been missing me. I, too, miss my earlier days at Trilogy.

"Not many people have got the gist of *The Vegetarian,* somehow," Ahalya ma'am says as she munches on her *farsan*. "But you are very impacted by it, Fiza."

"Yes," I say quietly, as I pick up my black diary to pen my thoughts, "I am."

Then I sit for a while longer at Trilogy and write in my diary with a fragrant rose ballpoint pen. Ahalya ma'am and Meethil sir go about their duties, interacting with patrons, selling books, guiding newcomers to the library section. Blaise reads a book for bibliophiles from the "reference only" section of the library, and I ponder over the plight of the protagonist of *The Vegetarian*.

I, too, live in a society molded and founded on patriarchal thoughts. The question of how to fight life itself boggles me like it must have boggled the protagonist's elder sister. How can women or people of other sexual orientations fight this system? Or will we, too, go "mad" in the eyes of the world and one day just want to turn into a tree!

As Ahalya ma'am and Meethil sir sit down to their lunch, when most of the customers are out, I look at the trees out of their windows. I look at the giant peepal tree opposite. The protagonist in *The Vegetarian* starts off by giving up meat, then vegetables and fruits, and then finally water; she thinks she will grow into a tree and that if she does, she will be free.

When will we all, men included, be free of this world of opposites created by patriarchy? I don't want to sound preachy, and once a priest did tell me that in my writings I can be quite "preachy." But I don't want it to come out that way. I'm just putting in writing the things I've been taught through books, and sometimes how real, and sometimes how unreal, they seem.

Han Kang's *The Vegetarian* is not meant for children or teens below the age of eighteen. It is a book that will shake the very foundations that you stand on, so it's definitely not for people who want a holiday read. It is a book about women, and it's a book about how far women have come or not come in this world they did not create. If you are willing to take the plunge, be prepared: you will be disturbed by it.

I have not read Han Kang's *Human Acts* yet, but I have read her *White Book*, and it was crushing and beautiful. Also, it made me numb!

ESSAY 37

Trilogy: The Eternal Library 2

I LOVE TRILOGY. I LOVE THE placement of the books in Trilogy's bookstore and library. I love the Indian fiction section best, but I read nonfiction and foreign writers too. I have read, written, and interacted with so many people there that I'm quite at home within its walls. When I was writing my LGBTQIA book, as well as abridging the classics for my children's series, I was spending time at Trilogy practically every day. This was between 2016 and 2017.

I wrote in longhand at my usual table for hours, living only on tea and biscuits, and then either going out for a vegetarian lunch or for a bit of chicken at Copper Chimney, Worli.

At times when I had written about five thousand words, I would get up, stretch my legs a bit, and then walk around the beautiful place. I would watch the parrot and parakeets coming to the bird feeders; I would lean on a bookshelf and go through a Hindi novel. I would go and try to talk to Meethil sir or Ahalya ma'am and quite irritate them with my prattle.

Ahalya ma'am one day started a book club for library members. It was a unique book club in the sense that no single book was chosen for reading and discussion, but we could choose and read any book from a category, like biographies, science, travelogues, historical structures, history, and we would talk about our various choices at the book club.

I really liked this system and was always the first one at Trilogy ready with diary and pen, to take notes. We had a variety of very interesting readers from all walks of life discussing their choices at the book club. There was a special language needs counselor, a chartered accountant, an economist, a virologist, a banker, a software engineer, and little old me, a humble teacher and writer who was totally excited to be talking about books.

Our discussions were fun and erudite. I managed to speak, actually speak, and that gave me a lot of confidence. One of the younger boys even complimented me on not being a wallflower, and I felt glad about it. I'd found my voice. I don't use it much, but it's there. I keep it under wraps, but it's there.

I loved taking down notes during these meetings, as the fruit bats flew across the darkening landscape outside and as Ahalya ma'am moderated club activity. I made two friends: Kanchana and Sravya. I'm no longer in touch with Sravya, but I am still in contact on Goodreads and Facebook with Kanchana. Kanchana was a dear friend, one of the only ones I've really ever had. She was good to me, but I'm so deep in my reclusiveness and loner lifestyle that I found it difficult to share my world with anyone else, even someone as loving and caring as my dear Kanchana.

I stopped contacting her after a time. This was when my LGBTQIA book was released. She tried her level best to keep in contact with me, but I was breaking off. I was breaking off all ties with the world and retreating into seclusion. I don't know whether you, dear reader, approve of this or not but this is my reality: I don't like people anymore. My students are fine, my angels. But that's it. I'd rather remain in the shadows, in this shadowland of bookishness and stories-a-plenty. And Trilogy provides for a lot of that shadow life that I lead.

The book club disbanded because some of the members were leaving town for good, and others couldn't match their schedules with the book club. I was sad for a bit when it ended, but I continued to write in my diary. Silent writer. Silent notes.

I am fond of Trilogy. I'm fond of its books and its ambience.

I love to buy boxes and boxes of books produced by niche publishers there. I have learned so much from these new publishers and their writers – they have educated me.

I love watching the people that come and go from Trilogy. I like imagining who these readers are and what their quirks are. I observe Ahalya ma'am and Meethil sir carefully, too, with my writer's eye. I note my observations. I miss doing all that these days since I'm so busy and haven't spent as much time there.

"Why are you looking at me like that?" Ahalya ma'am asks me as she places some new books upon the library shelves. She raises her beautiful eyebrows, enhancing her dusky gorgeousness. Her look says many things, but one thing is clear: she knows my writer self is figuring out a way I can use her in one of my books.

ESSAY 38

Fatal Accidents of Birth: Stories of Suffering, Oppression and Resistance by Harsh Mander

I PICKED UP THIS BOOK FROM A SHELF that holds many others of its genre at the Trilogy bookstore. Trilogy has always supported books that are different and inspiring, and that reveal the plain truth. In 2018, this was one of the best books I picked up from the store.

I bought the book at Trilogy but read it in my office-cum-writing hut. Suffice it to say that the title of the book attracted me – "fatal accidents of birth." The stories in this tiny book come from real life, and it's so strange that the people in the book were abused in the most terrible ways known to man just because they were born poor, or a particular gender, or into a certain caste or religion.

This is indeed a book of suffering, oppression, and resistance.

We need books like this to make us realize that we should not discriminate against people based on religion, caste, gender, social class, economic status, or the village or community they were born into.

Two stories left me with a very eerie feeling: *From Godhra to Una* and *The Many Deaths of Ishrat Jahan.*

Reading the chapter titles itself made my hair stand on end. The erudite reader will comprehend, therefore, my reasons for not dwelling on the contents of the book, and realize that I am glad there are people like Harsh Mander out there fighting for justice and human rights. And who knows, if not for the grace of God, there would go I!

The book is well presented, very relevant for our times, and should be read by all and sundry before India, God forbid, ends up like another Syria.

I may have not traveled much and am mostly an armchair scholar, but by reading widely I've learned of the most heinous behavior and cruelty of not only people in India but throughout the world. And to think that these horrible things are happening to the victims who suffer from this cruelty all because they were born in the wrong family and at a very wrong time in contemporary history.

"I'm glad you were born a girl, you know," said my mama the other day. "And that I baptized you as soon as I could and started living with you here in Bandra West."

I know what she was hinting at. She was hinting at the Mumbai 1992–93 riots, considered the deadliest in India after the Godhra riots of 2003 and the Partition riots in the early twentieth century, during India's struggle for independence.

Mama told me all about the riots in my papa's Byculla town. My papa had to close shop during that period, and my paternal uncle's shop was burned to the ground by rioters. My grandfather, Ibrahim, wore a large Mother Mary rosary around his neck whenever he had to go out. He pretended he was Christian to ward off the rioters. Papa lived in the heart of Muslim Byculla. He was scared, Mama was scared, but I was too young to comprehend.

"Riot," I said one day when I was two years old. "Riot-riot-riot-riot ..."

Blaise picked me up and shushed me.

"Don't say that word," he whispered, "or you will be killed."

I put my finger on my lips just as I had been taught. My future school, BSS, was in the heartland of the riots, and corpses, burned body parts, fire and blood were visible on every corner. I was not yet old enough to attend school at BSS, but Mama was there. Since the riots started while school was in session, the teachers had to ensure that all the children were safe and handed over only to their parents or guardians, before they could go home. Mama was the last to leave and tried to hurry home, as it was long past my feeding time. She walked, actually walked, all the way down that bloodied road back to Bandra West. Back to me. On her way, she saw rioters burning a jeep at the Mahim junction. She saw burn victims being transported to the nearest hospital. She saw dead-body parts strewn across the road home.

Communal riots had begun between the Muslims and Hindus in Mumbai. And against all odds, Mama came home safely to give me milk.

What I'm trying to get at here is that we live in the culture of fear and silence. The two go hand in hand. We are afraid, that's why we keep silent, and we keep silent because we fear what might happen to us if we don't. But books like Mander's tell readers that we must stop this culture of silence and fear. I'm not saying we have to love our family less, but that by being quiet all the time we are adding more fuel to the flame of despotism, religious fundamentalism, and sectarianism. We need to stop being silent and afraid before it's too late.

I, too, am quite a coward in practically every way. But after reading *Fatal Accidents of Birth,* I believe that enough is enough! We have reached the moon, but we can't cross the distance of caste, class, religion, etc., to our fellow brethren, whom we owe more than moon-dust; we have made footprints on the moon but have not spurned dogmatism with our heels.

If you also stand up for human rights and human dignity, then please read this book. It's not a pleasant read, but it's an inspiring and an educative read. Read it during class hours at college; read it if you, too, are working for human rights and justice for all; read it if you, too, were exploited just because you were born at the wrong place and at the wrong time.

"I'm glad God gave you to me, Fiza," Mama says as we sip coffee early in the morning. "I have loved my years with you."

I gulp down a large quantity of my BRU Gold coffee. I ask, "What would have happened if I were a boy?"

Mama shakes her head sadly.

"Then you would have been with them, of course. Maybe eventually they would have packed me off, but they would have never let a boy child go." She looks at me and smiles. "You would have been a father by now. The owner of the family business. Patriarch of the Pathan family, uneducated or maybe somewhat educated, you would have been a real man by now."

I lower my head and look into my mug. The light brownish-white liquid soothes me, makes me calmer when topics like these are discussed. I chug it down, invariably emptying the mug.

"I'm not a real man. Sometimes I don't even think I'm real."

"Why not real, *cuchu*?" Mama asks, her hand on my shoulder and her face wrinkled with worry. She and I call each other *chuchu*; she is chuchu Mama to me and I'm *chuchu* baby to her.

"Why not real, *chuchu*?" Mama repeats. And then I think of all these people I've read about who have suffered and are still suffering. I think about the harrowing tales I've read and actually lived through in my own lifetime in Mumbai. I think of my silence, my books, and my reticent relationship with the world.

Am I real? Or am I just like one of my books? Paper and gum. I've read so many stories, real and unreal. The real are definitely scarier than the unreal. Nonfiction beats fiction most of the time these days when it comes to horror stories.

As I type these words, the Lok Sabha 2019 elections are at hand. As a citizen of India, I still have my right to vote for the candidate of my choice. Will this be the last time I will be doing so? Such thoughts cloud my already muddled mind as I read and reread *Fatal Accidents of Birth* and books like it.

I am a silent, reclusive loner. But I don't like the culture of silence.

As we approach the 2019 Lok Sabha elections, things are just getting worse. Mumbai is becoming a more difficult place to live, as religious fundamentalism, poverty, unemployment, and rowdy behavior start to take precedence. Books that speak of justice, religious tolerance, minority issues, etc., are being banned and pulled off bookshelves. It's good that places like Trilogy are brave enough to keep these important books that are truly worth reading on their shelves.

But the tide is turning. And I've never loved tides that turn. Moving water in general has always caused me distress. Moving waters flow on, please.

ESSAY 39

The Victorias

IT WAS IN THE YEAR 2015, when I was traveling to town via L. J. Road, Mahim, that I noticed the Victoria Secondhand Bookshop and Circulating Library for books and DVDs had separated.

Instead of one bookshop, what I saw before me were two separate shops adjacent to each other and run by two separate people. They both were secondhand bookshops and had the facilities of a lending library.

But why had they split?

"Narayan," I called to my Man Friday. "Let's check these two places out."

Indeed, I found out that the libraries were run by two brothers of the same family, but that the businesses were separate. They had split and were unwilling to share the real reason with me then, and even now.

"At least take a look at the collection," said the elder of the two in a friendly manner. I looked and I liked what I saw. Wonderful paperback and hardback thrillers and horror books, Mills & Boon down the ages, a lot of historical romance novels, numerous Indian fiction books, and other secondhand books dating over fifty years or more – not to mention all of the classics!

The younger man's store offered a similar collection.

What was I to do? Well, I did the most natural thing I could do at that time. I took a year's membership at both places: one book could be borrowed for two weeks. From the elder gentleman I borrowed Dan Brown's *The Lost Symbol* and from the younger gentleman I borrowed Håkan Nesser's, *The Strangler's Honeymoon.* I remember the names of the titles so well because after that day in 2015, I was unable to visit both their shops. I was busy studying for one of those MA exams that I ultimately wouldn't appear for, and I was also preparing for an IAP Career exam in publishing, which I would manage to pass with distinction. So, I didn't have time to read both the books, and they just lay there, accusing me silently, on my study table, which was a mess of books, paper, and stationery – mind the tower of TBR books!

Then one day, exactly a year later, as I was trying to clear up the mess on the study table, I got a call on my cell phone. Yes, I was one of those few twentysomething millennials still using a cell phone in 2016. Well, it was the younger gentleman from one of the Victorias casually asking me whether I would like to renew my membership with him.

"Oh, sir, I'm so sorry," I stammered.

"What for madam?" came a very kind reply.

"Well, I didn't read your book, and I didn't come back to return it."

"Well, do you still have the book with you?" he asked in an even kinder voice. I pushed a few of my MA history guides and found the Håkan Nasser book underneath them, as well as the Dan Brown.

"I have the book, sir," I answered.

"Well," he said kindly as if he were instructing his child how to butter the bread, "come back then."

It was a call from heaven. I'd been given absolution.

"Oh, of course I'll come back," I gasped with joy and thankfulness into the cell phone. "I'll come right away. Oh, sir, how much money should I carry for the fine?"

The younger gentleman laughed like Santa Claus on Christmas, "I have found a lost customer. That's more than enough for me. Just come back, madam. Come back to the books here."

He was laughing, like St. Nicholas, and calling me to heaven, like Jesus. Of course, I went back!

Again, I told Narayan to head to the two Victorias. I was over fifty-two weeks late returning my books, and this is what I'd told Narayan, but then again, he was used to my eccentricities, stepped on it and there I was, back to the split Victorias. I renewed my membership in both the lending libraries and have remained their most regular member since, and most loyal in a very oddly disloyal way.

❋

I love both the Victorias. I love their thriller and horror paperbacks and the secondhand books they sell at cheap and/or reasonable prices. The elder gentleman's shop smells of jasmine incense sticks, while the younger gentleman's shop smells of rose-scented camphor balls. Both places are deliciously filled with all the books I love: Jeffery Archer, Stephen King, James Patterson, Mary Higgins Clark, Sidney Sheldon, Arthur Hailey, Tess Gerritsen, Robin Cook, Danielle Steel, James Rollins, Dean Koontz, Lee Child, Harlan Coben, John Grisham, Ken Follett, Dan Brown, Jo Nesbo, Leon Uris, Wilbur Smith, Anne Rice, David Baldacci, P. D. James and more, more, more!

As you can see, I'm a sucker for thrillers. I now live on the books lent to me by both the Victorias and have spent three years as an active member. I even sell my old books to the elder gentleman. He gives me good prices for the books. I save the money I make from books for the month of May when tutors don't get paid due to the holidays.

I go there practically all the time. The elder gentleman is now a friend of mine, and his wife and I have a hearty time together.

"You are reading so many books and yet you want more!" she stated incredulously one day as I dropped more books into my jute bag. "This girl is mad!"

"I'm mad over books. That's good madness," I said in response. Hearing that, we both doubled up with laughter while the elder gentleman, whose name is Mr. Iqbal Merchant, made a meticulous note of the books I have borrowed and the ones I have returned. Both Mr. Iqbal, and the younger gentleman, who I only know as Mr. N. A. Merchant (I've never asked his name), have learned my habits and allow me to borrow any number of books. They trust me and know I will bring the books back; really, they spoil me like the bookish brat I am!

I love their books and their spirit of keeping the reading public of Mahim satisfied. I see numerous people entering both libraries all the time and I hope this will continue as the years go by.

One day Mr. Iqbal told me his first name. I smiled as I counted the Stephen King books, I was borrowing that afternoon. I answered without looking at him, "My father's name is Iqbal as well."

"He is your father?" asked Mr. Iqbal pointing at Blaise, who was going through some old Alistair MacLean thrillers.

"No, he is my maternal uncle. Mama's younger brother," I answered as I put the heavy books one by one in my bag, I said in a matter-of-fact tone: "My father abandoned me at birth."

"Why would he do a thing like that?" asked Mr. Iqbal, not liking the nature of his namesake at all. Even his dear wife stopped short in her arrangement of magazines to hear what I was saying.

I sighed as I pushed the last Stephen King into my bag,

"He left me because I was a girl child."

"Bah!" said Mr. Iqbal now totally wanting to distance himself from his namesake. "He is a fool, that much is for sure."

His wife hugged me from behind, "Such a flower of a child, and he abandoned you. Whenever you come here you make us smile and laugh," and then she held my chin. "But you cry inside *na*?"

I nodded. Blaise hadn't noticed the exchange. She went on, "No siblings?"

"No," I said, "Just me, just little old bookish me."

Mr. Iqbal nodded in silent contemplation while his wife patted me on the back and said, “We all have problems. But I agree with my husband: your father was a fool.”

One day, when I had finished reading Mr. N. A. Merchant’s books I went up to his shop to return them. It was the month of Ramzan, the forty days of fasting period for the Muslims. The Aazaan went off, and Mr. N. A. Merchant opened a steel container filled with lady finger vegetables to eat and break his day-long fast.

I, after a lot of rummaging, found some Robin Cook books I wanted to read. I came to the front. Mr. N. A. Merchant offered me his food, “Want to break your fast, madam? Aazaan just went off.”

“Thank you so much, sir,” I said humbly. “But I’m not a Muslim.”

He stopped eating midway through his meal even though he was definitely famished. “But your name is Fiza Pathan in the book, madam?”

“I follow my mother’s religion. My mother is a Christian. It’s my father who is a Muslim, and he abandoned both of us.”

“What for?” he asked, looking quizzingly at me, quite taken aback.

“I was a girl child.”

“He left you because you were a girl!” said Mr. N. A. Merchant, his eyes narrowing in disapproval of my papa. And then I heard something that made me smile, “He is a fool, that much I can tell you.”

I left him with a giggle, which he did not understand the reason for, and waved him good evening.

Both the Victoria men are Muslims. Both are blood and flesh of each other in more ways than one. I hope one day I see them joining back again. It may seem queer to you, but the truth is, even I love happy endings.

ESSAYS 40

The Omen by David Seltzer

I WAS RUMMAGING THROUGH the clean but old paperbacks of Mr. Iqbal's secondhand books for sale when I stumbled across David Seltzer's horror book of horrors, *The Omen*.

"Whoa!" I fell on my knees in happiness. "I have actually found *The Omen*!"

Blaise recognized the book with the innocent-looking boy on the cover, the boy who was supposed to be the child of Satan. The child looked sinisterly at me – if looks could kill!

"You will get scared with this one," Mr. Iqbal warned me as he checked out the book for me. "Do you want to buy it or borrow it?"

I borrowed it. Naturally, I wanted others to have the opportunity to read it one day. Besides, I almost never (this is a really big confession) keep horror books and so-called satanic books in my personal library. I have issues; let's just leave it there and come back to *The Omen*.

I took four days to read *The Omen*. I took that long, even though it's a very small book, because as usual I was busy with tuitions. It was 2018, which was quite a busy year for me as the ninth- and tenth-year English language and literature syllabus had changed, and

I had to upgrade myself and write new notes for application questions as well as regular questions for comprehension purposes. Basically, even though I was busy at work, I spent much time thinking about Damien, the seed of Satan, born at an unholy hour, who was to be killed at any cost, though he be a mere child – but a child of hell!

I read most of *The Omen* sitting on my recliner in my office-cum-writing hut. I used to be alone there, as I used to wake up quite early in the morning, and go there to write after a very light breakfast, accompanied by a strong mug of BRU Gold coffee. You bet your life I was freaked out, especially when a coconut fell on the roof of the writing hut. It was a big BANG-DANG-DUM and during that part of the book when – wait, I'm not going to spoil it for you! If you love horror stories, you have to read this book. You are not a true fan of horror if you have not read *The Omen*.

However, if you are not much of a horror fan, and you have a weak constitution, by which I mean that creepy books petrify you and make you tremble all over, then avoid the book. Those who love their horrors, like me, please do read this book. You'll love it.

And, yes, point to be noted: it is definitely scarier than all the movie versions. The movies (sorry Hollywood) are NOTHING compared to the book! You've got to check it out!

I, sadly, was unfortunate enough to have seen one of the movies before I read the book. Don't make my mistake; read the book first and then watch the film or films later.

The story is about an American government official's child born in an Italian hospital. The child is stillborn apparently and the official is devastated because his wife really wanted this child badly. If she were to hear of its death, she would plunge into grief. That's where an Italian priest comes in with another baby. This baby is quite a sight, full of a lot of black hair and cute as can be. The official is told that the child's mother passed away during childbirth, and the child had no one to care for him.

The Italian priest urges Mr. Thorn, the American official, to accept this child in the place of his own. However, he is not to tell his wife about the exchange. And he should think himself blessed and lucky – for on that day, he had been given a son.

Mr. Thorn accepts the child as his own. And then after that, I'm not going to get into it, but it will blow your mind. Do read the book.

"Got scared?" asked Mr. Iqbal, when I came back to his store to return the book.

"Pretty much," I answered. The truth was I was shaking all over until I started my next thriller fix.

I am awed by the power of *The Omen* by David Seltzer. It is a page-turner and one of the scariest books to read if you are alone in the place you are reading it.

I love the books that were penned between 1960 and 1990. To me, these books and these writers are the best; they created fascinating and relatable characters, had a great sense of how to build suspense, wrote meaningful descriptions and powerful dialogues. There is quite a lot of patriarchy running through these books, but they are in substance the best of the best.

That's why I love these old twentieth-century thrillers and horror books. That is why I loved *The Omen* and that is why I keep going to the Victorias to get books that were penned during that time.

"Not wanting to take a movie?" asks Mr. Iqbal's wife, sliding open the glass doors of the DVD and VCD section of the library. Yes, I have mentioned that both the Victorias rent out VCDs and DVDs as well.

"I'll take *The Omen*. The old one," I say and Mr. Iqbal laughs.

"This girl loves old books and old movies," he says as he hands over the film. "She was born at the wrong time."

Could be. Mama was thirty-nine when she gave birth to me. That was in 1989, and that was revolutionary.

Mama and Papa were in love for a long while and actually wanted to get married in 1978. But since Nana was against the match, they waited and stayed apart for ten years, waiting for her consent. They received her consent in 1987 and were married that same year. I was born in 1989. Maybe I was to be born in 1979 – during the disco-pop era, when Blaise was still at college, just after my favorite singer of all time, Elvis Presley, went to his final resting place.

Yes, maybe I was meant to be born at another time. But as my mama is fond of saying, "Where you're dotted, there you're knotted." In other words, whatever is ordained will happen.

ESSAY 41

The Exorcist by William Peter Blatty

I WAS IN MR. N. A. MERCHANT'S SHOP at Victoria's in 2017 going through the old shelves when my hand landed upon a Tess Gerritsen novel. As I pulled out that book, I realized there was something behind it in the niche, and put my hand in.

It was an old book. I pulled it out; it must have been there for quite some time.

I was stunned. It was *The Exorcist* by William Peter Blatty.

"I see you've found *The Exorcist*," said Mr. N. A. Merchant as he flipped through the worn-out pages and dusted its cover. "It's very frightening. A spine chiller of the worst kind."

"I want it still," I said, as he handed the book back to me.

Blaise was petrified when he saw it.

"You are *not* going to read that," he said. "And even if you do, read it during the day and not at your usual time."

My "usual time," back in 2017, was midnight to 4:00 a.m. I was abridging the classics in the 'Rare Classics' series with my fellow author and colleague, Michaelangelo Zane. I was also teaching too many classes at one time. I was dying to read all the fiction and non-fiction that was piling up around my office. That's when I started a bad habit. I became a nocturnal reader, commencing reading only after I had completed my corrections, which was after midnight.

I then went on reading for four hours at a stretch, and only at 4:00 a.m. or thereabout would I go to bed.

I read *The Exorcist* at that dead hour of the night in mid-2017. No one in the house was awake but me. I read with the nightlights on, which were very dim and created spooky shadows with the curtains and the curios I had collected over the years.

As with the book *The Omen*, I had already seen the movie of *The Exorcist* before I read it. But, yet again, the book was more frightening than the movie could ever be.

The story is also well developed, suspenseful, and much more relatable to demonic possession than we in the Catholic church are used to seeing. The characters in the book are likable and some of them highly intellectual. The discussions that occur between characters about God, demons, and demonic possession are very well crafted. I should say that the movie (or movies) don't do justice to the book at all. It's sad to see so many good horror stories hacked to death by the film industry, which feels a need to fit such stories into a small timeframe of 120 minutes. In this way, they destroy horror books and the horror genre rather than building it up. I have a problem with that.

Yes, I've heard many people say that they were spooked by the movie. I was too. But the experience of reading *The Exorcist* by William Peter Blatty for two days during the silent hours of the night was far creepier – I was frightened out of my wits!

For those of you who don't know the story, here is a bit of the synopsis (my take) to intrigue you.

An American film personality is one of the main characters. She is popular, divorced, and has a twelve-year-old cherub of a daughter. She is contemplating her situation, whether she should marry again, when she hears sudden scraping sounds in the attic. She thinks its mice and orders an exterminator. But the sounds of scraping continue. Also, her daughter starts acting peculiar. Ever since she started playing with a Ouija board, she is too frightened to go to sleep. On the other side of the world, an archaeologist-cum-exorcist priest finds something odd in the sand. Something evil that should not be there. In addition, a young dashing priest is new to the location where the American film personality stays and is consulted for a case of demonic possession. How all this comes together, you'll have to read the book to find out.

I was sweating in a panic as I read the book. My heart thumped out weird sounds on my ribcage every time Blaise or Mama turned in their beds. I was a nervous wreck.

That is exactly what the book does to you. You will be frightened, guaranteed.

When I returned the book to Mr. N. A. Merchant, he was in conversation with another customer so he greeted me with the raise of his hand. The moment I put the book on the desk to return it to him, the middle-aged lady shrieked. It gave me and poor Mr. N. A. Merchant quite a turn.

"What – what is that?" she asked, pointing a trembling hand at my book.

"*The Exorcist* by Blatty," I said. I am very helpful where books are concerned.

"Oh, yes, it is," she said, all the while shaking like a leaf in the chilly breeze. "I saw the movie."

"The book is scarier," I said with a grin.

She was not gutsy enough to take it.

But I was and it was an earth-shattering experience in emotions. Now that's what I call a really good book!

Eventually all the reading I'd been doing between midnight to 4:00 a.m. would knock me out. In 2018, I was admitted three times to the hospital because of terrible stomach ailments, obesity, and most importantly, lack of refreshing sleep. I had ruined my own health by reading into the night, sleeping erratically, and not eating at regular intervals. End result, I was diagnosed with sleep apnea.

I was shaken.

"You mean that disease Michael Jackson supposedly died from?" I gasped into my hospital pillow. "No, I'm too young to die! I've got so many books to read!"

"Relax, you're not going to die," said the nurse, giving me a vitamin injection on my butt (that hurt and still hurts). "You'll just have to sleep with a sleep app machine, something like an oxygen mask to push fresh oxygen into your trachea."

"Why does the machine have to do it?" Mama asked, crestfallen at the news. "What's wrong with her windpipe?"

"It's not her windpipe," the nurse muttered. "It's the fat. The weight around her chest and neck is stopping the respiratory organs from functioning properly." She destroyed the injection tip in a sort of cutting device and dumped the remnants into a waste bin.

Mama was gulping down her emotions.

Blaise said, "Does she have to sleep with a machine?"

The nurse got another needle ready, this one to draw my blood. She rubbed antiseptic with a tiny ball of cotton on the area she would puncture. As she inserted the needle, she said, "If she doesn't start using the sleep app machine, she will one day die in her sleep from respiratory failure." Then she pulled the syringe so that my dark blood spilled into the vial attached to it. "According to the sleep report we took last night, she stops breathing at least thirty-four times per hour." She then removed the needle and placed a large ball of cotton over the pinched area. The blood didn't stop. She had to use the first aid kit.

"Jesus, Mary, Joseph," said the nurse, who was a South Indian Catholic. "She is so fat that it is difficult to find her veins, or close them once we do find them."

I fainted.

I would be admitted two more times to the hospital in 2018. All because of respiratory or breathing difficulty.

I now use a sleep app machine and a mask when I sleep. You can't even imagine how difficult it is to sleep with a mask on a flat mattress. We were going in for a hospital bed, but there was no place in the tiny 1BKH flat we lived in. Plus, there were too many books and bookshelves and bookcases in the house. It was either comfort or my books. I chose the books.

And all this because of my being obese, plus size, fat!

It hurt to know that even something as simple as a regular position of sleeping was now going to be denied to me because of my weight. I withdrew once again from society. I broke off ties with Kanchana, the friend I had made at Trilogy. All dreams of traveling, which weren't there but even if they had been, were all washed away, like the waves of the Arabian sea on the shores of the Mahim Bay.

My weight was literally killing me. I was losing my so-called respect among friends, family, society, and doctors.

Nobody wants to look into my case. No one. It's either I reduce 30 kgs and then we'll talk, or let's do a bariatric surgery.

No one is comfortable with my size. Not even my doctors.

Doctors were not comfortable when the twelve-year-old cherubic daughter of the protagonist in *The Exorcist* was acting weird. They couldn't understand or diagnose what was happening, and that made them uncomfortable.

My weight cannot be diagnosed. And that makes people uncomfortable.

Where did it come from? Why such a drastic increase in weight over the years?

Read on to discover the answers. Or discover if there are answers.

The book phoenix shall not be grounded!

ESSAY 42

Victorias 2

AS I HAVE MENTIONED BEFORE, I am a regular at both Mr. Iqbal's lending library as well as Mr. N. A. Merchant's. I go there whenever I want to churn my brain with a thriller or horror fix. I talk with the owners and always come back with my jute or cloth bags full of books.

In Mr. Iqbal's library, my library number is 2007. He himself one day asked me to choose a number for myself and so I chose the year 2007, the last year that I was thin. After 2007, I started putting on weight which resulted in obesity.

Mr. Iqbal has this year, indeed at the beginning of this very month of March, opened a secondhand bookshop near his lending library. He is selling old paperbacks – thrillers, mysteries, suspense, paranormal, historical romance, Mills & Boon, nonfiction titles, classics, old Indian fiction, literary fiction, and more at cheap prices.

"Come and rob me – Loot-Lo," says he and his billboard, which has attracted many customers to his new secondhand bookshop. I am one of the first patrons to have "looted" some of his treasures. For a sum of three thousand rupees I have so far bought more than forty books, mostly from the 1970s and 1980s, belonging to the thriller and paranormal genre. I've saved some of the money I received as birthday gifts to spend on more of Mr. Iqbal's titles.

"I robbed your husband," I tell his wife, every time I come back from the "Loot-Lo shop," as I love to call it. She laughs and says, "Be frank. Exactly who looted whom?" And we clap hands and laugh at the joke together.

But on a serious note, I don't think Mr. Iqbal, or for that matter Mr. N. A. Merchant, are charging a lot for the fantastic books they provide to us readers. It hurts me to see when customers haggle with them over the prices of books, precious-precious-precious books! It seems like some people have forgotten the value of books in this twenty-first century. When I see Mr. Iqbal or his wife struggling with an irritating customer, I feel like shouting, "Why this devaluing of books? Why?"

"It's the internet and Amazon, and whatever else there is," Mr. Iqbal tells me as I search through his Indian fiction collection. "They are hell for the neighborhood lending library and secondhand bookshops. People are getting everything on their Smartphones in a moment's time, who is going to bother about us?"

But people do come. There are still people who love to read printed books, and they come from all over the Mahim, Matunga, Dadar area to both of the Victorias for a good read.

One day, I was entering Mr. N. A. Merchant's store to return some Katie Fforde chick-lit books when I spotted someone I knew at the counter.

"Regina!" I exclaimed, quite surprised. She was in the same class with me at St. Andrew's College.

"Fiza," she said, and we greeted each other warmly.

"Why don't you both take a seat and chat away in a corner of the library?" offered Mr. N. A. Merchant generously. But I was in no mood to talk. I could see the shock on Regina's face, seeing me so bloated and out of proportion. She looked at me with pretty, raven-black eyes that showed both shock and concern. I managed to scoot away quickly; I didn't want to explain my sudden increase in weight.

When Regina last saw me at a college renewal, I would have been 65 kgs. Now I was 122.3 kgs – and only seven or eight years had passed.

"Why didn't you talk much to a long-time friend?" asked Mr. N. A. Merchant gently as he took my Katie Fforde books back and started stamping some political biographies I had chosen.

"It's because of the weight, sir," I said, twirling my fingers and avoiding his eyes. "I don't want to talk about my weight."

He nodded and didn't ask further questions. He understood.

The temple women selling garlands and feeding the sacred cows at the Sitladevi temple watch me as I come and go from the two Victorias. They always say under their breath, "See, the fat book girl has come again."

I hear them but swallow my anger and walk happily to the librarians that love and have accepted me for the avid and voracious reader that I am.

I have read so much in these three years at Victorias. The Mahim of my BSS years has changed, however. These days chaos and heavy traffic are present daily because of the Metro that is being built all along the L. J. Road and S. V. Road. The work goes on, day and night, with the never-ending sounds of CLANG-BANG-BOOM-CLANG-BAM-A-BOOM! The journey to the Victorias, which once took ten minutes from my home in Bandra West, now takes thirty-five minutes or more. There is noise, pollution, congested roads, and filth everywhere. And to think this will be going on for the next five years or so. Mahim was not like this when I was studying at BSS.

But I still go, because I love my books. I love both of my Victorias.

Mr. Iqbal treats me like his daughter. He's overprotective. One day I was going through some of the erotica fiction in the library when, *whoosh*, he came from nowhere and took the books from my hands gently, saying quite comically, "Er ... not meant for you. You are a good girl. Come this way. There are nicer books here."

I laughed loudly while he became red as a beetroot. He can't imagine me wanting to read erotica – ha ha ha! That was really cute!

Mr. N. A. Merchant is helping me build a collection of Busybee books. He keeps on finding the collections of the witty Mumbai writer of current events for *The Afternoon* newspaper of the 1990s and early 2000s. For those of you who don't know, Busybee was the pen name for the Parsi journalist/columnist Behram Contractor, who wrote funny little parodies on the happenings in India and the world. I only read *The Afternoon* for his Busybee column. He passed away quite a few years ago. But Mr. N. A. Merchant has his whole collection and keeps on selling parts of it to me at very cheap prices. He is spoiling me yet again!

"How is your father?" I ask Mr. N. A. Merchant when I overhear him tell an older lady customer about the hospitalization of his father, the real founder of the Victoria Bookshop and Circulating Library.

"He is not doing well," says Mr. N. A. Merchant in a faraway voice I've never heard him use before. "He is confined to the bed. We are expecting the worst."

Mr. N. A. Merchant lives with his father. Mr. Iqbal doesn't.

"Your father isn't well," I say entering Mr. Iqbal's shop.

He lowers his eyes and I can hear the choking sensation in his voice when he says, "I've heard about it."

"Did you go to see him?"

"Once or twice in the hospital."

"He is serious," I say in my most emotive voice.

Mr. Iqbal looks the other way. "I know."

That is something we have in common, Mr. Iqbal and I; we both have estranged fathers. But I pray and hope that someday the two brothers will join forces again and become one happy family.

I hope I live long enough to see that happen. It will bring me a lot of joy of the bookish kind.

I hope it happens before the brothers' father passes away.

I hope it happens before I pass away. Because with my continuous fat accumulation and difficulty in breathing, I wonder sometimes when my own fat will choke me to my sleeping death.

❋

ESSAY 43

The American Library

BLAISE OFTEN TOLD ME ABOUT two libraries he used to visit when he was in his twenties. One was the British Council Library at Mittal Towers in Mumbai's prestigious Nariman Point. The other he visited only once or twice because he couldn't afford it. It was the American Library at Churchgate.

In the year 2013, I had just finished publishing two books. I was working day and night teaching and trying to study for my MA. In the meantime, something happened.

The American Library, which was in the town area, had just moved to the Bandra Kurla Complex (BKC) where all the top business houses of Mumbai are located. I always wanted to visit the American Library. I once went to the British Library when I was in the ninth grade. I liked the place, but soon it shut down as fewer people were willing to visit the library. The British Council Library now only has an online lending library, something like Amazon's website, except that you pay a yearly fee and have your books delivered at your doorstep. The American Library was still a physical as well as digital library. I was keen on visiting it.

"Let's go this Saturday," I said, the first time I decided to go.

"Can't," said Blaise, as he scanned through the library's website. "It's Columbus Day on Saturday, and so the library will be closed."

"Oh, they celebrate both Indian and American festivals?" I asked, quite interested.

Blaise nodded. "They open late and close early; we'll have to go next Saturday, when you are free in the evening."

"Okay," I said, and we went.

That was in 2013. I was twenty-four years old. It was quite an experience.

There was tight security, so we had to carry our government photo identification, like our PAN card or Aadhaar card, to prove our credentials. Blaise was still working as an officer in the Bank of India, and so he showed the security his bank ID card. We were let in. Then the authorities searched us and, through a high-tech security computer network, scrutinized our watches and the insides of our bags. When everything was clear, they handed us a visitor ID card.

"Welcome to the American Embassy," the security head said, as we strapped our watches on our wrists. "The library is in the main building. Just enter it and ask for directions."

"Thank you, thank you," I said as I pulled my sling bag out of the security tray while trying to clip the ID card to my black T-shirt.

We were inside the American Embassy now, Blaise and I. We saw the flag of the USA in the distance. The area was pristine clean, there were security personnel everywhere, both Americans and Indians. The American personnel looked very handsome.

"Stop staring at them," Blaise cautioned me, pulling me along. "Don't attract unwanted attention. Just keep going."

I still looked at these security guards or officers, stationed here in Mumbai so far away from their homes. I wondered about their lives, about how they perceived us Indians. I had never spoken to a real-life foreigner before. Not even those tourist foreigners who asked for directions to whichever place they wanted to visit. I am weird, yes, but I would love to one day talk to someone who is from a foreign country and see how they "tick." But back to bookishness.

We entered the main building. President Barack Obama's picture was on the wall. I went up to the picture and touched it with reverence. "Hello, President Obama," I thought as I looked into his eyes.

His picture looked so welcoming. Some of the American guards saw me doing this and gave me a friendly smile of approval. They led Blaise and me to the library through a number of security doors.

"It's so complicated," I whined. "I'll never be able to find my way on my own."

"You will with practice," Blaise said in a whisper. "Remember this houses the library and the American Embassy; it is not just any office building."

We finally found our way to the library, which was vast, spacious, and full of computers, foreign magazines, DVDs, and American books of all categories.

"Can I help you, ma'am?" came the voice of an elderly gentleman who was at the librarian's desk.

I scanned through the multitudes of books. All were American titles, but that did not matter. I loved the books and the magazines. I took a four-book membership and left.

With practice, I got along very well entering and leaving the library. I used to even sit in the library, to write, read, or study there. I read *I, Phoolan Devi* there and fainted because of the gruesomeness of her sexual abusers. The librarians flocked around me and splashed water on my face.

"You are okay?" one of them asked.

"I'm sorry. I'm sorry," I said breathing with difficulty. "It was the book. It was too much to take."

"Read something better, ma'am, for a while. Have lunch and then you'll feel better."

"Thanks," I said as I found my bearings. *Read something better* she had said. But this was reality, the multiple sexual abuses and gang rapes of a low caste girl who went on to become the Bandit Queen of India, Phoolan Devi. I continued reading the book.

The library served tea, coffee, hot chocolate, juice, snacks, and lunch. I availed myself of their services whenever I was at the library; I really loved their chicken sandwiches and chicken sausage burgers. They used to serve beef sandwiches, too, which smelled delicious. They stopped doing so when the cow-slaughter ban was declared in the country. India that is.

I used to go there on my own. I loved their library books. This was before I started reading on the Kindle, and I looked forward to getting the latest hardback titles printed in the USA. All over the library were students, young and old, who studied there. Many Americans brought their kids to the library to pick a book or a movie to watch at home. I read a lot of YA fiction there as well as books by Ann Patchett, Ernest Hemingway, and a heck of a lot of books on business, writing, and American politics.

I used to take tea with sugar. Most of the other library patrons my age and older chugged coffee. The place was always spic and span. It was a great place to be in. I loved it – until 2016.

Then the security checking got longer and more time-consuming. The library was renovated and was renamed the Dosti House. Once I was waiting out in the sun for two hours where, in previous years, security checks were so quickly done that it took no more than a few seconds. When I was completely roasted in the hot summer afternoon sun, I just went back home. I have not returned to the library since.

"Why don't you try again?" Mama asked one day as our taxi passed the American Embassy. "You used to love it there, and the books you read there always gave you so much pleasure."

"It's not the same, Mama," I said as the American flag blew in the breeze as our taxi whisked by. "It's not the same at all."

I miss going there, no doubt about it. But a couple of years ago, I felt wanted there. Now I'm treated like an outsider, like a threat.

I didn't mention why I was kept in the sun for two hours. The security was having trouble with my name and religion.

"Muslim name but religion is Catholic," I heard one of them say. "Muslim? Christian?"

I was told to fill out some forms, several forms while some other dubious characters were allowed in without a security check. I was a regular here. What happened? I was a regular at the American Library from 2013 to 2016. Four years. Now why suddenly so much of fuss about my name?

Maybe one of these days during the month of May when I'm free I'll go back again. I'll fill out all their forms and see where it gets me. I'll wear pants and a T-shirt instead of Indian wear. Maybe it will help. I'll take Blaise along with his Christian name and Christian religion, and then maybe I'll get into the library I was faithful to for four years.

I will miss President Obama's picture, the day I do land up there.

The last I saw the picture hanging up there was just before the American election results in 2016. I touched President Obama's picture. I always used to do that, whenever I entered and left the library.

The last time I not only touched but kissed the picture. Two security guards came up to me, and one of them said, "You okay ma'am?"

I looked at them and said, "I'm okay."

ESSAY 44

Conversations with Waheeda Rehman by Nasreen Munni Kabir

I've mentioned that I'm eccentric. I have a number of eccentricities and one of them is related to Bollywood movies. The eccentric part about it is that I don't like watching Bollywood movies, but I like to read books about them! I like reading books about Bollywood actors, actresses, film editors, critics, screenplays, directors, music composers, lyricists – you name it and I have read or am planning to read it.

But I do not watch their movies. Not at all.

Mama finds this fascination of mine highly comical. Mechu feels I'm batty but is astounded that I know so much about Bollywood without seeing any of the films.

"But, dolly girl, how do you know all this information about Sanjay Dutt's TADA case?" asks Mechu in shock. "You were only a two-year-old at that time."

"I read about it in his unauthorized biography," I say with a grin.

"But you don't like watching his films," Mechu goes on. "In fact, you've not been to the theater in months."

I giggle and cup my hands to my mouth.

"I read about his movies in books."

"You're incorrigible, dolly girl."

"I am what I am. And besides," I say as I scan through a new set of Bollywood books I've borrowed, "if one can get all the information one needs in a book, why see the film?"

Mechu nearly spilled her tea hearing that one.

But it's true. I like reading books about Bollywood but nowadays don't see the films. And my main supplier for Bollywood books is none other than both of my Victorias.

"Try this one," says Mr. Iqbal, putting *Conversations with Waheeda Rehman* by Nasreen Munni Kabir in my hand. "You liked some Guru Dutt books, so I think you will like this one as well."

I immediately paid the lending fees for the book and took it home to read. As I was leaving Victoria's Mr. Iqbal's wife asked, "You've seen any of her movies?"

"Whose?"

"Waheeda Rehman, of course!" She slid open the glass door of the DVD and VCD collection. "Take a movie home. We have her entire collection in VCD form."

"I don't like watching movies," I said, shaking my head in anguish. "I just like reading about them."

"Oh God, this girl is mad!" said Mr. Iqbal's wife as I waved a goodbye to them and got into Narayan's taxi.

I read Nasreen Munni Kabir's book in a matter of a day or two. I had always wanted to read a book about the beautiful actress who was featured in so many of the black-and-white Bollywood movies of yesteryear, especially about the rumored love affair between her and her director and co-actor. I've seen one film of hers. That's it. But thanks to this book, I have a good understanding of the movies she appeared in for so many years and how difficult it was to be an actress in the 1950s and early 1960s.

The book is in a question-and-answer format that was easy to read, full of insights, and very enlightening. Of all the Bollywood eras I have READ about, the time of the black-and-white film fascinates me the most. I love to READ about the music of that era and love to READ about the movies especially of that time. I love to READ about S. D. Burman's music – according to Waheeda Rehman, he seems to be a good music director. I must READ about his music someday soon.

So, I read *Conversations with Waheeda Rehman* and was enthralled by the actress. In fact, my mama had taught her children at BSS, so I felt closer to her.

The book is well presented and full of information about Waheeda Rehman's early start in the Bollywood film industry: how she stood her ground for certain conditions in the movies she acted in and about how she thought about directing her own movie. I liked her take on actors like Guru Dutt and Dev Anand. It was a fun, dazzling read about a girl from a humble household who changed the way people looked at cinema. I highly recommend this book to all Bollywood buffs, especially those interested in the black-and-white era, and those who are doing research or studying the cinema of Mumbai film studios.

I loved the book, but it didn't make me want to watch Waheeda's movies.

"Finished the book?" asked Mr. Iqbal when I placed it on his desk. "Would you like some more?"

"Definitely, sir!" I said as I took my jute bag off my shoulder and made myself comfortable. I took in the jasmine incense sticks scent which prevailed in Iqbal sir's Victoria. Sir took out his ledger to cancel the book under my name and number 2007. His wife patted me on the shoulder while a young girl arranged old magazines at the end of the small space.

"How are you?" Mr. Iqbal's wife asked.

"Feeling filmy," I said, and she thumped my back with a giggle.

"Silly girl," she giggled. "You read so much about films but you don't take any. Now which Bollywood biography you want to read today?"

"What is your name?" I ask her.

"Why do you ask?"

"Because I am writing a book and I want to put your name into it." Then I clarified as the younger girl with the magazines looked up from her work, "I want to tell the world what good books you have been letting me read at Victoria's."

"My name is Munira," Mr. Iqbal's wife said shyly, while sir pretended not to hear. "His name is Iqbal."

"And your brother-in-law?" I asked pointing to the neighboring shop.

"Arif," she said with a melancholy tone in her voice. "The *N* in the name is Noorali, their father who started this business."

I say nothing. Sir cancels my name with a ballpoint pen he always has in readiness. I lean on their strong cast-iron shelves. Munira ma'am picks up a few Bollywood biographies and shows them to me one by one. I take the biographies on Dev Anand and the Dharmendra. It will be nice to READ about their movies and READ about their lives.

"Don't you watch TV?" asks Munira ma'am, narrowing her eyes with concern. "*Sirf padte ho kya*?"

"Yes," I say with a smile. "I only read books. I hate watching the TV. It makes me giddy."

She is taken aback with my answer. She has a hearty good laugh.

"What – what kind of a young girl are you? Who in the world ever feels giddy while watching television?"

But I am in earnest. I explain to her how I feel really giddy watching a host of people running from one part of the screen to another and how that brings on my spell of dizziness.

"It's better only when the English subtitles are on," I say quite baffling the young girl with the magazines. "Then I at least understand what's going on. I only read the English subtitles and hardly look at the movie."

"My God!" says Munira ma'am.

"My God!" says the girl with the magazines.

"Don't harass my best customer!" Mr. Iqbal scolds his wife and thrusts the Dev Anand and Dharmendra books in my hands. "Let her read. It's good that she reads. Read away."

And then I take my leave and am back in my taxi with Blaise and Narayan, with my borrowed Bollywood books.

I think of Waheeda Rehman as the taxi moves along. I think of how her father died when she was so young and how she had to act in movies to earn a living. She had to give up her education for that. Today she is one of the best actresses of the Golden Age of Indian cinema.

"Your papa didn't like Waheeda Rehman," says Mama one day as I'm talking about the book *Conversations with Waheeda Rehman.*

"Then who was his favorite?" I ask. Mama was in a mood to talk about Papa. This was as rare as the sighting of Halley's comet. I was going to get out as much as I could, because my mama has been so reticent about Papa that it's hard for me to understand why I'm so different compared to everyone else at home.

"His favorite was Mumtaz," says Mama, as if she was saying a cuss word. "He loved her the most."

"Another Muslim Bollywood actress like Waheeda Rehman," I say with a smile. Mama doesn't smile along with me.

"He liked her because she was so sexy," says Mama again as if she were uttering something blasphemous. "It was always Mumtaz where he was concerned."

Mama then looks at me as if reading the face of my father in my face. She then says, "We both loved Bollywood films, Iqbal and I. We went every Sunday for a film for ten straight years. If anyone tells him that his daughter hates the sight of movies, he'll never believe it."

"Did he like to read?" I ask. I was trying to glean as much as I could. Mama was very moody when it came to Papa.

She laughed sarcastically. "He didn't even read the newspaper or the Quran. He hated to read. He found it boring. Now don't go back into the past. Talk about Waheeda Rehman. Did she say her kids went to BSS?"

I crumpled in my place. The mood had passed, but I had gained sufficient knowledge to realize how different I was from these two people, my mama and papa.

Then I see Blaise across the room, attending a business call with a book in his hand, and I think to myself, "I'm Blaise's daughter."

ESSAY 45

The Mistress of Spices by Chitra Banerjee Divakaruni

I WAS AT MR. ARIF'S VICTORIA when I stumbled upon *The Mistress of Spices* by Chitra Banerjee Divakaruni. I had heard a lot about her from both Mr. Iqbal and Mr. Arif. They both said she was a really good writer. But I always wanted to start out by reading *The Mistress of Spices*. I borrowed it on my yearly account with Mr. Arif and immediately started reading the book in Narayan's taxi.

It took me a week to read the book because at that time I was reading several books simultaneously. My own purchases plus library books from MCubed, Trilogy, the American or Dosti Library, and both the Victorias. The year was 2018. I was a confirmed mad book lady of twenty-eight years, and I was no mood to change that.

I loved Chitra Banerjee Divakaruni's book. It made me weep, and rarely does an Indian book of fiction do that for me. The story of a real "mistress of spices" in the garb of an old woman and her love for "her American" made my heart bleed. As I read the book, I remembered the boy I loved at school. I knew nothing about him, just like the protagonist of *The Mistress of Spices* knew nothing about her American, but she still loved him and I still love my old love.

"You are not thinking of marriage in the near future?" Mama asked me one day when we were alone and I was reading *The Mistress of Spices* on our only sofa, "I'm not saying to marry right away. I married at thirty-eight so there is no reason to marry early. Take your time, but are you thinking in that direction?"

I opened my mouth and shut it. My grip on the book became loose.

"Are you waiting for someone?" asked Mama sadly. She knew I loved that schoolboy. She knew everything. She sighed and said with a firm voice. "He is not interested, Fiza. Otherwise by now we would have heard of something. Let him go."

Tears welled up in my eyes. The book almost fell but I clutched it.

The book brought me back to my senses. To reality, my reality. I had sold my soul to books. I couldn't marry anybody and I couldn't become a nun.

"I want to live out my life as a spinster, Mama."

"Are you sure?" Mama asked gently. "You're not old. You're twenty-eight."

I chewed my lip. It was an action of pain and not indecision.

"I want to be a spinster, Mama."

"As you wish," Mama said with a nod. "Is this book a love story?"

I looked at the book by Chitra Banerjee Divakaruni in my hand. "Yeah, it is, Mama – it's a love story."

I loved the book to bits. I loved the way Tilo, the mistress of spices, doled out medicinal herbs and spices along with sage advice to all who came to her shop. The American was Tilo's distraction from her life's mission: to be a mistress of spices. The schoolboy I loved would be a distraction for me: the mistress of books.

The book is written to perfection and the suspense is killing. I've read few Indian novels as good as this one – it keeps you guessing through to the end. No, dearest reader, you are not going to get any spoilers from me. To know Tilo, her mission, and her American, you will have to read the book. When you do, you will experience the spices through the wonderful prose of Chitra Banerjee Divakaruni. This is the perfect book for lovers of good Indian fiction. It's a treat that will cause a volcano of emotions to erupt within you.

I cried for the schoolboy I loved. But after that, I chose my mission. What Tilo chose will be revealed to you when you read this exotic book. I know there is a movie out there but PLEASE DON'T WATCH THE FILM – at least don't watch the film first.

You may think I have no other hobbies besides bookish delights, but you would be wrong. I have a few hobbies that blend well with reading, writing, and teaching, but which are different tasks in themselves. Did I say, "tasks"? What I meant is that they are blessings!

One of them happens to be aromatherapy.

Yes, the secret is out. I am a huge believer, and practice aromatherapy. I have a range of organic and vegan oils, perfumes, scented candles, soaps, and lotions that rejuvenate me and my senses. Aromatherapy gives me peace, helps me in my breathing, and is a sort of religion for me.

One of the aromatherapeutic soaps I bathed in the whole week I was reading *The Mistress of Spices* was made with South Indian spices and herbs. I bathed in it every night and then slept on my mattress in my nightwear and read *The Mistress of Spices,* smelling like the spices themselves.

I also love to perfume the air with reed diffusers and scented candles. I love flower smells – jasmine and rose being my favorites. I even love lighting a scented aromatherapy candle while writing and reading. I have candles from almost every brand.

"You are smelling like something I cooked," Rita often says when I come from a bath of South Indian spices and herbs. "Shall we add potatoes?"

We both love my aromatherapy hobby. Rita loves forest smells and sea-salt smells.

I read Chitra Banerjee Divakaruni's book every night for a week and returned it after kissing the cover.

"It was an awesome read, Mr. Merchant," I told Mr. Arif, who smiled kindly.

"It was a real hit back in those days when it just came out," he reflected. "We had a lot of copies of the book at Victoria's. But then came Amazon and e-books, and then ..."

He stared into the distance. His shop smelled of the pleasing rose camphor balls he sold on the side. Mr. Arif also sold herbal medicine and did a lot of other things like health insurance, etc. It helped his bookshop to stay in business.

I then went into the shop to pick another Chitra Banerjee Divakaruni. I chose *Oleander Girl,* which is about a girl living with grandparents who were silent about her parents.

"You are a serious reader," said Mr. Arif as he noted the books in his notebook under my library number 3220. "You don't like to read a lot of chick lit from what I have seen."

"I love books indiscriminately, Mr. Merchant," I said as another library patron, an elderly Muslim gentleman, entered the shop. "But, yes, I often like to read books on serious topics."

I take the book from the counter and leave, a lover of Chitra Banerjee Divakaruni's books for life.

ESSAY 46

Kindle Books

I'VE BEEN A SELF-PUBLISHED WRITER for the past seven years; I started publishing at age twenty-three.

Now, I'm twenty-nine years old. By the time this book is out in the market I'll be thirty. What I want to say here is that, thanks to my Kindle sales, I managed to remain in the book market for a long period of time. Kindle, CreateSpace, and Amazon have helped make my dream into a reality, and I am very much indebted to them.

And yet, it makes my heart bleed to see bookshops and bookstores that sell physical books close. I have to admit, however, that I do see a benefit to all of this. We have to change with the times, and Kindle and e-books are here to stay. Are physical books on their way out for good? I think that as long as there is a demand for them, they won't go anywhere. But if the demand goes away, which I have a feeling may happen in the generations that follow Gen X (Gen Z, Gen Alpha), then I can see physical books disappearing from the market.

I'm saying this because I've been a teacher for the past ten years, and I deal with children of all ages and backgrounds. The urban Gen X child is much happier reading a book on the phone, iPad, or Kindle rather than actually going to a bookshop and purchasing a book. On the other hand, in India, children from rural backgrounds cannot afford e-books or Kindles so there is a huge demand for physical books there – at least for now.

I've tried ways and means to get my students to pick up a hardcover book first but, as the years go by, the need of a physical book in urban India seems to be on a decline.

So, although I'm making a highly subjective statement, I'm going to say that, yes, digital copies will be the only books we'll see in the near future – if we have a future.

I have a Kindle, and I love reading books on it. I don't discriminate between the two. Neither does Blaise, though he is a twentieth-century baby boomer. In fact, he reads more on the Kindle than I do. When I ask him why, he has a straightforward answer: "It is a quick transaction, affordable and accommodating."

I end my philosophizing on that note. Now, back to bookishness that does not discriminate between a physical or e-book! As long as it is a book, Fiza Pathan is ready to read it.

I was one of those millennials who got a Kindle very, very late (just like I got my very first smartphone very, very late). It was 2013 (I was twenty-four) for the Kindle and 2016 (I was twenty-seven) for the smartphone. But once I got it, it was a boon to me where reading was concerned. I have read so many books on my Kindle. It's my buddy, and I love it to bits.

I started reading books about the book-publishing business on my Kindle. I read all night, finishing the book to the sound of the rooster from the neighboring Wadi *chawl* crowing at the break of dawn. Later, I would read fiction and creative nonfiction on it, but in the beginning, it was only for work purposes.

Blaise and I were working around the clock to take my publishing firm, Fiza Pathan Publishing, from a distant dream to a very big reality. We read books about the business, learned about software, learned the way to promote books, and so much more.

We finally incorporated the company in 2016 on the 4th of May. It's been three years of hard work, persistence, health issues, and the constant sound of our computer keyboards typing away. But it has become a reality, and now I am the director and chief executive officer of my own niche publishing company. I publish books under the imprint, Freedom With Pluralism®, which is dedicated to books of quality that deal with education and social issues, and encouraging children to read.

Along with books about the publishing business, I read other books on my Kindle as well. I love reading short story collections on my Kindle. I love reading books of essays on my Kindle. I love my Kindle.

"Your eyes are red as blood," Mama shouts when she wakes up in the middle of the night and finds me reading with eyes that would frighten even Dracula. "You will destroy your vision, Fiza, if you continue like this."

I pay no heed. I just dim the screen a bit and continue to read.

My friend Kanchana from the book club at Trilogy is very fond of reading on the Kindle and iPad. Whenever we met at Trilogy or at a bookish coffeeshop we used to patronize called "The Mocking-Bird Café," we talked about our latest e-book reads. Well, *she* talked about her latest e-book reads, and I mostly listened. People compliment me by saying that I'm a good listener. But I'm not any better than anyone else in that vein unless they're talking about something that makes me want to really pay attention. People do like to tell me things they wouldn't tell anyone else. It's not that I'm allowing them to "let it out," it's just that I don't know how to make regular conversation. I spent twelve years in school on silent mode, what do you expect?

So, yes, Kanchana and I are in love with our Kindles and iPads. She reads for pleasure only, while I read for both business and pleasure.

I appreciate the relaxed way I can buy a book on my Kindle. It's amazing, the *technology*, that is. As I said, I miss reading some books in the physical form, but we have to change with the times. If we didn't change, we would still be reading scrolls of papyrus, and that's not my kind of a thing!

ESSAY 47

You Are a Writer (So Start Acting Like One) by Jeff Goins

I BOUGHT JEFF GOINS'S BOOK on my Kindle. I read it in a day's time and loved every bit of it.

After I read it, I thought to myself, "Why didn't I have this book when I was starting out as a writer in my early twenties?"

Seriously, if I had read this uplifting, informative, and positive-vibe book when I was twenty-two or twenty-three years old, I would have been doing a better job with my craft back then.

I am a reclusive loner. I have issues related to inferiority complex and self-esteem. When I read this book by Goins, I had already become the director of a publishing firm, but I still suffered from a peculiar kind of denial. It was as though I had some sort of traditional book-publishing hangover where I didn't consider myself to be a real writer or a real publisher. This book took away that inferiority complex forever.

You Are a Writer (So Start Acting Like One) is a must-read for serious writers who are just starting out, to make them realize that even if you are self-publishing your book on Amazon, YOU ARE A

WRITER. You don't need a traditional publisher or a vanity publisher to dictate terms to you about your book. That is not how the writing business works in the twenty-first century. In simple language, with little or no technical lingo, Goins ORDERS us to start believing in our craft and in ourselves. It's as easy as that. If we do not believe in our craft and take our writing seriously, nobody else will.

The book also provides tips on how to go about building one's platform, to start using social media to create momentum, and to hone your craft, making it better as you go along. But nothing is as important as believing you ARE a writer. You don't need other people to tell you that; YOU need to tell yourself.

I read Goins book in my office-cum-writing-hut on my recliner with a lighted-scented candle by my side. The aroma was of Ponds Cream and baby lotion, a special mixture called "love portion." I guess this love potion made me fall in love with Jeff Goins's book because in no time at all, I bought another book he wrote called *Real Artists Don't Starve: Timeless Strategies for Thriving in the New Creative Age*. I read it right after finishing *You Are a Writer*.

Since reading these books, I'm a changed person. I have decided to look people in my business in the eye and say clearly enough for them to hear, "I'm a writer."

"What does Fiza do?" asks one of my building's neighbors. "She is always at home. Doesn't she intend to work?"

"She's a writer," Blaise says. "And a publisher."

"Yes, I know all that," says the intolerable neighbor. "But when is she going to really work and earn money? When will she go out for a job?"

We've got a sort of bureaucratic hangover here in India where you are only thought to be "earning" and "working" if you go OUT to work. No one in my neighborhood knows anything about my finances. They just assume that writers are not serious people, that they are just playing around and don't earn money. They don't even consider me to be a real teacher, even though I've been running my tutorial for the last ten years.

"Yes, I know all that," says another neighbor. "But when is she going to be a real teacher?"

"Real teacher?" Mama asks, flabbergasted. "She has been teaching children from grade five to twelve for the past ten years!"

"Yes, yes I know all that," the insufferable neighbor continues, "but when is she going to go out and teach in a school, earn a salary from an institution, and get a pension?"

Mama sighs with irritation. I feel like throttling the neighbor.

"If she knew your finances," Rita whispers to me in the kitchen as she reads a Chetan Bhagat thriller, "she'd quit her job and beg to join you."

"I'm not interested," I say as I switch off my Kindle. "A prophet is never recognized in his own country."

And so, it is. Even though I am more than financially stable thanks to my own hard labor for ten years, and an award-winning author, and a director of a niche publishing firm, I am still thought to be sitting in the house or office-cum-writing-hut doing nothing. It is so infuriating that sometimes I feel like screaming the building down.

I'm not the pushy type. I'm not the type to brag, not even in print. But to be subjected to these questions about a job that's paying my bills and running my household is getting on my nerves. That's when books like *You Are a Writer* give me the patience to take a deep breath and allow me to throw out the negativity and just focus on what I'm doing: my writing, teaching, publishing, and reading.

If you are a writer starting out, I suggest that you read this book before going any further in your writing career. If you plan to be a part- or full-time writer who does not bow down to traditional publishers, then this book will be even more valuable to you. If you are being harassed at home, by your peers or others, because they don't think that writers, especially self-published writers, earn any money, then please read this book and let your eyes (and theirs) be opened and the scales brushed off.

The most important thing one must remember when becoming a writer is to have patience.

A writer's life is a lonely one, in which we sit in our writing haunts, wherever they may be, for hours, days, weeks, months, years at a stretch, working on a project we believe in. We love doing this because we were born to do this. But traditional publishers and vanity publishers have killed writers' dreams and their works. On the other hand, indie writers and self-published writers are selling books and earning royalties. But, according to Jeff Goins, in order for that to happen you have to become an authorprenuer. An authorprenuer is a writer who sells books through her involvement with blogging, guest blogging, websites, radio talks, book conferences, *beta* readers, peer group book clubs, etc. As a writer friend of mine, Ron Yates, once said in a radio interview, "There is no free lunch out there." So we can't just self-publish and sit tight. We have to promote, and blogging, marketing, having our own websites, etc., is how we do it.

I know this is not what a writer wants to do. I certainly didn't want to become a businesswoman. I just wanted to write. But I realized, quite early in my teens when the first and last traditional publisher I approached rejected my book *S.O.S. Animals And Other Stories,* that I would have to do this on my own. Because I believed in my work. I believed that I could find the right audience who would love my work JUST AS IT IS. And today I have found my readers. It's a small group, but they are there, and they are paying me for my books – they want me to write.

So, yes, Jeff Goins says what I have learned in the seven years I've been writing: that writers are reclusive loners and solitary creatures but they have to get out there, at least on social media platforms and in book clubs, with their peers in order to start a life as an author who is paid for work.

I would also like to add here – and many people will disagree with me about it, but I'm still going to say it – don't leave your day job if you are planning on self-publishing in earnest. I'm dead serious about this. You've got to earn to feed your ambition and pay the many fees that you'll face: fees for good editors, fees for good proofreaders, fees to enter competitions, fees to enter book clubs, fees –

fees – fees! And where, pray tell, are you going to get all of this money if you have no bank balance or a day job on the side?

So don't quit your day job (or for that matter, night job) if you are a person who has little or no money and is starting out fresh in life.

I have my job as a teacher to fuel my writing. I finance my own publishing firm; I've not taken any loans. And certainly, none of my family members, let alone my estranged and deranged Papa, had anything to do with it. It's all been my earnings. HARD-EARNED, and don't you forget that!

It's almost 7:00 in the evening as I type this piece. I've just finished teaching, and now I'm here in my office-cum writing-hut working on this. I don't wait until "the muse" takes me; I work whenever I get the time, because, with all the jobs I do, I have no time and no excuses. I wrote my *Classics: Why We Should Encourage Children to Read Them* while teaching children biology. It was a bestseller on Amazon for a year and a half. Get over those excuses of needing a special place, time, muse before you can write. If you want to feed your empty stomach, then sit in front of that laptop and type!

Jeff Goins will teach you all this.

And your life as a writer will teach you many other things.

It taught me to write-publish-promote – the mantra of the self-published writer today.

ESSAY 48

Granth Bookstore

IN JUHU, THERE IS A BOOKSTORE called "Granth," which in Sanskrit means *book*. It's an awesome place that Blaise started taking me to in my last year of college.

The store is near the beach, so there is a lot of sea, sand, and activity in the area. A few miles away is the famous Juhu beach of Mumbai.

I don't like the sea, but I love Granth and visit as often as I can. If you want to spot your favorite Bollywood star in Mumbai, Granth is a good place to do it. Bollywood-actress-turned-bestselling writer, Twinkle Khanna, our resident Mrs. Funnybones, is a regular at Granth. Many other film stars and film personalities go there as well. I recognize them because I've read about them and also because they are all so glamorous.

Granth is a peaceful and welcoming home of books to me. They have two floors; the first is for the adults and the second is for kids. They have a huge collection of books and these days they are specially curating their books to suit the demands of their clientele.

I love shopping at Granth. The team there has known me for years. They have seen me grow from a teenager into a woman, and they feel proud when my books are displayed on their shelves.

Granth is a chic place and a hot spot of literary activities for the schools on that side of Mumbai city. They serve a large number of people from different walks of life. I go there at least once a month to shop for good books and to drink their delicious cappuccinos.

They have a coffee shop in the adult section of the library, where they serve black coffee and cappuccinos with cookies. Sometimes I sit in one of the well-placed readers' nooks and go through my purchases, write in my diary, and talk books with Blaise and the manager of Granth, Mr. Hiren.

I love the way their books are so clean and always smell as if they have been freshly brought from the printers. I love the coffee-table books at Granth. They have a huge coffee-table collection, bigger than any I've ever seen. It's a pleasure to go through them. They especially have a lot of coffee-table books on the subjects of art, music, and cinema. I buy most of my coffee-table books of the cinema and Bollywood from Granth. I buy Amitabh Bachchan coffee-table books for Mama.

If Mumtaz was Papa's favorite Bollywood heroine of yesteryear, Mama's favorite Bollywood actor is the emperor of Bollywood himself, the legendary Amitabh Bachchan. Mama loves him. She used to watch all his movies with Papa.

"Your papa hated Mr. Bachchan," Mama said as she combed my long hair for college one day. "He only tolerated him because he could then come with me to the movies. Mr. Bachchan is the real and only superstar of Bollywood."

"Why don't you just call him Amitabh Bachchan like everyone else?" I asked along with a tiny wince as a knot was pulled out of my then waist-length ebony hair.

Mama smoothened my hair and tied it with her own hands.

"He will always be Mr. Bachchan for me," she said in a sad voice.

I understood. I understood so well.

Mama became infatuated with Amitabh Bachchan when he first appeared on the Bollywood screen in the 1970s. She, like every other girl of her age, used to watch all of his films and read filmy magazines and gossip columns about the superstar. Mama was a movie buff and loved everything about Mr. Bachchan. And she was a lucky woman in more ways than one.

When she was a twentysomething teaching at BSS, both of Amitabh Bachchan's children, Shweta Bachchan and Abhishek Bachchan, were in her class. She used to meet Amitabh Bachchan, her superstar, during PTA meetings, along with his wife, a noted actress of Bollywood, Jaya Bachchan née Bhaduri.

Mama called him Mr. Bachchan back then, and she never stopped even after both the kids left her care.

Jaya Bachchan was aware of Mama's love for Papa and that they were seeing each other a lot. Jaya Bachchan, it seems, didn't like the idea of Mama dating Papa at all. She tried very hard to convince Mama to stop seeing him. But Mama didn't listen. Jaya Bachchan said it wouldn't last. It didn't. Jaya Bachchan was right.

I buy coffee-table books of Amitabh Bachchan at Granth for Mama. I buy them because Amitabh Bachchan is the man my papa could never be for Mama. Especially when she needed him the most, when I was born to both of them. Mama was beautiful, petite, and fairer than my laptop screen. She still is, though a bit older. Amitabh Bachchan, though he still rocks the screen with his great performances at age seventy-six, is also old – but gold for Mama. She will never forget her Mr. Bachchan.

The coincidence of it all is that Amitabh Bachchan lives in Juhu itself, just a few miles away, near Juhu beach. We pass his two bungalows, Jalsa and Pratiksha, whenever we visit Mechu at Malad. Mama always likes taking the inner roads to Malad, though I and every other sane person in Mumbai prefer the Western Express Highway. She likes to go through the inner route on S. V. Road because she gets to see Jalsa and Pratiksha. My Bachchan-crazy Mama!

And my papa, who hated the man but who loved Mama, who still loves mama in fact.

It's me he doesn't love. I got in the way of his beautiful love story. I, that annoying girl child!

At Granth, I buy their special classics series from their huge classics section. They even have those old-fashioned pocket-sized hardback replicas that used to be printed in the Victorian Era when a book was made to fit in a Victorian man's waistcoat pocket, ready for reading at any time.

I've bought quite a few of those in my time, and they're so cute that I prominently display them in the hall on a special shelf that I bought from the Mecca of book lovers in Mumbai. You'll have to read a bit more to learn about that.

I love drinking cappuccino after cappuccino at Granth. I have made some of my biggest business decisions there and have taken risks most twentysomethings wouldn't dare take.

The place smells of paper. And they grow money plants as well as sunflowers, which is a sight for sore eyes for a plant lover like me.

"What are you working on?" Blaise asked me the last time we were there, which was the 31st of December 2018.

I shook my head, "I plan on writing a lot in 2019. I would like to do a better job of my memoir with the libraries and the bookstores that have made me into the reclusive reader and writer I am."

"Why a memoir so soon?" Blaise asked over his coffee cup. "People write their memoirs later in life when they are much older."

I fold my hands over my large chest and look out the floor-to-ceiling glass windows of Granth.

"I don't have time," I say as I watch the swanky BMWs and Mercedes go by in the dark of the tropical winter's night.

Blaise chuckles. "You have a whole life to lead. What do you mean you have no time?"

I keep on staring at the vibrant street below us. The waitress at Granth asks if we want more coffee, and Blaise says no.

"Because I stop breathing thirty-four times per hour when I am asleep," I think to myself. I don't say it out loud to Blaise.

ESSAY 49

The Bunker Diary by Kevin Brooks

I PICKED UP THIS YA BOOK at the American Library in the year 2016. I went there on my own because Blaise was at work. Narayan dropped me at the entrance gate of the American Library and I entered on my own. I had to pass through many doors. I was in a hurry as I had to get back to the tuition house – exams were coming up and I hadn't finished some of the middle school portion yet.

I went to the shelves that displayed the latest books that had come in. Every week new books and magazines arrived at the American Library, and I loved to borrow and read them. As mentioned before, I loved reading YA fiction and non-fiction. Who doesn't? Besides, they stock some of the best and unique writings in American YA fiction.

The Bunker Diary by Kevin Brooks was displayed on the new arrival shelf. It was almost lunchtime and the librarians were ready to take their lunchbreak. I read the synopsis and without a second thought borrowed the book.

I read the book in a matter of hours. It was dominatingly spellbinding and hideously frightful. It tore me to shreds.

The Bunker Diary is about a group of people who have been mauled in the street, somehow kidnapped without remembering who their kidnapper is and how they were kidnapped. They are shut up together in a bunker, a nuclear bunker most likely, with cameras everywhere, even in the bathroom. The story is about how the people of different age groups manage themselves in a whitewashed concrete bunker, with no windows and no doors; just an elevator that is not in their control which sends down food, water, and sometimes unwanted surprises.

I was awestruck by the power of the book and how Kevin Brooks had wielded his pen. Though the book is for young adults, it is really suffocating and horrifying. I was numbed by it. The ending is completely out of the box, something I'll not forget.

"Miss, what are you reading?" one of my students in the eighth grade asked while she and others around the table were doing a picture composition.

I let out a long breath. "It's a really frightening book."

"Worse than the movie *The Conjuring*?"

"Definitely worse," I said. "Continue writing your composition, please."

Why did I think the book by Brooks was worse than the movie *The Conjuring*? Because it was suffocating and disturbing. It is something we all pray should never ever happen to us, but at times it does. And then what? How do you preserve your dignity as a human being? How do you react to such a situation? What would you do if you were locked in a bunker with no way out, no one interacting with you from the other side and when you feel something creepy is going on around you; nothing to do with ghosts or the paranormal, but with the kidnapped victims stuck in that bunker with you? How do you remain human?

All this reminded me of my own life and the lives of the people in my country. We are, all of us, common men stuck in a bunker where there seems to be no way out. Everyone in power, be it government ministers or business tycoons, is watching like those cameras in *The*

Bunker Diary; they are watching everything we do. How do we reclaim our rights as a democracy? How do we get out of the bunker?

The Lok Sabha elections will be over by the time this book is out in the market. I will be voting in April, and I don't know whether I'm going to be freed from a sort of neofascism in the city and country at large, or whether I'll be suffocated like the people trapped in *The Bunker Diary*.

I may not be a big talker, nor am I very well read, nor am I a great intellectual to discuss certain matters close to my city of Mumbai – I am a writer, a plain one, but I am one and this is my reality. We are all afraid what will happen in the next five years, whosoever be elected in office.

I read *The Bunker Diary* in 2016 and I will never forget it. Symbolically, that YA book is so close to my reality and the reality of Mumbai and India that it sends chills up and down my spine. For the worst tales of horror are the ones that are real.

"Who are you going to vote for?" I ask Mama as she drinks her hot tea with brown sugar to keep her diabetes in check.

She looks at me, flabbergasted. "You know who I'm going to vote for, so why bother asking?"

"Because I do not want to vote for anyone," I say with my coffee mug in my lap. I'm just waiting for the coffee to cool down a bit, to become lukewarm. My mouth can't stand boiling hot liquids.

Mama sighs and takes a sip of her tea. "You know we have to vote. We have to go out and show up."

"I am going to vote but ..."

"But what?" Mama asks, putting the cup on the coffee table.

I shrug.

"I'm going to press that button. The one that says that no one is capable."

"Don't do what the Germans did," Blaise says as he checks his mail on his smartphone, which is more high-tech than mine. "They got Hitler."

We maintain a moment of silence. We don't want a Hitler. Definitely not a Hitler.

"You'll be voting for the second time in your life for the Lok Sabha general elections, Fiza," Mama says, and we laugh. The point of the joke is that by now I should have been voting for the third time in my life for the general elections of India. But the last time I was busy being filmed for a documentary on the day of the elections in Mumbai. The documentary was called *Black Sheep* (I mentioned it earlier in the book), a documentary about the Kinnar, or eunuch community, of Mumbai.

On that day, I got up late and had to speed with Narayan to the hotel where I was to be filmed. The transsexuals came very well decked out compared to my khadi-kurta and black jeans. They were astonished when I said I would miss the voting that day.

They had all got up early to vote before they came for the filming.

"Look," one of them said, putting up her index finger. There was an indelible blue ink mark on her nail, showing that she had voted. "You ought to be ashamed of yourself for not going to vote before you came here," she said, but in a friendly way that sounded funny, so we all laughed.

The filming ended long after the election in Mumbai was over. I had missed it.

"Make sure you vote next time," another Kinnar said, pointing her inked finger at me. "Your vote can tip the scale in certain circumstances. One vote can be the cause for your own victory or defeat."

That was in 2014. After the shoot, I drove to MCubed Library to sit and read. The adult section was full so I had to sit in the kids' section. I was reading a book called *A Conspiracy of Paper* by David Liss. I sat there, oblivious to all the activity of kids and parents running around.

I remembered all this as I tried to cool the BRU Gold coffee in my mug. No, I hadn't voted in 2014. I'm sorry.

"You will have to vote," Mama says, finished with her tea and getting ready for class. "It matters little what button you press. Just show up, okay?" She looked over her shoulder as she left the room. "People are watching," were her parting words.

Was it a warning or a statement?

I don't want to suffocate.

If you want to feel the thrill of *The Bunker Diary*, you should make it a point to read this book. It's YA, so teenagers, too, can read this book and become educated about the realities of our existence. It's not a comforting read, so it's not recommended for those who spook easily and those who are faint of heart. If you do read it, get ready: the book makes you ponder some serious stuff.

ESSAY 50

The Suragi Tree by Prabhaker Acharya

I DON'T TRAVEL MUCH. I'm a recluse to the point where other people would lose their sanity.

But I used to travel to Karnataka at least. Karnataka is a South Indian state just below Maharashtra, where I live. We used to visit Bengaluru and Mysore where one of my favorite writers, R. K. Narayan, used to live.

We visited Bengaluru because we had a family friend living there, Mrs. Shirley Hamilton Noronha, who had a huge two-floor cottage in the suburban part of town. She lived there with her daughter and younger son. She had four kids total: three older boys and the daughter was the youngest. The youngest of the boys was called Sunil, and he was the inspiration for the teacher in my children's book *Raman and Sunny: Middle School Blues.*

The place was cozy but we used their hospitality only once, on our first holiday. Most of the time when we visited Bengaluru we lived in a hotel the bank had allotted to Blaise, as he was an officer there.

In Bengaluru, I shopped for books at the various bookstores, malls, and secondhand libraries. One of the books I happened upon was *The Suragi Tree* by Prabhaker Acharya, which sounded very much like an R. K. Narayan-style book.

I read it in 2011, when I was teaching in a regular school, which was during my hurting years. I read it every night after a meager dinner and after doing a lot of paperwork and preparation for class for the following day.

If you are a lover of R. K. Narayan's books, *The Suragi Tree* is worth a read because it's written almost in the same style, which I appreciated very much. If you like good Indian fiction along the lines of literary fiction (not chick lit), then this is a book you will enjoy.

The book gave me a lot of peace from the turmoil in my life at that period of time. I lost myself in this South Indian family that I was reading about and whose members felt a deep sense of bonding with the suragi tree growing outside their home. I loved the protagonist, who spent most of his time reading under the suragi tree. I loved the part where he moved to Mumbai and the life he led there.

It was a smart read and very much like the Indian fiction that I favor.

Shirley ma'am loved to go through the books I had purchased from bookstores. She was a rigid Protestant by faith and didn't like my fondness for Hindu philosophy and literature. I was like a daughter to her. But she found me pretty weird and too bookish.

I liked her youngest son, Sunil. He had this cute chocolate-boy look with the intelligence of Einstein, and he loved to read. He fascinated me as a character. Shirley ma'am was thinking of getting me married to one of her boys. If I had the choice (which I don't), I would have loved to have married Sunil. He was a very nice guy, four years my senior.

"You like him?" Mama asked in a teasing fashion. "Shirl will drive all your Muslim, Buddhist, and Hindu philosophy books out of the window if you marry her son."

But I was in my hurting years and I was also ambitious about my career as a teacher and writer, and later, a publisher. A mountain of books piled up between me and relationships with men, a mountain I had built of my own accord. Books are better than boys, as an old

Facebook meme said. Besides, books don't get up one day and say, "I'm leaving you because you gave birth to a daughter."

I don't go to Bengaluru anymore, though one day I hope I will. I want to visit those bookstores again.

I want to find another awesome read like *The Suragi Tree*.

Traveling. Going to other places. Sightseeing. Meeting new people. I don't do these things well at all.

But I liked my few trips to Karnataka. I liked living with Shirley ma'am's family and seeing what life was like in a city other than Mumbai. Someday, I hope to travel to London, Paris, and the USA to shop for books, especially rare, old editions.

But that's a long way off, just like the protagonist of *The Suragi Tree* felt a long way off from the places in which he would later live. His home near the suragi tree would always be best of all.

But one day, this reclusive reader and writer will travel. Will go to the places she loves. Which will be more bookstores and secondhand bookstores where she feels right at home, even if it is somewhere far away from Mumbai.

"Have you ever given the thought of settling down abroad?" Mama asked me off and on when I was in my early twenties. "You are well qualified and maybe you will want to do so once you are in your thirties."

I am twenty-nine still. A year to go to make such decisions.

These days when I tend to the neem trees in my modest garden, I think of the Prabhaker Acharya book I read a long time ago, seems like another time altogether. What happened to that thin twentysomething girl with long ebony hair? Where did she go? And now instead of her, when I look in the mirror, who is this gigantic monster I see?

"Monster" did I say? No, I'm not a monster. Just a plus-size woman dealing with books, students, and more books on the side.

I wish I, too, could read under a suragi tree for hours on end someday.

ESSAY 51

Landmark at the Infinity Mall

AFTER I JOINED A REGULAR SCHOOL in 2011, I was told of a bookstore chain called Landmark, which was a bit off the beaten track but a great place to shop for books. So, one evening, Narayan, Mama, Blaise, and I made our way to the mall where this bookstore chain was situated. This place was at Andheri, in Mumbai, a place of constant traffic, pollution of both air and noise, high-rise buildings and, to cater to the high-rise buildings: a number of malls.

This was the first time in our entire lives that we were entering a mall. The year was 2011.

"Please let's take the stairs," Mama said. "Or the elevator, please."

Mama was terrified of the escalator, though it was the fastest way to get to the second floor where the bookstore was situated. Mama wasn't the only one who was scared stiff; even I was perplexed by the escalator. In particular, how would you get off it?

"No, no, no!" Mama headed back to the taxi. "I'm not going up. You and Blaise go ahead. I'll wait for you both in the taxi."

"We were supposed to be having a family trip," Blaise glared at Mama. "Okay, we will take the elevator."

The elevator was jammed packed with people and the queue extended right up to the entrance. From the looks of it, we were in for a very long wait.

"The stairs," Mama suggested meekly.

We looked all over for the stairs, and almost jumped off the fire escape, but we didn't find the stairs. When we asked for directions, the mall helper seemed as stupefied as we were. Where were the stairs? Nobody knew.

"Mama, we have to go by the escalator," I said, quite deflated. "Even if we die trying to do so."

"Don't be so melodramatic," Blaise scolded me. "It's easy. We'll all just hold hands and watch what the ones in front of us do. That's it."

"What if those in front of us are equally clueless?" I ventured.

"Oh Lord Jesus protect me!" Mama murmured as she eyed the escalator with mounting fear.

Blaise pondered the matter. "We'll stand behind some youngsters. They'll know how to get on and off."

We agreed. Well, I agreed. Mama tried heading back to the taxi but Blaise stopped her.

That escalator petrified us. Blaise said that he and Mama would get on first, and I would get on behind them. But in the end, Blaise was on one step, Mama two steps below him (while she held on to his hand), and I was right below Mama, clutching the banister for dear life.

We each tripped as we got off.

"See," Blaise said, breathing heavily. "Nothing to it." And Mama hit him hard on the shoulder.

We entered Landmark and were blown out of our minds with excitement.

"This is a bookstore?" Mama asked quietly as we passed through security. "It looks like a shopping center for everything: toys, Xboxes, computer games, board games, skateboards, designer bags, chocolates and sweets, Blu-ray movies and DVDS, stuffed toys, school stationery, scented candles, guitars, pianos ..."

"Where are the books?" I asked at the help desk. They told us to go down past the DVD collection. We did, and we were again stunned.

The bookstore section was huge.

"Books-books-books-books-books-books-books," I chanted under my breath.

❋

Landmark was massive. It housed and sold everything, but its main commodity was books. Infinity Mall at Andheri offered a huge space with packed bookshelves and cozy nooks in which to sit and read to the sound of Justin Bieber or One Direction or Taylor Swift blaring on the loudspeakers.

Whenever I wanted to shop for books big time, I used to go there. Mama accompanied us on these trips, but she never got used to the escalator. On the other hand, I got used to it really quickly and so did Blaise.

I would be carting a lineup of baskets behind me as I went from shelf to shelf, picking up books. The place sold every genre you could think of, and if you took the trouble to search for it, you would find what you were looking for. Landmark at Infiniti Mall had a large International literary fiction section, a whole aisle of it. Can you believe that? I had so much to choose from! It also catered to teenagers. That was the time Stephenie Meyer came on the scene with her Twilight vampire books. The store's YA section was even bigger than the literary fiction section, dedicated to YA and vampire literature.

The place was swamped with the latest bestsellers at discounted prices. I bought most of my Shashi Tharoor books from there, maybe sometime around 2013.

I never sat back and read there because the blaring Western pop music was just too loud for comfort. The nonfiction section was the biggest section of all, and I literally picked everything in sight. I especially loved their Indian fiction section. They had a whole row dedicated to it, and I bought a lot of good books from there. I can still picture myself, on one knee in front of the Indian fiction shelf, going through some of the best Indian fiction I've ever read in my life.

By the time I was done, the workers there had to pack my books in two to three giant shopping bags that could manage two humans inside each.

My all-time record for books purchased in a single day is 106. I counted each book before billing, and while I did, all the other shoppers gawked at me and some actually approached me to ask their peculiar questions.

"Are those books for a library or just for you?"

"You mean you are really buying all those books?"

"You must be loaded to be able to afford all that, aren't you?"

"But what are you going to do with so many books in your house?"

"Are you from a foreign country? You look kind of from Saudi?"

I didn't know what to say about the last one but, yes, people were shocked by my hunger for books. And, yes, by this time I was buying my own books with my own money.

"Why don't you try our toy section, madam?" said a Landmark salesman with a pearly white-toothed smile. Seriously, toys? At the time, I was a bit fond of stuffed toys so I would buy one or two teddy bears to go with the books.

Whenever I went to Landmark at Andheri, I was so excited because there was always something new to read. And their discounts were unbelievable.

When I started a kid's book club at the tuition house and called it Born to Read, I shopped for the children's' library at Landmark. The salesmen and women thought I was having a baby because of the way I was shopping for kids' books.

"Good news on the way, madam?" one of the regular salesgirls asked. I looked at my large tummy and then back at her. "I'm not having a baby. I'm plus size. And I'm not married."

She looked at me quite puzzled.

"Then who is that man with the funny moustache you come with?"

"That's my uncle – maternal uncle."

She stood shell-shocked for a while and then face-palmed herself. She and the whole Landmark crew thought that Blaise was my husband. Blaise took it as a compliment. Mama took it as an insult to her cute young daughter. And I took it that people will remain people; because I am a girl, none of them assumed I could buy my own books.

"Your uncle is very generous to give you so much of money to buy books," said the salesgirl. "You are a lucky girl. Must be the darling '*laadli*' of your family."

"It's my money and I'm paying," I said irritably. "Why can't I buy my own books?"

Still, it was a joy to visit Landmark at Andheri. And, alas, it was a joy that couldn't last. In 2015, we went up the escalator of Infiniti Mall only to find that the Landmark had shut down. The other franchises on the floor said that they had shut for repairs but, after two or three more visits, one of the managers of the mall informed us that the place had closed their outlet forever.

"Now, now, Fiza, be a brave girl!" Blaise cooed as I bawled in the taxi like a heartbroken brat that I was.

Narayan tsk-tsked all the way back to Bandra West.

"Now, now, Fiza," Blaise went on giving me his handkerchief to cry in. "Be a good girl and don't cry. It's not like anyone is dead. It's bound to happen in business. Be a good girl and don't cry."

I would mourn the loss of Landmark for months to come. I still do. It was a magical place, and I'll never get over it being shut down.

Do you know what has opened up in its place? A stupid damn branded outlet for clothes. CLOTHES! Why is it always CLOTHES, and those never of my size, so what's the point!

Where did the reading public of Andheri go? There were so many people who used to visit and buy and read at Landmark; where did they all go? What became of those readers? Does Amazon feed their needs now? It's just so sad that I feel like crying again, even after four years.

Landmark's demise in Andheri would prepare me for something worse later on. Because in 2018, another bookstore would close down for good, and it would make a tear in my bookish soul forever.

"Cheer up, chin up," Blaise said as he googled Landmark one day, "They have one last franchise in Mumbai."

"Where, where?" I asked desperately almost jumping on poor Blaise.

"Vashi," he replied fending me off. "Vashi at the Infinity Mall there."

"Vashi!" Mama said totally aghast. "That's at the other end of the world. It will take us hours to go there."

"We are going," I declared.

Mama shook her head in frustration and Blaise sighed deeply.

"Here we go again," Narayan said a few weeks later when we made our way toward the Vashi Infinity Mall in the deepest suburban part of Mumbai, literally in the salt pans of Mumbai.

"I've never been this far," Mama said. "I mean, look at it." She was referring to the wilderness and the lack of streetlights around us. "We are going to die out here if we don't leave before it is dark."

She needn't have worried. We left even before the afternoon could start, because the Landmark at Vashi was a poor excuse for a bookstore franchise. The place was crammed with toys, sweets, computer games, technology, stuffed animals, gift curios – and hardly any books. The bookstore section was as big as MCubed Library, and the literary fiction section was only one tiny shelf.

"At least you tried," Mama told me as we made our way back home in the early afternoon toward Bandra West. We passed salt pans, rice fields aplenty and a large number of slums with too many people in them. Though most of the slum shanties boasted dish antennas, I doubted these families would have the money to spend on books.

It took us more than two hours to get back home. In all, we spent four hours on the road. That was in 2015. Today, if we were to take the same route, we would have to spend five hours going and four hours coming; that's nine hours on the road. In nine hours, I could type about nine thousand words on my Dell Inspiron 11 laptop. What has happened to Mumbai in just a matter of five years! The Metro project and falling bridges have made traveling in Mumbai a hellish nightmare. Since no one is getting to work on time by the road, many commuters and students are taking the trains to get to work, college, or school. With the large population of people taking to trains (the "lifeline" of Mumbai), railway queues and overcrowded trains are at an uncomfortable and dangerous all-time high. Commuting has become a mess, so I have stopped even thinking of going toward the suburbs.

I'll always remember my fun days at Landmark, the great number of books I bought there and read. I used to go there every Diwali season, the Hindu festival of lights celebrating Lord Ram's return to his kingdom after defeating the king of the demons, the ten-headed Ravana. Diwali doesn't seem like Diwali without Landmark. But life has to go on, and one has to keep on turning the page.

You will have to turn this page, too, to find out about another place close to my heart that shut its doors forever. It was a Mecca to book lovers in Mumbai, and this Mecca's prophet was a man called Shanbaug.

And one day, Mecca would come home to me.

ESSAY 52

Strand Bookstall and a Man Called Shanbaug

THERE ONCE LIVED A MAN called Shanbaug. Shanbaug had a dream. He dreamed of starting the best bookstore in Mumbai.

He started by selling two shelves of books at the Strand cinema. Then someone gave him a place at Fort area in the town area of Mumbai. There, Shanbaug collected a few salesmen to whom he taught the book-selling business. And then, with shelves of Burma teak wood filled with books galore, the Strand bookstore, which has nothing to do with its namesake in New York, was born.

People of all walks of life came to the Strand in great numbers. The place was always packed to capacity with readers. Shanbaug and his salesmen worked hard to give their customers the best of the best books and always at discounted prices. Shanbaug never believed in "sales," which is the common theme of every franchise in Mumbai. No, Shanbaug didn't believe in sales, but he believed in discounted prices for every book every single day of the year.

The store was set up in the middle of the twentieth century. Within a few years, Shanbaug had achieved his dream. Strand bookstall became the Mecca of book lovers in Mumbai. Foreigners and

Indians from all over Mumbai and beyond flocked to the Strand bookstall just to see the place.

Back when Blaise was twenty-one, he worked in the Fort area as a clerk in the Bank of India. That's how he first heard about the man called Shanbaug and his legendary bookstall.

Long before I was even a thought in my parents' heads, young Blaise went to Strand. He was bedazzled and made friends with the salesmen there: Jagat, Sanjay, Virat, Anand, and so many others. Don't forget their names, for they will be important from now on in this book of bookish essays.

Well, the twentysomething Blaise made friends for life. But Blaise was not earning enough then to buy the books even at discounted prices, so he used to stand in the middle of the two-floor bookstore and read the books he loved, especially books on philosophy and the mysteries of life – alchemy, the pyramids, extraterrestrials, reincarnation, Edgar Cayce, Ascended Masters, Ascension, the Bermuda triangle, past lives, theosophy, etc. The Strand had it all.

Blaise rarely spoke to the man of the moment, Mr. Shanbaug. Shanbaug never interfered with Blaise but made sure he was fine, and when Blaise would purchase any book, he would be the one to write the bill for them with great discounts.

Blaise says he was fascinated with Shanbaug. He wondered why, Mr. Shanbaug allowed him to stand in his store and read for free even though he rarely bought any books. In 2018, he got his answer. A news article that ran when the place closed said that when Shanbaug was in his early twenties, he too could not afford the books he wanted and used to read books standing up at bookstalls. One day he was kicked out of a prestigious bookstall because of this. It was then that he swore he would build his own bookstore where poor young students and the common man would be allowed to stand and read without being questioned.

The Strand was the hub of bookish activity for the longest period, over something like sixty years, and was at its peak in the '70s through the '90s. Shanbaug, the avid reader and connoisseur of books of all categories and genres would win many prestigious national awards and trophies. The Strand was always packed with people, and there was hardly any place to breathe. And new books, cartons of them, came in every fortnight. The Strand was certainly a book lover's paradise.

But then, one day, Shanbaug passed away. Due to certain unforeseen circumstances, most of his salesmen and managers left him. Only a few remained to hold the torch. But there were no more crowds, new books came in rarely, and the old books were not getting sold. Customers who used to come in their hundreds dwindled in number and fewer books started to be sold.

It was the year 2005. That's the year I passed out of BSS. That's the year Blaise would introduce me to the Strand bookstall.

❋

"You mean to say you knew there was this marvelous Mecca for book lovers and you didn't tell me about it?" I said to Blaise in 2005. I was a teenager and I was using my frustrated voice. "How could you do this to me?"

Blaise patted my head. "I wanted to take you to the Strand, but you were so quiet. You hardly ever spoke, I thought you wouldn't be interested. And besides," he added as he pulled out his cell phone to check messages, "we didn't have the conveyance or the money when you were little to travel all the way to Fort. And you hated to travel, you know that."

"But if only you had told me..." I was inconsolable. "I never got to meet Shanbaug."

"She is right," Mama said as she comforted me. "The least you could have done was told her about it. I had some money. We could have gone on Sundays."

Blaise shrugged as he leaned on the wall of our home, which back in 2005 badly needed painting.

"I was in my thirties," Blaise said. "I didn't gauge Fiza properly. I didn't know she would love to come."

"Drat," I said and then I threw a temper tantrum. "I WANT TO GO THERE NOW!"

Blaise looked at the time on his cell phone.

"It's 6:30 pm. By the time we reach the place it will be closing time. They close at 7:00 or 7:30 p.m. But," he put his cell phone back into his pocket and smiled a whiskered smile. "The Strand is having a book fair in Juhu next to Amitabh Bachchan's house. It's on till 10:00 p.m. for the next few days. Want to come and have a taste of your first Strand book fair?"

I jumped for joy. Something was better than nothing.

We went there by rickshaw, which was cheaper than taxi.

"Oh, look! Do you see Mr. Bachchan's bungalow?" Mama asked, totally excited.

"I don't care about Amitabh Bachchan!" I groaned through the handkerchief protecting me from breathing in the gas fumes on the polluted road. "I just want to see the book fair."

"I think Mr. Bachchan is at home this week," Mama went on like the true Bachchan and Bollywood fan that she was. "He will greet his fans at 9:00 p.m. sharp."

I rolled my eyes and looked out of the rickshaw.

We came to the Kaifi Azmi park and grounds. Behind the park was a large hall where the book fair was being held.

"Hurry up," I screamed with excitement as I jumped out of the rickshaw.

"Take it easy," Blaise said while Mama paid the driver.

I ran into the hall. I fell in love!

The place was packed and had a number of books that were to my liking all over the place. I picked and chose my books and navigated myself under Blaise's supervision. Blaise told me how to navigate during a book fair in Mumbai and how to identify which tables to go for the specific books of choice. Today, I'm an ace at book fairs. I can navigate through any book fair in any part of bustling Mumbai and come out with treasures every time.

I bought several books that day at the Strand book fair. I still have those books, and I'll never let them go. Especially my old 2004 revised *Roget's Thesaurus*, paperback edition, which I still use for writing. It was in a miserable state a week ago, but I took it to an all-purpose store called the Paras Stationery Store around the corner of our lane. The store sells everything from toothbrushes to box files, and they fix the binding of books.

The owners who handed the newly bound thesaurus to Blaise said, "I think the person who has used this book, used it a bit too much."

I have it right here on my writing table as I type this essay. It's been with me through my whole writing career. I wouldn't sell it or give it away for a world of books!

When we had to go back home that day, we had to take a cab because we had a box load of purchases.

"This girl is showing the signs," Mechu said when she saw my purchases the following weekend.

"Showing signs of what?" Rita asked as she stirred a curry on the stove.

Mechu smelled the curry. "A bookworm-for-life type of sign. Philo (Mama) won't have to worry about Fiza spending money. I know the bookworm type. The girl from now on will spend money only on books. Everything else will be of minimal or no importance."

"What are you saying?" Rita said quite astonished. "She will become another Blaise!"

"Looks to me she'll be worse," said Mechu over her horn-rimmed glasses. Then, as an afterthought, she added, "The curry you are cooking needs more lime."

I was so fascinated by my book fair purchases that I stared lovingly at them for over a week before I even got down to reading them.

The next month, Rita, Mama, Blaise, and I all made our way to Strand. It was a joy ride. The taxi driver was an old man and his taxi was older than he was. We got a good look at the Colaba area where the richest of the rich stay in Mumbai. We watched the sun setting over the Arabian sea at the Chowpatty sea face, which was the most bustling seaside spot in Mumbai.

It was raining by the time we reached the Strand. It was beautiful, and the books smelled of vanilla extract, wood shavings, and camphor balls. The ground floor was full of nonfiction and fiction books for adults. The first floor had books for children and coffee-table books. I bought a lot of books that day. I was still not earning, so I was springing a leak in Blaise's pocket.

The salesmen were quiet, though they recognized Blaise. There was no sign of Jagat, Sanjay, Anand, Virat, or any of the familiar faces and friends Blaise had known for years.

"I can't understand it," Blaise said as he looked over a Lewis Carroll omnibus. "Where have all of my friends gone? All of your classics came from here and all my esoteric books," he said as he looked around the store and then sighed sadly. "But it's not like how it used to be. It's too empty and too quiet."

The salesmen who remained were familiar with Blaise (though not close friends), and they saw me and put two and two together.

"So this is the child for whom you used to buy Goosebumps for all these years?" one of them said as I placed hardback after hardback on the counter where Shanbaug had sat. "We were wondering which child you, an unmarried man, had suddenly adopted."

I bought my books, mostly classic omnibuses, like the complete works of Lewis Carroll, Edgar Allan Poe, H. P. Lovecraft, Jane Austen, the Brontë sisters and a partial collection of Charles Dickens's books. I had access to all the books at the BSS library, but I wanted copies of my own.

"Well," said one of the salesmen with big, friendly gray eyes. "Here's a big discount for you."

It really was an excellent discount. I went home a happy book phoenix, and Blaise needed to borrow money from Mama for the cab.

Going back home was a bit dangerous because the place was pitch dark at night. So, until we found our trusty Man Friday taxi driver, Narayan, we went to the Strand only in the early mornings on a weekend, mainly on Saturdays as Sundays were packed with sightseers who wanted to visit the Mecca of Mumbai's book lovers.

I loved my visits to the Strand. But I missed Shanbaug. It's so strange for me to miss a man I never knew. I used to look at his photographs under the glass tops of the desk counter where the cashier at Strand sat and say a small greeting by petting the place where the photograph was.

"Hi, Shanbaug uncle," I said silently. "I'm here."

I continued to visit the store from 2005 to 2018. A town area visit meant I had to visit the Strand.

"I don't like Fiza coming here," said Mama to Blaise once in 2013.

"Why not?" he asked.

Mama resented answering in my presence, but she said it all the same.

"They are going to close down. Those are the same books on the shelves since we've last been here. I just know it's going to close down soon. And it will break her heart."

Blaise shrugged it off like a lizard. "The Strand shutting shop – never!"

"Mark my words," Mama said. "The Strand will shut down and that will break my daughter's heart."

We all then remained silent in Narayan's cab. It was late afternoon. It was raining cats and dogs.

We drove home.

ESSAY 53

The Collected Works of A. J. Fikry by Gabrielle Zevin

I LOVED MUSING OVER MY THOUGHTS at the various book haunts I had adopted as my own. It was in 2014, in the hot season of October, that I read *The Collected Works of A. J. Fikry* by Gabrielle Zevin. I had borrowed the book from MCubed and was reading it in haste. A book discussion was going to take place soon at MCubed, and I wanted to take part in it. So, I read the book sitting at the round table at MCubed in the adult's section of the library, turning pages faster than I usually did.

There were good-looking, upper middle-class college students sitting all around the adult section of the library reading their textbooks. And there was I, a bit older than all of them (twenty-five) reading a wonderful book at top speed.

The place was quiet. The sound of librarians talking to children could be heard on and off, and readers were interrupted only by those entering the adult section to pick a book to read.

There were two girls sitting up in the nook near the ceiling, too. They were studying for an IAS exam. I saw their textbooks. One was studying history while the other was studying economics. Seeing them made my heart sink: Here I was, a rookie writer and tuition teacher trying to earn some money to feed my family, and I couldn't even make time to take a board exam for an MA.

I didn't even have time to read a book on a subject of my liking for a book club discussion at MCubed. And it was and is a really marvelous book.

I consider Gabrielle Zevin's book as one of the best fiction books I've read about a bookshop. What I call "a bookish book."

It is the story of an owner of a bookstore that is not doing too well who receives a baby at his doorstep with a note. What happens after that is emotionally beautiful, and I will not spoil it by mentioning the details here. All I want to say is that it's an inspiring book and a redemptive one concerning love, unconditional and pure. I especially love the book launch that takes place and the mystery of who ends up being the real author – no, no spoilers from me. Read this literary fiction masterpiece to discover the rest.

As I said, I was reading it at top speed. I so wanted to be part of a group of like-minded people. I was going through a phase in 2014 where I missed talking to people – a bit. So I joined the book club at MCubed to get myself some friends. And it worked, too. I met a friend. She is forty years older than I am, and I know where she lives. Alas, even after knowing her since 2014, I don't know her name. I know her favorite genre of books, her love for journalism, her erudite nature, but I don't for the life of me know her name. That's me for you.

I managed in that one day to finish *The Collected Works of A. J. Fikry,* and I was an emotional ball of wool by its end. I knew that, just like the bookstore owner, I too was a solitary soul. At the end of the book, I wished I had taken my time and read the book slowly, imbibing all the lessons of love, acceptance, and bookishness it had to teach me.

The book is an excellent summer holiday read. You already know by now that I don't often read books that can be considered relaxing holiday reads. Well, Gabrielle Zevin's book is one of those, and I read it during the Diwali vacations. I'm sure everyone who loves literary fiction, love stories, and bookstores will love this book as well.

I did make it to the book discussion, but I didn't say a word at the club meeting. I was silent from beginning to end. As I have mentioned before, it was only at Trilogy's book club meeting that I actually started speaking to people after a very, very long time – especially to people of my age.

After I finished reading Gabrielle Zevin's book that evening at MCubed, however, I was totally drained. The sun had set, and it was around 6:45 p.m. The yellow lights from the lamps were soothingly bright, a soft breeze blew through the library, and the evening librarian (who was not Oliver sir) went to the cooler for a drink of water.

I sat there, stupefied and exhausted, torn to shreds by a paperback.

I asked myself, "What is my life? Writing and reading and teaching all day and all the time, that's what! When will I study for an MA? Will I ever study for an MA? I'm twenty-five years old. I'm old. The last time I checked I was 45 kgs and still a teenager – WHAT HAPPENED?"

The bookstore owner of Gabrielle Zevin's book was a widower. I felt like I was already a widow. I felt something was lost in me among the many folds of my added flesh, as if I were fat, tired, and beyond everything.

That's when I made a decision. That's when I knew I would never fit in. I would never be anything but a book phoenix, and I didn't care.

The librarian finished her drink. One of the students sauntered into the toilet after shutting down his laptop. People were going about their regular work while I had been torn to shreds by a paperback.

Many questions have not been answered that have come to my mind. Questions about my past, my father, myself, my existence, all of which I've sublimated into the books I've written and the books I've read and drowned in over the years.

But those questions do come to me. They come like book dust and settle on my bones. I dust myself off but some still remain.

MCubed doesn't have book dust. It doesn't have dust at all. It's cleaned every day, including the bookshelves.

ESSAY 54

Strand Bookstore 2

I WENT TO THE STRAND Bookstore whenever I could. When I was in college it was difficult because we had no conveyance. But by the time I was teaching and writing, we had Narayan, and I headed there as often as I could.

I used to watch the faces, the sallow and sad faces of the salesmen. The customers had stopped coming in droves. Even the Mecca of Mumbai book lovers could no longer attract the tourists and regulars who had once flocked to the bookshop. But in those dark times, I still went there. I always did.

I used to roam the shelves of the adult books section. A salesperson always handed me a chair to sit on as I perused. I purchased some of my best books, finding them displayed on the Burma teakwood bookshelves that were the pride of the Strand. The bookshelves were very strong and smelled delicious. The books could be stacked vertically, making the whole stacked get-up look beautiful as well as convenient to see and read.

I used to go around to every bookshelf, taking my time. I even sat in the same place Blaise had sat ten years before my birth. Whenever I used to stand like that and read a book, the salesmen had a sort of déjà vu experience.

"You are just like your uncle," the gray-eyed salesman said as I placed book after book on his counter.

I loved the book arrangement on the shelves, nonfiction and fiction and classics mixed to make the book-searching business more interesting. There were other shelves, of course, strong shelves loaded with books on politics, political science, global terrorism, social sciences, vampire fiction, erotica, philosophy, et al., all to be savored as I went in a circular motion around the whole bookstore. Blaise and Mama used to accompany me. Mama sat in the taxi and prayed the rosary while Blaise joined me inside the store.

But the years went on and for some reason I don't know, old books were not being bought and no new books were coming in. There was an antique Parsi bookshelf right in front of the store about seven feet high where, according to Blaise, the new arrivals used to be displayed. By 2016, no new book stood on that beautifully carved stand. But I continued to visit the store, still.

"When will the new books come, *chacha*?" I asked the salesman billing my purchases.

He didn't answer. There was silence in the store.

"I said when will the new books come, *chacha*?"

He looked at me with the most sorrowful eyes I had ever seen. I was reminded of that saying in the Bible in the book of Isaiah, "a man full of sorrow and acquainted with grief."

I left the store that day, a very dark and cloudy day.

"Don't go there anymore, Fiza," Mama said, cautioning me, "I can't see you getting depressed every time you come out from there."

"Mama, but it's Shanbaug –"

"Shanbaug is dead," declares Mama flatly.

Her voice hit hard against the walls of my paper heart.

"Shanbaug will never die," I said, looking out the rain coming down in torrents as Narayan moved the cab toward Queens Road.

The news came via newspaper from the daughter of Shanbaug. It said that Strand would be closing its shutters forever on the 27th of February, one week later. For all those who had been influenced by the man called Shanbaug, the patrons of the bookstore that was once called "the Mecca for book lovers" this was the last clarion call. The daughter of Shanbaug requested that we all visit Strand during its last week and buy at least one book from the Burma teakwood shelves for the last time. Give the book a home and keep it forever as a memory of Shanbaug, the man who built the best bookstore in Mumbai.

The clarion call was heard.

During the last week, hundreds of people, old, middle-aged, and young came to the Strand. They came in their cars, taxies, buses .... wheelchairs! The Strand was full of book lovers who had come one last time to say goodbye.

Blaise and I went too. We had to wait in a long queue to get in. We'd have a hard time getting in to purchase our last Shanbaug book. The place was packed. The AC was off and everyone was sweating it out – pushing and pulling for a book.

"Was this what it was like during your time, Blaise?" I asked him. He didn't reply except in the form of a nod. His eyes were red with tears.

In this swirl of things, I noticed one of the salesmen. He was sitting with the others in a corner, crying woefully.

"Uncle, please give me a memento," I said, hoping for a poster or maybe a photograph of Shanbaug. "Please memento uncle. I won't be coming again, uncle, please, a memento."

But my cries were not heard, or were they?

We bought our books (I bought a John Galsworthy's omnibus, and I can't remember what Blaise bought) and exited the building. Then we clicked a couple of selfies outside as news media journalists reported on how the Mecca of book lovers had come alive after almost twenty years. I held the omnibus to my chest and stifled my sobs.

We then got into Narayan's taxi, took one last look at the Strand with its shutters up, and drove off.

I thought that was the end of it.

But it was not. Because in life sometimes the little prayers of unwanted girl children are also heard.

"Memento please uncle – MEMENTO!"

ESSAY 55

Kitab Khana: The Best Bookstore in Mumbai

IT WAS IN 2011 THAT BLAISE came to Mama and me with the news. He had found his old Strand friends.

"They have opened a new bookstore at Somaiya Bhavan, owned by the Somaiya family, under the able direction of Amrita Somaiya."

"Where is it?" Mama and I asked in unison.

I was so excited.

"At Flora Fountain, in the Somaiya building. It's nearby to the Strand."

We immediately drove that Sunday, when I was free from teaching, in Narayan's taxi to Flora Fountain in Mumbai. It was a busy area, what with the Mumbai University and the High Court just opposite us. But since it was a Sunday, the roads were clear and no lawyers were on the streets in their black robes and white neckbands.

I entered the store. I smelled books. I fell in love.

"Hello Jagat sir," said Blaise. "So here you are. And here is Sanjay sir too."

In fact, the missing salesmen from the Strand were all here at Kitab Khana.

"Welcome to our new venture," said Jagat sir, shaking Blaise's hand, "We are obliged to Somaiya ma'am for thinking of us. Welcome to Kitab Khana."

Welcome indeed. The place was a dream come true.

It was exquisitely, bookishly beautiful. There were as many bookshelves as the eye could see. Very solid teakwood and polished bookshelves, some bookshelves going up to the ceiling, which had to be thirty feet high! The flooring was marble and the tables colonial Parsi-style. There were British colonial sculptures of androgynous people on the walls, which gave the magical place an elegant feel. There were dainty staircases leading to the balcony where philosophy, religious, and classics were shelved.

"I feel like a princess from a Disney movie," I said to Mama as I climbed one of the stairs to go to the balcony.

"So, this was the baby you used to shop for at the Strand," said Sanjay sir to Blaise as they shook hands, pals of old. Anand uncle was at the counter, the cashier. Shailesh, whom I call my brother, was the right-hand man of Jagat sir, who was the manager of the store. Blaise looked around and recognized all his old friends from Strand.

"But why?" Blaise asked while I strutted across the place like I was in book heaven, as I was! Jagat and Sanjay sir explained to Blaise the difficult circumstances they had faced at the Strand since Shanbaug passed away. No new books were coming in and they were not being paid. They had families to look after and so when this opportunity came, most of them took it. Now they were here at Kitab Khana, running the place for Amrita Somaiya.

I bent down and waved to Mama from the balcony. I saw that the place even had a vegetarian café attached to it. What more could I ask for in a bookstore?

I bought many books that day. Since then, my life has not been the same.

Kitab Khana made me the writer I could only dream I could be.

Thanks to the Kitab Khana team, I have become the writer and niche publisher I am today.

I owe them more than I can say. I owe them my whole life.

Since 2011, I've been a regular at Kitab Khana.

I've seen it grow into a bookstore loved by everyone in Mumbai. At one point in time, I used to visit the bookstore every Sunday to pick up a new read. Kitab Khana's selection is eclectic and all-encompassing. It has something for everyone. It has a vast nonfiction and fiction section that covers every genre. It has a huge section for history, sociology, politics, economics, logic, and other social sciences that just take your breath away. Its classics section is always updated and extremely vast, mostly showcasing Penguin classics, both modern and old. But shoppers can find many other books from publishers small and large throughout the store.

Kitab Khana strives to inculcate reading, especially among children, and its children's section is unlike that of any other store in Mumbai. It has special kiddy rugs and bean bags where children can sit and read or be read to. Jagat sir goes out to bookfairs abroad to bring back a wide selection of new books of all genres every year. In fact, just like the Strand when it was doing well, new books come to Kitab Khana almost every week.

It was here, in 2011, when I was a teacher at a regular school, that I said to myself, "I'm going to be a writer for real, and my books will one day be placed here at Kitab Khana."

Now that dream has come true. But it wouldn't have, if not for the faith and love of Jagat sir, Sanjay sir (whom we all love to call Sanju sir), Shailesh my brother, Sandeep the efficient, Anand uncle with a smile on his face practically all the time, Deepak my biggest help, and so many others who have educated me in books and in the business of books.

It was here at Kitab Khana that Jagat sir accepted my first books to be placed on their shelves. He is the most quiet and soft-spoken man I've ever met, and he has a heart of gold.

"Best of luck," he wished me when I offered *S.O.S. Animals And Other Stories* to be placed on Kitab Khana's regal shelves. I was not worthy, but he had trust in me and my talents. My first book launch, which was a jam-packed event, took place at Kitab Khana. Sanju sir still swears that my book launch had one of the largest crowds ever.

"It was like a wedding," Sanju sir tells Blaise. At that book launch the Kitab Khana team made me very comfortable. Fr. Joshan was my chief guest, and Ratan uncle was looking after the affairs of keeping it all peaceful.

"Fiza has to be comfortable," Ratan uncle said to Blaise as they were helping out with the arrangements. "This is her big day and she should be comfortable to speak."

And speak I did. I would like to mention here how Kitab Khana makes it a point to start every writer's profession, whether coming from a big publisher, an indie publisher, a niche publisher, an academic, or a self-published rookie like I was back in 2012, the same way. Kitab Khana believes in helping writers get a good start. They hold events all the time, and Kitab Khana is an important event space during the famed arts festival of Mumbai, the "Kala Ghoda Festival." Kitab Khana keeps up with the times and believes in freedom of speech. It uses its platform to shelve books pertaining to humanitarian issues that are fundamental reading at the bookstore. Kitab Khana is always on its toes and always updating their catalog and the quality of their books at their store. It has seen me as a rookie writer and a niche publisher.

"Look, madam's advertisement is in the Biblio magazine," says Deepak holding up for all to see the advertisement for my company's books in a nationally famous book newsletter. Everyone crowds around Deepak to see.

Jagat sir is silent but is like a godfather to me. Sanju sir is like my foster father and always worries about my health and takes care of me as if I am his own daughter. Shailesh is my brother.

"You will always be part of our family," he tells me. "And I am always there for you."

Deepak and Sandeep are my greatest well-wishers. Deepak knows well my taste in books and what I love to buy. Anand uncle the cashier is always cracking jokes with me and I with him. He is like another maternal uncle to me.

The whole Kitab Khana team has made me one of their own. And all this wouldn't be possible without the aid of ma'am Amrita Somaiya.

"You've come a long way," Blaise says to me as I sip my lemon iced tea in the Kitab Khana café. Even the café waiters and manager are fond of me. "What are you planning to do next, Fiza?"

I look at Blaise, wipe the fizzy froth moustache off my upper lip, and place the glass back on the table.

"I don't know," I say at first slowly then a bit quicker, making me out of breath. "Everything has happened so suddenly. I never planned to be doing business, especially not the publishing business, but now I am. I just wanted to be a teacher and do writing on the side. I'm not that good a writer, but I try my best."

Blaise leans back on his chair. He rolls his eyes.

"You have in a span of seven years won more than seventy book awards and counting, including the 2018 Digital World Book Award for Short Stories for your LGBTQIA book *The Love That Dare Not Speak Its Name*. You were there competing with the likes of Chanelle Benz, and it was YOU that won."

I shake my head and crack my knuckles, "I'm not anything special. I'm just a girl wanting to earn money from her writing and teaching so she can buy more books to read."

Blaise drinks his hot mocha coffee and chuckles to himself.

"You still have not answered my question. What are you planning on doing next?"

"I want to write a few magnum opuses," I say rubbing my hands. It's a bit cold in the café.

Blaise chokes on his coffee. "A few? Writers only have one!"

"I've got a few," I say seriously, looking away out of the cafeteria glass into the bookstore, "And one magnum opus which is a real magnum opus which, after I write, my writing duties will be complete."

Blaise finishes his coffee. He can finish hot coffee with brown sugar very fast.

"I want to shock people," I say as I pick up my drink.

"Why?" he asks.

"Because I can."

Blaise changes the topic. I order another lemon iced tea, and he orders bun *maska* (bun and butter), the specialty of Mumbai.

It's the 21st of March 2018. I have just celebrated my twenty-ninth birthday. We are at Kitab Khana talking to Jagat sir and Sanju sir about the release of my book *Nirmala: The Mud Blossom* in the Mumbai market. A month ago, on the 27th of February, the Strand shut down for good.

We were busy talking books. It was a weekday and so there were many lawyers in their black robes and white neck-bands in the bookstore.

Suddenly, a medium-height, thirtysomething, strikingly well-dressed lawyer comes up to me, me alone, and says this: "The Strand is selling its Burma teak bookshelves."

And that's it. He leaves me and our group and moves deeper into the bookstore.

I tell Blaise what he said. We ask Jagat sir and Sanju sir for confirmation. They nod.

"Oh, yes," said Sanju sir face-palming himself. "How could I have forgotten to tell you that? Yes, the Strand is selling their bookshelves."

"Burma teakwood," adds Jagat sir. "Beautiful pieces. You will never see the like of it ever again in Mumbai. Vidya ma'am is selling them at throwaway prices."

Vidya is Shanbaug's daughter.

"Beautiful bookshelves, all of them. And no white ants problems ever."

"Do you want some of them?" Sanju sir asks, pulling his smartphone from his pocket. "I can talk to someone there for you."

I look at Blaise. Blaise looks at me. We implore Sanju sir to make the call immediately. We were going to drive there right away and take whatever we could.

"His life was in his bookshelves, you know," says Jagat sir.

"Who?" like a dimwit I ask as Blaise exchanges numbers and messages with Sanju sir.

"Shanbaug," Jagat sir says, raising his eyebrows. "He got them made himself. Looked after them himself. His heart and soul were always on them. They were his life. Those shelves. It's your good fortune if you manage to get them. Then you truly are a lucky girl."

Sanju sir finished his exchange on the phone. Blaise called Narayan to get the taxi ready. I ran around the store in search of the lawyer, the medium-height, well-dressed lawyer who told me the news. But he was nowhere to be found.

He had vanished.

"Where did he go?" I begged Jagat sir.

He, too, seemed perplexed.

"Where indeed did he go?" he echoed as he looks all over the store to no avail.

"The man just disappeared," I said to Blaise clutching his shoulder. "The lawyer disappeared."

"Never mind him." Blaise pulled me outside. "The bookshelves are selling quick and if we don't get there soon, we won't get the best."

We hurried. When we arrived, we found that it was true. Indeed, Vidya ma'am was selling her father's bookshelves.

I bought four of them. If I had my way, I would have bought them all. It's sad that I have a small house to live in! I bought two of the largest Burma teaks, one of the smallest Burma teaks (used to hold the pocket books), and the oldest Burma teak there in the store – you guessed it, the Burma teak showcase that stood right as we entered the store, where the new books were displayed.

Vidya ma'am kissed each bookcase as she stuck my name on those I had selected. She then gave me a blessing. She was into esoteric religions and blessed me with the power of her Master, Jesus the Christ.

Blaise whispered to me, "She looks exactly like Shanbaug."

As she opened her eyes after the blessing, she said, "Long way to go, my dear. And many more books to read and write."

"I hope so," I said humbly. This was the best day of my life. A part of Mecca was coming home with me.

We organized the delivery and went back to thank the Kitab Khana team for aiding us as they had always done.

Deepak told me in Hindi, "You really are very fortunate ma'am. One day, you will open your own bookstore."

"My luck is certainly good today," I said cheerfully. "All thanks to an angel disguised as a lawyer."

I never did see that lawyer again.

Shanbaug came home. Delivered in one piece. It felt like he was meant to be here. That's how well his biggest Burma teak bookshelves fit in my bedroom side by side. The oldest one adorns our hall and the smallest one, which I call my "*chotta* Shanbaug" is in the inner room of my office, where Blaise and sometimes my co-author Michaelangelo Zane work. I call all my bookshelves my Shanbaugs.

Whenever Blaise looks at the biggest cases, he says, "I used to love these shelves when I was younger. I thought I would never be able to afford something like this." Then he looks at me and says with pride, "But my baby has earned her money well, and she bought a miracle of a bookcase home. God bless you, Fiza, for being our baby."

I stand still and look up now at the biggest bookcases, full to capacity with my collection (a small sample), with books on Bollywood, philosophy, thrillers, social issues, economics, medicine, ethics, globalization, sociology, travel, graphic novels, horror story collections, essays, history, English literature, Hindi, etc.

When I look at them, I think of Papa. I feel like telling him, "See, Papa? See what you have missed? You want to go for Haj, but I have Mecca at my nana's home."

This is my way of fighting back the prejudice against girls, by being just me, only me, nothing new, just little old bookish me!

"Uncle, memento – uncle, please, memento."

At times when I am sick in bed due to my sleep apnea or spondylosis, I feel an old man's presence in the room. He speaks in Konkani and strokes my fevered brow or aching hunchback soothingly, saying words of encouragement which I can feel but not understand. He also puts me to sleep on days when I've overworked or if I am having, due to my sleep apnea, what they call "out-of-body experiences."

"Shanbaug used to talk to Jagat sir and the rest in Mangalorean Konkani," Blaise informs me when I first started having these experiences. "Jagat did say that Shanbaug's life was in his bookshelves."

I nod and drink my BRU Gold coffee, finishing it off. I place the cup back on the coffee table, tie up my hair, ready to start a new day at the publishing office.

ESSAY 56

Gone Girl by Gillian Flynn

Before I knew the Victorias, I would always buy my latest thrillers from Kitab Khana. We customers would always be given a discount of 20 percent on the MRP; just like the Strand, Kitab Khana doesn't believe in sales only. It was the year 2013, when practically everybody was talking about this book, a thriller of thrillers called *Gone Girl.*

"It is selling like hotcakes," said Deepak to me as he handed me the book. "*Bahut chal raha hai.*"

I read the synopsis and was totally into the book, so I bought it.

The following Sunday, at Kitab Khana, Deepak asked, "Madam, did you read it?"

"No, *yaar*! I didn't get the time," I complained, rubbing my eyes which were swollen and red due to writing notes and English language worksheets late into the night. "More books went this week?"

Deepak pointed to the table where it was kept. "Only one copy left and ten went today alone."

"Ten!" I exclaimed stopping short.

"And four piles of ten each gone since last Sunday," continued Deepak. "This has never ever happened before, madam. I tell you, read it. It will be made into a Hollywood movie soon, I tell you!"

I was stung in place. Fifty books gone in a week at Kitab Khana! It must be quite a book. Tuition work or no tuition work, I would be reading this thriller that very night.

I got back home that Sunday at around 8:00 p.m. I had an early dinner of chicken curry and picked up the book to read, and boy did I read it!

For those of you who read Gillian Flynn's book before it became a blockbuster Hollywood movie, I raise my coffee mug to you. For those of you who haven't read the book yet, or who have seen the movie but not read the book, then you are missing out on a thriller that will send the worst kind of chills racing all over you, not just up and down your spine! I envy those who haven't read it yet, because you will enjoy the thrill of reading the case of a missing wife (the gone girl) and a perplexed husband who doesn't seem to be all that worried about his wife's disappearance. He's been cyber shopping for some very expensive objects, has a history of physical abuse, had an affair with a student, and thus becomes the number one suspect. But seriously, asks the author in the last line of the book cover copy, "What happened to the missing wife indeed?"

This was one of the creepiest thriller synopses I have ever read! And the book is equally scary and thrilling. But don't read it if you are not into a lot of gore and shocking scenes. During the time the book was making the rounds in 2013, I read a very weird news article on my Facebook page. It said that people who were having heart trouble or cardiac issues were dropping dead or having serious heart attacks while reading the book. Of course, we can't believe everything we read on the internet, can we?

Well, I didn't have a heart problem in 2013; so I read the book and I'm alive and still talking about it. If you are spooked easily, don't read the book with immersion reading or with the help of an audio CD of the book or the Audible version. You will be screaming at the middle of the book, believe me. Those of you who have stouter hearts can go in for an Audible or you can let Alexa read it for you; either way it will really spook you!

After I read the book, I placed it on the side of my bed and couldn't stop thinking about it. So, I didn't get sleep till six in the morning and had to get up by 9:00 a.m., and that was a pitiful day with sleepy me going around telling my students not to read *Gone Girl* until they were eighteen.

The Hollywood movie was a disappointment to me. Blaise couldn't understand what was going on, Mama understood everything and couldn't believe she was watching such a movie, while Narayan was texting throughout the film, except during the scary sections.

Later, I was cruising around during 2013 Christmastime in Narayan's taxi. I was getting out of the taxi at Bandra's Crosswords when a hot guy came out of it. He was a lot younger than I was, but he sort of smiled at me and showed me his purchases, which he held in his tattooed hand. Both the books he had chosen were thrillers, but not *Gone Girl*.

I said, "Have you read *Gone Girl*?"

"Should I?" he asked in a bass voice. He was really good-looking and friendly. So, I decided to do him a favor.

"You got cash for another thriller?" said I, the mother hen-cum-teacher instinct acting up.

"I've got some, yep," he said.

"Go get *Gone Girl* right now and read it tonight."

He went back in along with me. I picked up a copy of *Gone Girl* and handed it to him, and we both moved toward the counter.

"Hey, my name is James," he said putting out his right hand.

"I'm Fiza."

"What?"

"Fiza- Fizz-ah!"

He pulled back his hand. "It's a Muslim name. Er, see you, Fiza."

And that was it. He walked off in the other direction. Well, at least it was not me being overweight that ruined it all. Just the name, a Muslim name, which James was freaked out by. At least he got a good book to read. I thought this to myself as I looked for something new in the fiction section. I had got a lot of Crossword gift vouchers for Christmas and wanted to spend them.

But no thriller I bought that day could match the brilliant Gillian Flynn's *Gone Girl*.

I remember after that everyone was asking at bookstores whether the store had anything more deadly than or as scary as *Gone Girl*. It was like the world suddenly had divided into before *Gone Girl* and after.

"Madam," said Deepak the following Sunday when I entered Kitab Khana. "Are you also going to ask if we have a good thriller like *Gone Girl, ha*?"

We both laughed. We sorted out the books I wanted and then I went to the café for a glass of lemon iced tea. Blaise was visiting the toilet. I thought about James and what he must have thought of my book. He must have definitely loved it. Maybe he felt sorry about his behavior upon hearing my name. But this was not the first time something like this had happened, nor would it be the last. Even where my own books are concerned, I am at the receiving end of communal hatred.

I was of the same religion as James. But he didn't even give me a chance to explain, let alone hear the full name – Fiza Josephine Pathan.

I wonder what James is doing these days.

ESSAY 57

In Other Words by Jhumpa Lahiri, Ann Goldstein (Translator)

"MA'AM, THE LATEST BOOK has just come."

"What?" I said as I looked up from my usual black couch in the magazine section of Kitab Khana. It was Deepak, and he was holding a book with what looked like to be Jhumpa Lahiri on the cover.

"Madam, this is the latest from Jhumpa Lahiri, but it is nonfiction."

"Ha!" I was shocked as I took the book from Deepak. I had read Pulitzer Prize–winning Jhumpa Lahiri's *The Namesake* at Trilogy and was fascinated by her mastery over the English language. I had ordered the rest of her works from Kitab Khana, which I brought home and kept in my new shelves in my office-cum-writing hut. I've yet to read them.

The year was 2016. I had just started my own publishing company and through the help of Jagat sir and Sanju sir had managed to get a good, well-known Mumbai distributer to distribute my first book to be published under my imprint Freedom With Pluralism, which was

Classics: Why and How We Can Encourage Children to Read Them. By the following year, I was to take up distribution myself.

But coming back to the book, I was fascinated by the photograph of the beautiful author Jhumpa Lahiri on the cover of a nonfiction book called *In Other Words.*

I was surprised to read the synopsis of the book, which stated that the author had actually written this book in Italian and had an English translator translate it into English for her, huh!

Needless to say, I was intrigued.

I went over to the café at Kitab Khana for a vegetarian pizza and to drink lemon iced tea. I read *In Other Words* while eating the delicious pizza there. As I read with Blaise and Mama, Jagat sir came personally to the café to call me to autograph my book and talk to a reader who had bought my book.

"My Fiza has become a celebrity," Mama said as I came back closing the nib of my Bally Big B ballpoint pen.

I sat down. I said, "I'm not a celebrity, Mama. Come on, don't say that – I'm just little old bookish me!"

But my mind was stuck on a for-real writer celebrity, Jhumpa Lahiri, wondering what in blazes had gone wrong with her. As I read on, my eyes began to bulge. If what I was reading was correct, then Jhumpa Lahiri wouldn't be writing in English for a long time to come. Maybe even forever, and I just could not accept that!

"She is besotted with Italian," I said aloud before shoving a bite of vegetarian pizza in my mouth.

"With Italian pizza?" asked Blaise as he ate his bun with butter, along with a lot of jam this time.

"No," I whined almost on the brink of tears. "With the Italian language."

"Fr. Joshan is learning Italian in Rome, right?" Mama asked as she ate her vanilla ice cream. "He learned it in a matter of months, he is so brilliant."

"Is anyone even listening to me?" I said in mock frustration. But that statement of my mama's got me thinking. According to the book *In Other Words,* Jhumpa Lahiri has fallen in love with the Italian language. She is so besotted by it that she has even shifted to Italy to live there and learn the language, write in the language, and be one with the language. She has given up everything, including writing in English for the time being, until she is proficient in the language.

Why all the fuss? Because Jhumpa Lahiri has never been a part of another culture in the form of a language. She wants to feel at one with a culture and language other than her own, and so wants to learn Italian.

That is why she wrote *In Other Words* in Italian and didn't translate it herself. It is a challenge for her to excel in the language, but she is taking the time necessary to grasp it.

I thought of myself. I personally can read, write and understand only two languages fully in spite of living in a country that's overflowing with languages. The languages I know well are English and Hindi, ranked in order of comfort.

Mama knows almost four languages, and Blaise knows six. Language learning has never been a problem for my family members, but somehow I have never been able to pick up any regional language other than our national language, Hindi.

Papa always spoke in English to me and so did Mama and the rest of the family, so I never learned Konkani or Urdu, the regional languages of my mama and papa respectively.

I can understand Jhumpa Lahiri's longing to belong to a language. But I wouldn't go to the extent she has to learn and be one with it.

"The bill, sir," I say, and instead of handing the bill to me, the new waiter hands the bill to Blaise, the only male at the table. *Why can't I pay for my own food?*

We leave a huge tip and go out into the bookstore. A book launch is going on. I remember the famous writer, columnist, and literary celebrity Shoba De being there, discussing a younger writer's book that she was there to launch.

"Had your pizza?" Sandeep, a good and efficient salesman at Kitab Khana asks me.

"I also almost finished the book I just bought here," I said with a smile. Sandeep also likes to read. He is older than me by a year or two. He is one of the only salesmen at Kitab Khana who had not been with Shanbaug or worked at the Strand.

I say goodbye to everyone at Kitab Khana as I always do and then make it to Narayan's taxi. All the books I've purchased are there in four cloth bags with the Kitab Khana logo imprinted on them.

"Home now, Narayan," I say as I flip open *In Other Words* and continue reading.

The book is hypnotizing, just like all of Jhumpa Lahiri's books are, but the richness is missing. She is struggling, but her love for Italian comes through and you feel for the writer and her beliefs as you read the book. You seem to agree with the convictions of the writer. And, most importantly, you realize that some things are beyond fame, fortune, and everything advertised in this world – advertisements always creating a lack when there is abundance!

"Mama, what language did you and papa converse in?" I ask, hoping it's one of those days she is ready to talk about him. I'm lucky, it is one of those days.

"We used to speak in English, of course," Mama said as if to say she was almost insulted by the remark on papa's behalf. "He was educated in the same school as Blaise, you know that."

"Was he fluent in it?" I venture to ask. Blaise is eyeing me with a look as if he's trying to warn me to stop the conversation.

"His English was good enough for me," Mama said. Narayan was busy listening to our conversation too. "We spoke in English all the time. Even when I was married to him. I used to speak to his family in Hindi. They were not that fluent in English, especially not your witch of a paternal grandmother."

"Mechu says my paternal grandfather spoke English very well," I say.

Mama thinks, looking out of the window.

"He was a very different man, your paternal grandfather. He was not educated but was very good and fluent in English. In your papa's family, you would have been the second graduate in the family and the very first postgraduate. Your paternal grandfather, if he was alive, would have been proud."

"How many languages could he speak?" I asked, and Narayan looked at Mama from the corner of his eye. I guess the fact that this "English-Christian madam" actually once lived in a house of uneducated and orthodox Sunni Muslims was shocking him.

"How many languages could he speak?" I asked again. But I was out of luck, the floodgates closed back up on me yet again.

"I don't go into the past," Mama said sternly. "I have left my past behind me. You should too."

"What past?" I say aloud quite irritated. "What past do I have but silence?"

Everyone is quiet now. Narayan drives faster. I read *In Other Words*. I think of Jhumpa Lahiri. I think of her, and I smirk.

Dearest Jhumpa Lahiri: What would you have done if you were in my shoes? I have a whole paternal blank in my life, apparently for a sin I did not commit. But whenever I ask for reasons, I'm reminded of the breakup rudely, curtly, and like a slap on the face. That's why I believe what I believe.

I believe I broke up my mama and papa's perfect marriage. And that they hold me responsible for it.

I ended a twelve-year-old love story. I'm the scum of the earth. And my penance is silence. I'll therefore always be silent.

In regards to *In Other Words*, if you are a true fan of Jhumpa Lahiri and believe in her, you will not be disappointed by this, her first foray into Italian. The translator has managed to keep Jhumpa Lahiri's voice intact so you can expect sheer excellence from what you are reading. If you, too, are in love with a particular language and you are loving it as you learn it, then this is the book you should be reading. And if you find yourself in Jhumpa Lahiri's situation, feeling like you don't really belong anywhere, then this is the book for you.

I went home that night and finished the book. I have not finished my own story yet.

ESSAY 58

The Transition of H. P. Lovecraft: The Road to Madness by H. P. Lovecraft

THE FIRST TIME I CAME ACROSS H. P. Lovecraft was at the Strand in the year 2012. I was then twenty-three years old and had just published my first book, *S.O.S. Animals And Other Stories.* I had also started blogging on Insaneowl.com, originally hosted by WordPress and currently hosted by me on WordPress through SiteGround. Yes, I regret that I chose such a weird name for my blog. But how was I supposed to know at twenty-three that I would become a director of my own publishing company at twenty-seven? Things just happen and so did insaneowl.com.

I was reviewing books and analyzing them on my blog on a regular basis. I picked H. P. Lovecraft's book because I had just purchased it from the horror section at the Strand and the cover looked bizarre.

When I read the book, I realized that I was reading the best horror fiction I've ever read in my whole damn life! The book was fantastic, and I couldn't stop singing its praises the next time I visited the Strand.

I was taken aback when I read on the back cover of the book that Lovecraft had inspired many of my own favorite authors of the macabre like Anne Rice, Stephen King, and Clive Barker. As I pored over the stories at night UNDER my study table with the table lamp on, I was transported to a realm quite different from my own understanding of terror and fantasy. Lovecraft's ideas were not only macabre but also quite morbid and blood chilling. True, his works are steeped in grand descriptions which normally put a casual reader off, but a true lover of literature and horror will certainly realize after reading Lovecraft's *At the Mountains of Madness, Reanimator, Imprisoned With the Pharaohs* that the descriptions are all meaningful and necessary in order for the reader to completely realize the horror behind it all.

As Barbara Hambly stated, H. P. Lovecraft struggles to express his ideas to the reader. His ideas are powerful and extraordinary. His pseudo-Poe short stories get more original and more bizarre as his writing years go by. Lovecraft's characters, too, undergo transformations and at times reappear in other stories. As a result, he has created a niche for himself in the horror and fantasy genre – one that no other writer can ever embody.

He is excellent, as I have observed in first person accounts of the story, making the reader grip the book tightly in a cold sweat as he administers the opiate of fear into our system... almost like his warped character Herbert West does by administering a special powder into the veins of dead bodies or organs to bring them to life in the *Reanimator* (this was better than *Frankenstein*). Most of Lovecraft's protagonists, I have observed, are men (it's always men!) who are well educated; intelligent; believe in the dark forces; and have very sinister personalities (e.g., the constant repetition of the book *Necronomicon* by the Arab, Abdul Alhazred, who was a genius par excellence). They also have a bad habit of getting into trouble in spite of their intelligence.

I loved the book. I loved it so much that I did something that I normally would never have thought of doing in my wildest dreams. I started watching the horror movies based on H. P. Lovecraft's books.

I had practically no time to do this during the day so I would sit up after midnight and watch these movies on YouTube. I would watch the whole thing, which went on till 3:00 or 4:00 a.m., but I never stayed up beyond 4:00 a.m. (oh, I am such a psycho!). Soon I was watching other horror movies starring Vincent Price, Christopher Lee, Peter Cushing, Boris Karloff, Peter Lorre, and others who acted in movies based on horror books.

Those were the nights of shrieks, screams, and wailing wolves in the dark of the night.

"Can you please turn the volume down!" Mama would yell at me from the mattress on the common bedroom floor. "The movie is giving me a fright and that scream is too loud."

Silence is the loudest scream of a child left in the hands of books.

I chuckle, it's a Vincent Price kind of laugh, as I turn down the volume on my Philips computer speakers.

At this time, I read so much horror and watched so many horror movies that it reminded me of my *Dracula* days at BSS when I used Bram Stoker's book as a comforter for my harsh reality – the reality of silence.

It was also during this time that I started increasing in weight. I was watching monster movies on YouTube at the dead of night while all at Symbol Apartments were asleep and now, as I looked at my jowls in the mirror, I felt like I was turning into one. It was at this time that something very important came to me in the form of a dream – my *real* magnum opus.

I saw my whole story, the story I was born to write, in the form of a dream. It was a series of different scenes from the book and, somehow, I was able to fill in the blanks. So, now I had the ultimate magnum opus, which would be a horror story in three parts. No, I've not written it yet, but I'll start it the day I feel I am ready to do so. It is my masterpiece, and after I write it, I will have completed all I need to complete – all that started the day I walked up to the BSS library and pulled Bram Stoker's *Dracula* from the shelves.

Blaise gets spooked when I tell him all of this.

"A horror story? What's it all about?" he asks, half afraid. Blaise doesn't like to hear horror stories.

But I couldn't tell him then nor now. Not until I feel I've done my research and am capable enough, not until I have then typed it or written it in longhand.

The H. P. Lovecraft book from Strand sparked the flame in me and stoked the fire. It has stoked that fire for the past seven years. But I'm not ready yet, some more time and then I will write a tale like no other.

I owe Strand many things. I also owe it my dreams of horror and terror that have given me a sort of macabre peace in the macabre world that is my reclusive mind.

I stopped watching the movies after I took on more tuitions.

For all horror book lovers, your life is certainly incomplete if you have not yet read H. P. Lovecraft. *The Transition of H. P. Lovecraft* is a good introduction to his seminal work in the genre of horror. Those of you who have felt disappointed with *Frankenstein* by Mary Shelley or with *Dracula* by Bram Stoker (blasphemy-blasphemy-blasphemy) will find H. P. Lovecraft's book a substantial and horrific read. Don't watch the movies first, without reading the book. If you do, I think you will realize, like I did, that the movies pale in comparison.

I have in my possession, since the year 2016, a complete volume of H. P. Lovecraft's works, which was provided to me by Kitab Khana. It was Deepak who remembered my fascination with his works and put the gigantic tome aside for me in spite of another customer's wanting to buy it. I was grateful to Deepak as I always am, and I have since gorged on the book like a ravenous heathen.

On another visit to the Strand, I bought another volume of H. P. Lovecraft called *The Best of H. P. Lovecraft: Bloodcurdling Tales of Horror and the Macabre*. It's produced by the same publisher as my other book (Del Rey Books).

"It's the last H. P. Lovecraft we have," said the Strand salesman as he placed the book in front of me. I stood in front of one of the giant

Burma teakwood bookcases that would one day land up in my bedroom.

"When will another one come?" I asked without looking up. No answer.

I then walked through the Strand bookstore. I had a pattern, in fact, I have a pattern of walking in every bookstore and library that I visit. At the Strand I moved in a clockwise circle. I would focus my fresh attention on the books in the left-hand corner, which displayed the best stuff and rare stuff. I would pass the pile of nonfiction and a bookcase of erotica and then move on to the back of the store where lay philosophy and religion. Then I would move to the nonfiction section, which was a large bookcase (but not original Burma teakwood), where I spent quite a lot of time. Then I would find myself near a revolving bookcase with a few rare editions of old hardbacks like *The Little Flowers of St. Francis of Assisi, The Tibetan Book of the Dead, The Selected Poems of Robert Frost*, that sort of thing. I would end up in the right-hand corner with the fiction collection (common paperback fiction I used to call it) and only go for the rare ones. I would end my day in the classic section where there was plenty of room to sit and where I would often find Blaise mooning over a book of poems.

The Strand. Shanbaug. My heaven.

I would then leave with my purchases. Narayan would be waiting patiently, thinking he knew me by now, a sort of peculiar but informed connoisseur of books. Believe me, I'm not, but people think I am. I would like to make it clear that I don't know much about books like some other people do. I am not a literature graduate or postgraduate of literary studies, and I think that has limited my knowledge where good literature is concerned. But I do try my best. Let's also not forget that I dabble in all sorts of horror fiction and terror fiction, which is not to everyone's taste. Who cares, I say! One man's food is another man's poison.

ESSAY 59

Devdas by Sarat Chandra Chattopadhyay

LOVE. THE ONLY WORD IN MY LIFE that I really don't know what to do with. But if love is anything of substantial value, then my love for that boy from BSS is a love full of substance, meaning, and a variety of longings. I've loved him silently, like I do everything else, for the past sixteen years. He doesn't know I exist. He might never read the words I type here. But as sure as I love books, I've loved this boy, now a man, far away from my world and yet ... so close. You would laugh maniacally to know just how close!

In the year 2014 I bought a volume of the famous Bengali writer Sarat Chandra Chattopadhyay's work in the Penguin edition from Granth.

"This is the first one, and where is the second?" I asked seeing the number one on the volume.

The manager, Mr. Herin shrugged.

"Actually, after that one volume a second has not been translated."

"Oh, that's too bad," I mused, selecting the book and putting it on the glass counter.

"It contains the most famous of his books," Mr. Herin went on. "*Devdas* is there I believe. The story of unfulfilled love."

He turned his back as he answered the query of another customer. I looked at the index. Indeed, he was right, *Devdas* was there: the story of unrequited love.

I bought the volume and went home to read it. To be frank, this was not the first time I was reading *Devdas*. I had read it in Hindi in the year 2007 when I was in the FYBA at St. Andrew's College Bandra West. This would be the first time I was reading it in English.

I read it in the tuition house as Mama taught first graders math.

I was wanting to cry. Every word in the book seemed to be slapping my face, trying to make me wake up – but from what or for what – was it, love?

I excused myself to go to the toilet and cried there. My eyes were blood red at the end of the crying spell, but I got a hold of myself. I'm good at that. Wasn't that good in my early twenties but now I'm pretty good at hiding what I really feel.

I really had the most tender feelings for this boy I loved at school. But like the fictional story of Sarat Chandra Chattopadhyay's *Devdas* my love is unrequited, unfulfilled, and very bleak where prospects of an amorous nature are concerned.

Devdas is the story that tugs at my heartstrings. Sarat Chandra Chattopadhyay is good at doing that with his awesome dialogues, which even when translated to English or Hindi don't lose their richness and intensity.

Devdas was a Bengali landowner's son, who as a child was infatuated with a little girl called Paro or Parvathi, his neighbor. The landowner father one day sends Devdas away from their village to Calcutta, to the city, to study. Paro remains in the village pining for her Devdas. He returns when he is nineteen and when Paro asks him to marry her, he refuses as she is not of his class or caste. So Paro, heartbroken and quite humiliated, marries a widower, who is wealthier than Devdas's father. She becomes the stepmother to children who are older than she is; it's quite a peculiar thing in the story. Devdas realizes his mistake, but it is too late. He takes to alcohol and excessive drinking, always pining after his childhood love, Parvathi, even till his last breath.

Devdas is one of India's most famous stories. I consider Sarat Chandra Chattopadhyay to be one of the greatest novelists of India, and of the West Bengal region, like Rabindranath Tagore. *Devdas* in India is the symbol of unfulfilled and unrequited love. It has captured the minds of readers, scriptwriters, Bollywood, and soap operas. Everyone has tried their hand at re-creating this love story of stories. And whenever there is a fellow whose love has not met with acceptance, people call such a man "Devdas" or such a woman "Paro."

Paro never consummated her marriage with the rich widower, because he couldn't forget his first wife. So, Paro pined and lived and maybe died with Devdas on her mind and in her heart.

There is this one place in the novel that always makes me think of my little love story. The cousin of Paro, called Manorama, brags about marriage and talks all sorts of rubbish about being a wife and such when Paro says: "You only wear the sacred beads of a wife and the sacred red vermillion on your head in the name of love. What it really means to be someone's wife, what do you know about that Manorama?"

Patni kya hoti hai, yeh tum kya jano Manorama?

It sounds better in Hindi. Sorry to say I don't know Bengali, the language in which he actually wrote. It is painful, the wiser of us say, to hear or read these dialogues in Bengali.

So, I have been a Paro for the longest time ever. I am a sort of Devdas as well. He sold his life to alcohol; I've sold my life to books. Trust me when I say I have the traits of both Paro and Devdas inside me!

I've read *Devdas* in Hindi and in English several times, but every time I read it, I remember a boy who now is a man of worth. I wrote my love poetry books for him. I remember him every day. I've killed fascination in me to be ever faithful in love to him. What it really means to be someone's wife, what do you know about that, Manorama? What do you know?

I've grown wiser and older. I've realized that pining is not worth it, but I've grown so used to pining that I now do the pining for "the Word" my only God. He is my Francesco, St. Francis of Assisi. He is a sort of amalgamation of everything in the category of "love" that I possess in my bookish being. He is the only one I yearn for. Where my old love is concerned, who will ever love a book?

"Liked Sarat Chandra Chattopadhyay, madam?" asked one of the salesmen at Granth the next time I visited.

"It was great. I hope they bring out the next English translated volume," I say with a smile as I lean on the cashier's desk, which is decorated with white sunflowers. The salesman shakes his head.

"I don't think the second volume will ever come out, ma'am. Don't keep your hopes up."

I nod slowly. "I won't then."

"Want to see what we have new here, ma'am?"

"That will be nice," I say, wiping the corner of my eye before I look at what he has for me. He shows me some excellent volumes of Ruskin Bond, Yashpal, the Feluda series in two volumes and some new nonfiction books. I buy the lot and go over to have a coffee in my usual corner of the bookstore. I write a piece on the boy as I drink my cappuccino.

The sun sets and I linger there. I write almost four thousand words in my diary. Speaking of diaries, there is a special diary I have kept for the boy in question. After my death, I shall bequeath it to him. Then he will know that he once had a silent lover. I write to him in it every once in a while. It's like a last testament. It goes to him when I go. And if he goes before me, then I, like Paro, who wasn't even given a chance to see Devdas before he died, will be the most wretched book phoenix in the world.

Let's stop the sob story and come back to books and bookishness. Basically, if you want to read a really good Indian love story from a very early era in our literary history, *Devdas* is a good place to start. If you know Hindi and English, I recommend you read it in Hindi first. It sounds oh so awesome in Hindi.

We couldn't really write sex scenes at all in the late nineteenth and early twentieth centuries in our literary novels, novellas, and short stories. However, there are sexual elements in *Devdas* – though the love was basically of an esoteric and platonic kind – or as some literary critics I've read say, "of a higher kind." One of them being when Devdas hits Paro just before her marriage and creates a permanent wound on her forehead. Some of our more melodramatic Bollywood directors have shown the scar on her head to depict a sort of permanent vermillion mark which is worn by a wife to show the world she is married. The act of physical violence is a sign of frustration and passion, and it is the one and only sexual act committed between Paro and Devdas. Even though Devdas visits a courtesan called Chandramukhi, an older woman, he doesn't have a physical relationship with her. But worse than that, he makes the courtesan fall so much in love with him that he ruins her business because she can't be anyone else's courtesan. In this way, the book camouflages sexual passions and emotions.

Sarat Chandra Chattopadhyay is a master of his craft. If you want to read an out-of-the-box love story, then *Devdas* is the book for you. It's going to be terribly sad, so avoid it if you are already in a depressed state. The book has never depressed me, though it makes me contemplative.

I last read Devdas in 2017. Maybe I shall read it this year as a form of remembrance of things gone by. And things have really gone by very fast. But even in our fast-paced lives, some things remain eternal, especially great works by awe-inspiring masters of literature. The British have their Romeo and Juliet, and we Indians have our Devdas and Paro.

ESSAY 60

Still Alice by Lisa Genova

IT WAS 2015. I WAS at Kitab Khana, as always, on a Sunday. My book *Classics: Why We Should Encourage Children to Read Them* was still on the bestseller's list on Amazon. I was going through the shelves and tables full of the latest titles.

I remember that day very well. I was feeling great because of the success of *Classics*, which was another one of those "time pass" books I had written. I was roaming the vast expanse of Kitab Khana, inhaling its delicious bookstore smell and the smell of new books.

"Madam, latest."

I turned around as Deepak placed a book, a paperback, on the table next to me.

"It's selling like hot cakes. And now it has the cover of the movie. You should try it, madam."

He then took the books that I was lugging about to the counter.

"Chai, ma'am?" he asked. He always asks, the sweet soul.

"No, I'm good," I said. "I'll be taking this one too." I placed the book in his hands and went off deeper into history, sociology, economics, and politics, my favorite section of Kitab Khana.

I read *Still Alice* about a week later. I had heard through Goodreads that it was a great read about a disease people don't like to talk about.

Alzheimer's. Early onset Alzheimer's especially.

Many people who have read the book are people whose families have been affected by this dreadful disease, and I was one of those people. Nana had the disease. She completely lost her sense of self and memory, as well as control over her bowel movements due to the dreadful disease. I was a child when Nana used to scream at everyone, telling them she wanted to go to her mother. She used to run out of the house, too, but thankfully Rita or Blaise always managed to catch her before she got away. She hated the dark and cried for her mother. I remember covering my ears when I was four years old while Nana roamed the small flat screaming in Konkani for her mother: "*Mai, muje mai*." "Mother, I want my mother."

When I read *Still Alice* about a fifty-year-old brilliant Harvard professor succumbing to the onset of Alzheimer's I was reliving my early life with Nana, who by the time I was in the second grade had forgotten who I was, the girl child she had saved from being abandoned.

"Who is that child?" she asked Rita in anger. "Why is she living with us? Where is baby Fiza? This is not baby. This is someone else. Where is baby Fiza?"

As I grew up, she deteriorated. She forgot most everyone. She never forgot the baby me, however, and until the last, she never forgot her youngest son, Blaise. He was her favorite.

When I read *Still Alice,* I cried a lot. I cried due to the way the protagonist was losing memories, losing words. The book read like a thriller, because what could be more frightening than losing yourself while you are still alive? While you are – *Still Alice*?

Before the dreaded Alzheimer's disease ruined her life, Nana was the matriarch of our household. She ruled the roost according to a strict timetable: There was a time to sleep, a time to get up, to go to the church, go to work, come back from work or church, eat dinner, pray the rosary, etc. No one did the housekeeping except for Nana;

her children were only to concentrate on their work at the office, school, workshop, bank, etc. When I came along, she watched over me carefully. She made sure I had my way always, and that I was well fed.

I was her only grandchild. She was protective of me. She studied only till the third grade but spoke to me in English the best she could.

When the protagonist in *Still Alice* can't remember how to get back home, I cried more than ever. When she, an intellectual, is later ostracized by her family, my heart felt peace to know that our family never did that to Nana. We all looked after her. Even me, though I was the first person she forgot. Rita cleaned and bathed her, Mechu visited every week and took her out, Mama tried to talk her into behaving properly, David uncle prayed for her, Blaise always stayed close by, and I sometimes slept next to her and told her what I was feeling, how school was not going well, how I was being left out. Even in that state, she "sort of" understood me. I loved playing with her blue rosary beads. That was my solitary activity as she slept on her waterbed.

Still Alice made me remember Nana all over again. It's difficult for people who have not experienced the ways in which Alzheimer's ruins family life to begin to comprehend the small things that matter to such families, which Genova documents in her book: a small smile of recognition, a name remembered, a face recognized – a grandchild lost and found when the grandchild in question was there all the time.

Nana passed away in 1997 just after her seventy-sixth birthday. I sobbed my heart out. Many came for the funeral and to see the hearse.

"Stop crying, Fiza, or the principal of your school will think you are mad," Mama said, sternly, but I couldn't be controlled. This was my very first death, and I was a precocious child, well aware that I would never see my nana again.

"Look, Papa has come," Rita cried in an attempt to divert my attention, but seeing my papa only made me cry more bitterly. I thought now that Nana was gone, he would take Mama away and leave me in a dustbin or an orphanage or boarding school like Oliver Twist or David Copperfield.

When he tried to gather me in his burly arms, I kicked him away from me.

"Get away from me – get away – get away!"

He got the message. Mechu took me in her arms and glared at Mama. Her glare seemed to say, "I'll look after dolly girl for the night. In the meantime, you get rid of your husband."

I wanted to get into the coffin and lie with Nana, but Mechu carried me off. Blaise gave me some homeopathic pills, and Mechu put me to bed and slept next to me the whole night as the others said continuous rosaries, cried softly, and kept vigil at Nana's coffin.

In *Still Alice,* the children of the protagonist are so worried about their own futures that they take the gene test to see if they may develop the disease. One of them finds out she doesn't have the gene – she's the pariah of the family – but she is also the one who ultimately looks after Alice. It doesn't matter whether she has the gene or not, her mother was losing herself but she was still her mother, still the wife of her father – *Still Alice.*

I woke up next morning for Nana's funeral. Papa had gone and I was lightheaded because I hadn't eaten the whole previous day. Mechu fed me milk in a sipper bottle and changed me. I was unusually calm that day, and quiet. I was just happy that Papa hadn't taken Mama away while I was asleep.

I prayed the rosary. All of Nana's five children wept bitterly. I was not allowed to touch the coffin.

Nana was buried that afternoon at St. Francis of Assisi Church Bandra West.

Nana. Nana whose name was Gracy Martis, and who gave me shelter when I was an abandoned baby. She did so much good, so why did she have to suffer at the end?

These and other questions will bob up in your head when you read the heart-stirring *Still Alice* by Lisa Genova. It's a book that does more than provide an unusual or entertaining read; it creates public awareness. I think that is Lisa Genova's intention, because all of her books create an awareness of diseases and injury that can strike anyone – things that are beyond our control.

If you have a family member who is struggling with Alzheimer's or dementia, this book will make you feel like you're not alone. If you want to become more aware of the disease, *Still Alice* is a good place to start. Either way, it will make you cry, so go into it only if you are not the kind to get easily depressed. I don't want to give away the ending. But believe me, the ending of this book is full of hope and love and so I really don't think that after reading *Still Alice* you will ever get depressed at the end of it.

"Madam," Deepak comes to me the next Sunday I am at Kitab Khana, "that *Still Alice* book is out of stock. Jagat sir is ordering more. Thank God I gave you the book before we were out of stock." Then with a sad smile he says, "No one should suffer like this ever."

"Yes, no one should," I say and go up the stairs to the classic section. As I browse through the modern classics, I remember a mentally well Nana watching over toddler me as I scribbled on paper. She always used to love me to use a pen or pencil. "Write," she used to say, "and don't worry, I'm right here."

I am still writing, Nana. And you will always be my Nana. Still Nana.

ESSAY 61

Kitab Khana 2

KITAB KHANA SOON BECAME THE place where I could get the best books at reasonable, discounted prices. Like the BSS library, the place had a soul, and I found myself coming back again and again in search of my next great read.

I love the large Parsi colonial tables with their intricate designs and the books that lay upon them. Jagat sir is always bringing new and unique books to Kitab Khana, attracting every reader in Mumbai. It is such a busy place every day of the week that the team has its hands full meeting the needs of the customers.

The wooden flooring on the upper floor creeks like in old Victorian houses, and I love that. I feel regal and grand when I am at Kitab Khana. Their shelves are sturdy and strong. The ground floor, which has marble flooring, is pristine clean, and the warmth of the salesmen is more than I deserve. They are like my uncles or older brothers spoiling me silly every time.

Jagat sir has been a real support throughout. He has been like a godfather to me as a rookie writer and niche publisher. He says little, but his heart is made of gold. His camaraderie with Blaise is a sight to behold. Sanju sir is a man with a lion heart. He is always promoting my books and spoiling me with the best of books that come into the store. He is also very jovial and tells great jokes.

In December 2018, when I handed these men my book, called *The Reclusive Writer and Reader of Bandra: Essays,* all at Kitab Khana became teary eyed. Not because of the love I showered on them in prose, but because of the very first line of the book: "My father didn't want me because I was a girl."

Since then, the whole team has become softer with me. Anand uncle gifts me bookmarks silently with the tender smile of a doting maternal uncle. Shailesh watches over me and always takes the heavy books from my hands so I don't have to carry them.

That's Kitab Khana for you; a bookstore with a heart – not a paper heart like mine, but a blood-red, beating heart.

Sandeep, the bespectacled young salesman, is always cracking jokes with me. I like him, but only as a buddy.

"Coffee or chai?" Deepak asks when I sit down with a pile of books. Deepak, my savior and the one who always gets me what I want.

"Here, madam, give me that book." Deepak pulls an old copy of a book from my hands. "There is a fresher copy upstairs, I'll get that one for you."

"Ma'am," Shailesh my brother will say the moment I enter the store, "The Man Booker Prize books have arrived. Fresh copies. Take the best."

"I sure will Shailesh sir," I say, and he helps me pick.

When I see my books being placed at Kitab Khana and being sold, I feel so elated. I feel complete.

But Kitab Khana means a lot more than impeccable service to me.

It has allowed me to continue my education, through reading, especially books of social importance and history books that have made me a bit smarter. I have read books on global terrorism, fiscal policy, the budget, the tracking of a democratic election, analysis of William Shakespeare's plays, the fundamentals of Indian history, modern contemporary classics, letters of great writers and politicians, the Brexit poll, the Dalit Panther movement, the history of Russia since Lenin, communism, socialism, freedom of speech, the writings of Ezra Pound, the letters of Sylvia Plath, the London underground, the works of Sigmund Freud, the life of Graham Greene, and more.

I eat and drink at the café while my books are being packed. I love my lemon iced tea and the wonderful cakes they sell: blueberry cheesecake, ginger cake, apple cake, truffle chocolate cake, mud pie cake.

I eat, drink, and read. Blaise talks about books and the business of publishing to me. I love these talks and consume everything there is to learn.

It's 2019, and I'm going to turn thirty soon. I've come a long way and I have miles to go. I have to continue building up my businesses and writing more books.

But wherever I will go and whatever I will do, this family at Kitab Khana will always be there looking out and for me. And I think we are going to go a long way together, while we make this world a well-read place.

It was the 1st of January 2019, the current year.

I had finished my Goodreads reading challenge of reading 100 books in 2018, and I was happy as a drunk book phoenix on BRU Gold coffee can ever be. We were free from teaching that day so Mama, Blaise, and I went to Kitab Khana to start our new year at a positive place.

As I was talking with Anand uncle, a good-looking and vaguely familiar man entered the store with a backpack. He started talking to Sanju sir, and I then recognized him.

"Isn't he Jerry Pinto?" I whispered to Anand uncle. "The famous Sahitya Akademi award winner and the best-selling writer of *Murder in Mahim*?"

"That's him all right," said Anand uncle. Then, in an undertone, he added, "He comes here all the time. He loves this place and loves to read."

I went up to him and introduced myself. I was so excited to actually meet Jerry Pinto in person. I was gushing, and I'm sure he felt uncomfortable. Without my mentioning that I was a writer myself, he picked up my book *The Love That Dare Not Speak Its Name: Short Stories* from the table in front. He was attracted to the book because my latest prestigious award for the book, the 2018 Digital Book World Award winner in the category of short stories, was mentioned on the cover.

"That is Fiza ma'am's book," said Sanju sir, ever ready to promote my book.

"You mean, this girl?" he asked, pointing to me.

"Yes, sir. It's her book and her publication," added Jagat sir with a twinkle in his eye. "As you can see, she won the Digital Book World Award for short stories."

"That's what caught my eye," Jerry Pinto said, looking at the picture of Oscar Wilde on the cover. He then handed the book to Sanju sir, "I'm taking this and," he looked with a handsome smile, "will you autograph the book for me, please?"

I was shell-shocked.

Jerry Pinto. "The" Jerry Pinto of international and national excellence in letters was asking little old bookish insignificant me to autograph a book FOR HIM!

My hands were shaking as I penned the autograph, pen provided by Shailesh like a proud elder brother.

Jerry Pinto bent down to look at my mama.

"You must be a proud mother," he said to my tiny mama. Jerry Pinto's mother had passed away after struggling with bipolar disorder. He wrote about it in his bestseller and award-winning book *Em and the Big Hoom.*

"My daughter is a very simple girl, sir," Mama said humbly as she hugged chubby-checker me. "Very simple."

He smiled, still looking at Mama though he was speaking to me.

"Keep on writing, my girl, Fiza. And NEVER stop."

I nodded. I had heard the Master's words.

"I'll never stop, Jerry sir," I said, and I handed him the autographed book and allowed him the privacy to peruse the shelves. Blaise was teary eyed as was the rest of the Kitab Khana team.

I was on top of the world.

Jagat sir shook Blaise's hands as if to say "well done." And Shailesh, I guess, was looking sad, gazing into the distance, probably remembering the first line of *The Reclusive Writer & Reader of Bandra,* which I, too, was remembering at that moment on the first day of the new year: "My father didn't want me because I was a girl."

Dreams of unwanted girl children do come true.

ESSAY 62

Baluta by Daya Pawar, Preface by Shanta Gokhale (Foreword), Jerry Pinto (Translator)

"MADAM, how are you?"

"Hey, Deepak, where were you? Did you hear the news? I met Jerry Pinto sir!"

Deepak was the only one from the Kitab Khana family who had not been there when I met Jerry Pinto. But he had heard about it and was very excited for me. He pointed to the table where Jerry Pinto's books were kept. Next to his books were my *NIRMALA: The Mud Blossom* and *Amina: The Silent One*. My books were sharing the same space with JERRY PINTO's!

It took me back to that morning of meeting Jerry Pinto on the first of January 2019. I remember gushing over him as if he was a pop star or a Bollywood superhero.

"I read your translation of *Baluta* in 2017," I said. "It was so lovely."

"Really, thank you," he said and then turned to the modern classic books. He picked one, cracked it open gently, and inhaled the scent of its pages.

"Told you he was just like you," Anand uncle chuckled, as I stood with mouth opened like a character on Cartoon Network.

But, yes, I really loved Jerry Pinto and started liking Jerry Pinto's books after I read his translation of the Marathi book *Baluta* in 2017. I was reading a lot of Dalit biographies from the early phase of my MCubed days, and one day at the Trilogy library I saw *Baluta* on the shelf in the Indian fiction section.

I borrowed the book and read it while sitting at a restro-bar I liked, called The Mockingbird Café. It was a cozy place, dedicated to good food, drinks, and books. I was introduced to it by my Trilogy book club friend, Kanchana, and made it my place to read in when I was in the Bombay town area on my days off.

I read *Baluta* there after drinking peach iced tea after peach iced tea.

The memoir is about the writer in Mumbai in the 1940s and '50s, when casteism was at its peak in the city. It is considered to be the very first Dalit biography ever penned and motivated other Dalit writers to pen their own Dalit memoirs, either about themselves or their families. I was shocked and stunned by the book's brutal truths, and it only added to my respect and love for this community of people.

"You know Shanta Gokhale was my professor," said Blaise over his third cup of coffee at The Mockingbird Café.

"What?" I asked, not hearing him. I was too engrossed in the book.

"Shanta Gokhale, who has written the preface to the book you are reading, was my English professor when I was studying at H. R. College in the 1970s."

"No kidding!" I said, placing my bookmark in between pages so I wouldn't lose my place. I picked at the white pasta on my plate. "What was she like?"

Blaise wiped coffee off his moustache. "Very passionate about her work. Loved to write and was a great professor."

"Really?"

"Yes," said Blaise as he took another large gulp of his mocha coffee. "She would have liked to have met you."

"I don't have much to say," I said leaving the pasta for Mama, who was busy with some note-writing. I clinked my tall glass of peach iced tea with Blaise's coffee cup. "But, yes, I can see that the world is a small place indeed."

Shanta Gokhale is now in her eighties. She has touched the lives of many like Blaise, and, yes, it would have been nice to have met her, but I'm too much of a recluse.

I read *Baluta* in three- or four-days' time at The Mockingbird Café with iced tea and coffee passed from Blaise to Mama to me. Kanchana used to meet us there, too. On one of her visits, she disclosed that she was getting married.

"Congratulations, babe!" I said clinking my tall glass of peach iced tea to her mocktail bottle. "Here's to your coming marriage."

"And to yours, too, someday soon with that BSS boy you love," Kanchana added cheerily.

Mama looked at me, and I pretended to be busy reading the menu.

Baluta is a shocking book, originally written in the Marathi language by Dagdu Maruti Pawar, and translated into English by Jerry Pinto. It is a unique memoir because it speaks of the troubles of the writer, who after being well educated was still living on his mother's earnings. The book is a quick read and an indictment of the caste system that is still very much a part of Indian society, and especially Mumbai society. I often come across reviews on Goodreads and Amazon from readers who say they are not moved by *Baluta,* and more specifically, Daya Pawar's tale. To such reviewers, I say if you are not from the Mahar caste or another untouchable caste, convert yourself to a Dalit at once and start living the life of one for real. Come on, I dare you to do this! I cringe when I see apathy in response to a brave man like Daya Pawar, who has managed to inspire many Dalit biographies just with the grace of providence. The lower castes have been suffering for ages; if some good is coming their way, can't you just be human and give them a chance?

So, if you are a TRUE believer in the complete emancipation of the Dalits and in the complete eradication of this evil of evils known as the caste system of Indian society, then read *Baluta*, the biography revolution among Dalits and the people of India, especially Mumbaikars.

It's books like these that make me work harder at my own publishing firm and make me strive to create better books featuring social issues and education for everyone – Freedom With Pluralism.

"So, when are you thinking of settling down?" Kanchana, from her magic world of love, asked me at The Mockingbird Café' as she took a big swig of her pomegranate mocktail.

I tap the tall, empty iced tea glass in front of me.

"I'm not settling down. I want to focus on my work and my career and my books."

Kanchana nodded and said, "Best of luck!"

I smiled. "You too, babe. You too."

ESSAY 63

Wayword & Wise

IT WAS 2016 AND THE TORRENTIAL RAIN was beating on our taxi as we made our way to a new bookstore we had just heard about. They said the bookstore sold curated books and was housed very near the Chhatrapati Shivaji Terminus (CST) in Mumbai.

With my pink ladies' umbrella, which by now was convinced she was only meant to be an umbrella for the rest of her days, I emerged from the taxi and looked at the bookstore hovering over me with its gold lettering and blue background – Wayword & Wise.

"Cool!" I was excited to visit a new bookstore after such a long time. I got out with Mama and Blaise. We entered, and the first thing I sensed was the magical smell of books. I also noticed that Western classical music was playing in the background.

A man was walking toward Blaise with his hand out. Blaise smiled in recognition. "Virat, it's you!" Blaise joyfully shook hands with his old salesman friend from Strand. Yes, the missing link. The only Strand salesman who had not joined Jagat sir was at Wayword & Wise working as a manager. He was in charge of looking after the place and choosing the curated books.

Virat's history with Blaise began at another elite bookstore called "The Lotus Book House" in Bandra West during the 1990s. I was too young back then to join him, but Blaise often bought books at Lotus.

By the time I learned about Lotus, the bookstore had closed down. Virat then started working at Crossword's, where he came into contact with our common friend Sandeep from Kitab Khana.

"This is your ...?" Virat asked Blaise as he pointed at me. I literally was grabbing all of the books placed standing up on the "New Arrivals" section.

"My niece," Blaise said.

"She lives with you?"

"Yes," Blaise said as I continued to shop in the literary and biblio sections. "I used to buy the kiddie books for her."

"That explains a lot." Virat nodded happily as he saw me filling baskets with books. "She has good taste."

I bought so many books that day – and with my own money. I'd been paying for my books with my own money for a while by then.

Wayword & Wise has a vast collection. It mainly caters to the erudite reader, especially those who love foreign writers. The shelves are strong; most are carved into the walls. The walls are made of stone; the building is of the colonial era. The Indian fiction section is small, only a single bookcase. But what the place lacks in Indian fiction and nonfiction, it makes up for with all kinds of international fiction. It has some of the rarest books anywhere, and it is the only bookstore that actually has a separate section of books for the LGBTQIA community.

It has a giant graphic novel collection, a large collection of rare and uncommon nonfiction, the international titles I earlier spoke about, and new content coming in almost every week. The new books are curated by Virat sir, who is a connoisseur of books. I know that I'll always find different books from those sold by the rest of the bookstores in Mumbai. He is a voracious reader and wants only the best for Wayword & Wise.

I walked through the store that day as if I were walking through an enchanted forest. The sound of the recorded Western classical music concert was soothing to my ears and whenever a music piece ended and the audience started clapping, I felt at ease. The place is very chic and breathes refined taste.

Whenever I want something different, I come to Wayword & Wise. I know Virat will always have something for me. From bibliophile books to books about art to books on Hollywood to books on poetry to tomes filled with literary criticism, I can find books I've never seen before at Wayword & Wise.

Virat sir loves to get into conversation with customers about books and the authors of the books. I have been greatly educated by the books at Wayword & Wise, especially where literary criticism and essay writing is concerned. I've read the essays of Zadie Smith and Albert Camus, which I picked up from here.

Mama doesn't come into Wayword & Wise as the air conditioners there are very powerful. But she is always happy when I come out with my treasures.

Blaise loves the place: the décor, the motif, and of course the books.

When we are alone in the bookstore, Blaise and I have a conversation with Virat sir. He has a lot of fascinating stories to tell. He remembers when Blaise used to go to The Lotus Book House.

"You were into esoteric literature at that time, right?" he asks Blaise and Blaise nods. Virat muses over that.

"Your niece seems to be a bit different."

"She was always different," Blaise says proudly, and I blush. "She is devoted to her books."

And being at Wayword & Wise has made me even more devoted to books than I was before.

When Blaise and I told Virat sir about our Shanbaug bookshelves, he was in agreement with the team at Kitab Khana about Shanbaug. "His life was his bookcases, I'm telling you," said Virat sir. "If you got the Burma teak ones you are a lucky bunch. Like you, my house is full of books. The shelf space is over. There are now cartons of books. Books I just do not want to give away. Most of the books at Wayword & Wise are bought by me before anyone else has a chance to buy them."

We all three laugh and then I walk out with my purchases. I love to come here, especially when I am in need of refreshing myself after a week of classes or a new project I'm working on. I am able to declutter my mind in the company of the great masters of prose while Virat sir browses through a new carton of books as a Western piano concerto plays in the background.

❋

"I've seen your mother but who is your father?" Virat sir asks one day when Blaise is perusing the young adult section of the bookstore.

"My father doesn't live with us."

"Your parents are divorced?"

"No, they just live separately, and I live with my mama's family."

"Oh, okay," Virat sir says, and then he changes the subject as quick as the buzzing of a bee. When he read the first line of *The Reclusive Writer and Reader of Bandra: Essays* he, too, was shocked, but didn't comment. That's what I like about Virat sir; he doesn't get personal. He allows me to be anonymous.

The year I discovered Wayword & Wise was the year I discovered the last "new" bookstore in the city. I am such a frequent visitor that it doesn't seem like it is only about four years that the bookstore has been in Mumbai.

I've grown into a quiet, contemplative, and very good listener at Wayword & Wise. I sit on the cane stools and sometimes stare at the wonderful books on display, happy that I can afford them and happy that I'm welcome here, in this place of refined intellectuals. I've overcome old sorrows and painted a life for myself. I've grown into the silent person I was meant to be, like I was at BSS. I am at the peak of my silence, and I want nothing more than to be left alone.

I've been slowly shutting doors. It's like that story by Anton Chekhov, about how a young lawyer shut himself up in a room for fifteen years with only a piano, books, and alcohol to fill his days. He did it to win a lot of money from a bet, but at the end of fifteen years, he had read so much that to him all the money in this world had no relevance. He ran away without claiming his reward for the fifteen years he spent in confinement.

I've grown into such a person. If given a chance, I would like to retire from the world and devote myself to books. The world has left me cold. People don't have anything in common with me. Society thinks I'm odd. My mind doesn't fit in with the norms of Mumbai life and, even though I live in the city of dreams, my only dream is to pursue the twilight that descends on my being with every page I turn of a really good book.

And I love the books at Wayword & Wise. Because they have made that fact clear to me. I am meant to be all alone. Forever.

"Mama, sometimes I feel that after I die, you and Papa will unite again," I say one day as I enter Narayan's cab after a good contemplative day at Wayword & Wise.

"Why do you talk such rubbish?" Mama scolds me, tears forming in her eyes. "When you say things like that it pains me."

"And me too," Blaise adds.

"Me too," Narayan adds, and we all laugh. Narayan loves going around with me; he says so to everyone he knows.

"Baby only goes to libraries and bookstores. Nowhere else," he says to his uncle as they sip their hot milky tea in private (but not so private considering I can hear them). "But she is troubled by something. Something we shall never know."

That's right, no one can know. Only silence can scream out an answer in a babel of more quiet sounds.

ESSAY 64

Ashish Book Center and Book Fair

FOR THE PAST SIXTEEN YEARS, I have been religiously attending the half-yearly Ashish Book Fair. The Ashish Book Center is a large depot bookstore in Mumbai in the CST station area very near Way-word & Wise. It has been hosting book fairs of secondhand and new books for the longest time ever. And I have been faithful to it ever since I graduated from BSS, in 2005.

It was Blaise who took me to the fair at the famous Sunderbai Hall, Churchgate, where many book fairs are held.

The people at Ashish know me well. They have seen me every year since I was sixteen years old. We've had the longest relation-ship in books ever. I took that relationship to the next level when I started visiting the Ashish bookstore in 2012.

No one understands my needs like the Ashish team.

"Chai, madam?" they ask as I visit them these days, obese and quite different from the slim and pretty girl from college they knew in the first decade of the twenty-first century. "Hey, Peon, bring madam some hot tea, *garma garam chai*!"

I sometimes accept their hospitality. They are a pioneering lot of booksellers, and I love their taste in books. But before I talk about

Ashish Book Center and its fairs, let me tell you something which you might have noticed by now if you have been reading this bookish memoir from the beginning.

You may have noticed that basically this area of South Mumbai is a hot spot of books. All the major libraries and bookstores are concentrated in this part of bustling Mumbai. There are numerous libraries dating back to when the British were here in India, and new stores like Kitab Khana, Wayword & Wise, Bargain Book Hut, Satyam Bookstore, Sterling Book House, The Examiner Bookstore and even a whole lot of booksellers who sell their books on the roads. Yes, you read that right, literally on the pavements of Flora Fountain near the Kitab Khana, Fort, area. It's also the former location for old stores like the Strand and Oxford Bookstore.

This area of Mumbai is the best place to find any books that you want at decent prices. This is also where a large number of tourists flock to see British heritage structures. Basically, this place is book heaven – you cannot die hungry for books in Fort area, Mumbai, that's for sure.

Now, coming back to Ashish Book Center, they have been hosting their fairs for the longest time ever and I've been going to these fairs also for the longest time ever.

This team of book sellers knows me as a reader with varying tastes and as someone who buys without bargaining about the price. They give me the best service and the best books at reasonable prices. They pack books in boxes for me as I drink their tea and discuss books, publishing, and when the next book fair will be happening.

"Madam Pathan's books have to be packed *chaka-chak*!" says the manager at the counter in Mumbai lingo. "The *maal* has to go all the way to Bandra West, so use the best packing material." And then, turning to me in a softer tone, he says, "Madam Pathan, some more chai?"

Once when I attended the Ashish book fair, I went home with five boxes. The workers had a time packing the wide, tall, and deep cardboard boxes. But they know I'm a woman of my word, and they do it "*chaka-chak*." I feel warm, welcomed, and loved at Ashish, whether at their book fairs or at their store, where I am a regular. I always feel fulfilled and satisfied with my purchases.

These days they have their book fairs in Thane, Andheri, Navi Mumbai, and other places, but as long as they don't go out of the city of Mumbai, there I go, to get the best books at the best prices.

"Madam always comes," says a worker as I pick through books like a professional. "She has always been faithful to us."

The people running the show in Mumbai are lovely, decent, and always ready to serve. They don't stand on formality. They don't have to ask. They know.

"The way you talk about Ashish, I think you are talking about a drug dealer," says Mechu over her horn-rimmed glasses. "Dolly girl, are books your passion or addiction?"

I look my godmother squarely in the eye and say, "It's my life force. Without it, what is life but just – life!"

"Dolly girl! You are incorrigible!"

I know that, but if I have to live life, I need my fix. And the Ashish team, from the managers to the workers, know that. MADAM NEEDS HER FIX!

When I am done reading my books from Ashish, I either keep them or I sell them at good prices to Mr. Iqbal at Victoria's.

"All your books have this Ashish Stamp on them," Mr. Iqbal complains as he sifts through four blue garbage bags of books that I have sold to him. "What is this Ashish and what do they do?"

I look at him with a naughty smile. "They pump me with books, the only 'crack' I am addicted to."

Mr. Iqbal says "tsk-tsk" and happily goes through the great books I've given him. Munira, his wife, thumps me on the back and says, "With the number of books you have, you can open your own bookshop. Why haven't you thought about that?"

I nod and look out at the teaming traffic that whizzes past us.

"I've not yet thought about that. I'm too busy writing my own stories and selling them to think about selling anyone else's stories."

"These books are marvelous," exclaims Mr. Iqbal, and I have to agree with him. Ashish sells the best of the best.

I have been going to all the Ashish Book Fairs. These day's they call it "The Bookish Affair," and I love the way they are handling the book business.

When my co-author and writer, Michaelangelo Zane, and I started on our project to abridge classics in our Rare Classics series, I went to the next Ashish book fair and the bookstore to get the volumes of classics that we needed to refer to and then abridge. Ashish sells these well-bound and decently priced classic collections. Most of my classic omnibuses and the collections I own are from the Ashish book fair. They are right in front of me as I type these words in my office-cum-writing hut:

- Jane Austen collection
- Robert Louis Stevenson collection
- Henry James collection
- Charles Dickens collection
- Thomas Hardy collection
- George Eliot collection
- Maxim Gorky collection
- Anton Chekhov collection
- Virginia Woolf collection
- Sir Arthur Conan Doyle collection
- The Brontë Sisters collection
- Mark Twain collection
- Kahlil Gibran collection
- John Buchman collection
- Franz Kafka collection
- H. G. Wells collection
- Jules Verne collection
- Rudyard Kipling collection
- Plato collection
- Anthony Trollope collection.

Michaelangelo and I have worked over these many volumes to create our Rare Classics collection. And the funniest part of the whole thing is that our Rare Classics series are doing extremely well in the international market. All this thanks to the volumes I used to buy over the sixteen years at the Ashish book fair and book center since 2005.

When I go looking for old, rare books, I go to Ashish. Their prices are ridiculously low but their books are out of this world. I have this craze for old leather-bound books and the pre-World War I and II novels that Ashish has in their depot. The smell of the leather-bound books reminds me of my BSS library, which had many leather-bound books back then.

"Madamji, are you okay?" asks one of the workers at Ashish as I pet an old book tenderly, as if it is a wounded swan. Papa, my long-lost papa. The following is a poem I wrote on this subject:

There is a silent voice in death without you papa,
It's painful to hear the silence of pages gone papa;
I am so forlorn and this will be a dirge paged here forever more,
Silent screaming in the library of books gone to their disturbed rest.

And, yes, I cry. The workman doesn't pry. He leaves me for a moment and returns with boxes filled with old books for me to pick through.

I look forward to Ashish book fair events like some people look forward to their birthday or Easter or Christmas. Earlier, in the good old days, they used to send their book fair brochure by mail. Now they advertise via social media; how time has flown by.

"You are very nice, madam," says one of the managers who helps me select my books. "I have not seen anyone who respects books like you, as well as human beings."

Yes, I love and respect and worship books. Humans? I think I'm just nice because that is my nature. But my sweet editor, Kim Catanzarite, thinks otherwise: "You have written many stories about people who are treated unfairly due to their sexual orientation, religious beliefs, etc. You stand up for those who don't have a voice. This is no small thing. And it shows that you do care. You care a lot!" Sweet of her.

But humans, on a personal level, have not been very good to me. Especially since I've gained weight. It seems like after I gained weight, I lost everything. I've become an object of fun and mockery. The moment a bit of my tummy fat started to show up, people in college began to humiliate me verbally, emotionally, psychologically, and physically. I was called all sorts of lewd names, and some girls pinched me on the tummy, which really got on my nerves. Lata would humiliate me time and again about my obesity, making my life miserable when I was with her. Everyone I meet, even today, comments on my weight and my plus-size body. Everyone has free advice to give.

Books have never treated me differently, and neither have the people who work at Ashish. They respect me for who I am, and I respect them in turn.

In my hurting years, my plus-size body was a source of jokes for many people. It seemed as though I had become subhuman or not human at all. No one cared that the jibes they continuously took at me hurt me to the core.

To some humans, I'm not anything else but fat. I'm not a director and chief executive officer at Fiza Pathan Publishing, I'm not a multiple award-winning author, I'm not a successful teacher, and I'm not a good daughter. I'm nothing but a fat thing meant to be the butt of ridicule for the rest of my life.

So be it.

I've rejected people the same way they have rejected me. I hate company and go to bookstores only with family members. I have basically gone into seclusion. Maybe it was meant to be. I may be leading a very hectic and active life, but all of it happens behind closed doors because I can't take this shit about body shaming anymore.

You are disappointed? You are disappointed about my decision? You feel my seclusion and my anonymity is a sign of a disturbed soul? Well, to you I say that the world is quite disturbed, and you've got to live with it. If the major disturbances in the world don't disturb you and my seclusion does, then you need to analyze your reality and your perception of what is a problem and what is not. I was never a problem, but the world made me a problem – a big fat problem they hate to see. So, leave me alone with my books and let me live my life.

I always seem cheery at Ashish events. I always seem cheery to all the people connected to Ashish Book Center. I am loved here and wanted. And I'll remember their love and their books all my life.

You will always find me at their book fairs, with their long rows of fiction and nonfiction of the highest tastes, searching through boxes. People often feel lost at book fairs. Not me. In that vastness, I find peace. I get to choose enough books to keep me happy for another good year, or at least several months, of reading.

"Baby, should I bring yet another basket?" Narayan asks me at one of the Ashish fairs. I smile like an imp, and he understands and happily gets another. Yes, it takes two and sometimes four people to help me out as I purchase books from Ashish: Narayan for the baskets, Mama for the guarding of the baskets that are filled, Blaise with my cash to pay for them, and me to supervise it all. It's just me, silly old bookish little me.

Narayan strolls with me at the fair like a devoted elder brother. I pick a book and then place it in his hand, and he places that book into a basket neatly while I move along the row. We are partners in delightful bookish crime at Ashish.

The other day at the Ashish fair, as we just entered the Sunderbai Hall, Narayan's first act was to collect some three or four baskets.

"I'm just being prepared," he told the Ashish team, and they all had a hearty good laugh of a bookish kind.

It's a delight to watch them pack the books into boxes. They do it so well and with such respect for the books that it heartens me.

"The very best boxes for madam!" says the manager, and other book fair patrons look at me with awe at both my insatiable thirst for books and the way I am looked after so well at Ashish. Then the workers who have packed my boxes carry them on their shoulders to the taxi. Narayan asks to help them, but they don't allow him to lift a finger.

In addition to the fairs, I often visit the Ashish bookstore at CST.

I'm greeted with dignity, and whether I buy one book or a hundred, I am always given the best service and tea and an easy chair to sit in for more comfortable perusal.

Thus, has it been my journey with the Ashish Book Center family. I hope to retain their goodwill until the end of time.

But I have lost my hope for people in general. It's a useless cause, and I don't want to please anyone anymore.

By the time you read this book, I may have gone completely into seclusion. I may have distanced myself from regular society forever. But don't worry about me; as long as I have my books with me, I will be happy. Don't drop by to meet or greet me. I'm not worth your time. You could be in happier company with someone more communicative. I only communicate well with a pen in my hand or under compulsion to earn money to put food on the table. I am not meant for this world, and this world was never meant for me. From the time of my birth, I was an unwanted person, and maybe I will depart even more forgotten than in someone's memory.

But if I do leave this plane of existence someday, you can be sure you will find a pile of Ashish books on my reading table, still waiting for its devoted reader to read its illuminating combination of twenty-six letters of the alphabets.

God bless you for rejecting me!

God bless books for adopting me. I will ever be at their bidding!

ESSAY 65

The Holocaust as Culture by Imre Kertész, Thomas Cooper (Translation)

"NEW BOOKS HAVE JUST ARRIVED," Virat sir says as he passes me in Wayword & Wise on his way to help another bookstore patron find something in the philosophy section. "Take a look near my table."

I go to Virat sir's desk. Classical piano music is playing on the music system, and the bright lights of Wayword & Wise make this hot, dark, rainy September day a bit less gloomy. I'm ready to read something new and to discover a different writer, which I always do when I am at Wayword & Wise.

I check the bookshelf near his desk. I reach for a tiny book and stare at the title: *The Holocaust as Culture* by Imre Kertész.

"Well, this promises to be something new," I say in my mind as I hug the book to my bosom and look out for another. That day, I would buy a whole boxful of Seagull Publisher books and some rare philosophical books, and leave with a genial smile on my face.

I would read Kertész's book, two months later, in December of that same year, 2018. The book was over in a matter of minutes but the impact it had on me was more than overwhelming. Books do this to me sometimes, especially if they show me a different angle of looking at events and things. What I had read changed the way I think of the Holocaust and the reasons it took place. It made me realize that the Holocaust was not a "historical event." Moreover, it was a culture, a deviant culture that grew in Europe until its final culmination in the Holocaust. The Holocaust as a culture – that idea blew me away! I had never read such a take on the Holocaust. The dialogue between Kertész and his interviewer is amazing, one that deserves reading and contemplation.

After I read Kertész's book I went on Amazon and bought some of his other books to read in the near future.

As I closed the book in December 2018, I got up and ran to Blaise. "You have to read this. It will change your life," I said.

He smiled and took the book. His eyes were tired from a long day of work.

"You have changed my life," he said and put the book in the Shanbaug shelf. "I'll read it later."

Blaise.

Blaise Martis. The only person who has really understood me. The only person who I can relate to on an intellectual level. A person who has done so much for me. A person who loves books as much as I do. I think maybe he and I share many of the family genes.

Fathers come in many different shapes and sizes in one's life. I lost a Papa on the nineteenth of March, 1989, at 3:45 p.m. I gained Blaise a few minutes later, when he with Nana came to the hospital to see newborn me.

Blaise. Blaise who had told me about the Holocaust, who taught me that we must learn from the past and never let such a thing happen again. Kertész died trying to tell the world the same thing.

But just like there is no sense in abandoning a child because she was born a girl, there will always be no sense where racism, communalism, sexism, anti-Semitism, and all the *isms* put together are concerned. There will be no sense until we see humanity before we see the human, till we realize that individuals are more important than humanity as a whole.

Blaise listened to me as I told him about the book. I poured my soul out to him, something that I have never been able to do with any other male. He listened as I told him about the amazing interview between Kertész and Thomas Cooper, and how Kertész talks about his books, racism, history, and the individual.

This book taught me about suffering, pain, and rising up again into a new form – like a phoenix!

This book is only about 112 pages of Holocaust literature, and it will give you a new way of looking at that terrible scar on our twentieth century, reminding us that we must never let it happen again.

I was teaching my tenth-graders about the Holocaust the other day.

They had never heard of it. They didn't know what I was talking about.

"You mean you have never been told about World War II or Hitler or Nazism?" I asked incredulously.

They looked at me as if I were something from out of space.

"Is Nazism an app?" one of them asked. "I always thought it was either an app or a heavy metal band from the 1930s."

A moment of silence for that wonderful answer!

Sincerely, everyone, what's going on? How can a fifteen-year-old not know about the Holocaust? And if parents, teachers, education ministers, and the powers that be are thinking this is some part of the history syllabus that shouldn't be highlighted, well, the joke is on you. Because when you forget about the Holocaust and the fact that it was a cultural act and not a historical event, you and your loved ones are the losers. We are all the losers.

But it looks like people have clean forgotten about the evil that was the Holocaust. I can see it in the way things are going around the world. People have forgotten. Or are being led to forget by the ghastly junk that predominates our globalized world's agenda these days.

In my country, too, people, especially kids, have forgotten the Holocaust. They have forgotten about wicked men like Hitler and leaders who are bleeders, who make us bleed, suffer, and die with the fact tattooed sometimes on our left hands and sometimes in our hearts. No one cares about humanity anymore. No one cares.

Normal human beings are now declaring themselves to be a god in my country – humans who are not even worthy of being called humans let alone gods or even demigods.

I'm not here to preach because, as I have said before, I've given up on humanity. But I have humanity in me, and that humanity is making me type these words as I seclude myself from a world that never was mine.

I'm no preacher. I'm just me, little old book-crazy me. But I matter, don't I? You matter, don't you? Your Muslim or Christian or Dalit friends matter, don't they? The Holocaust matters, doesn't it?

And if there is a negation to all stated in the previous paragraph then there is no need for me to urge you to read this book. But if there is one tiny 'yes' in response to even one of the above, then please read *The Holocaust as Culture*. Read it because the Holocaust happened and must not happen again. And people matter, even if they are so dehumanized that they can't see the humanity in the human in front of them.

"New books came in just yesterday," Virat sir says, the next time I enter the store in January 2019. I nod but take my time to move to the bookshelf. Blaise is with me and is checking out the latest arrivals in front of the store. I can see my book, *The Love That Dare Not Speak Its Name*, in the LGBTQIA section, and I'm happy. As long as we can include everyone in our scheme of happiness, then never again will another Holocaust take place. Never again will I have to explain the need to read a book about the Holocaust to parents and students who seem to be living in an ivory tower of their own while people burn humanity in my country every day, bit by bit.

I tell Virat sir about the book and that it was an eye-opening read. He nods. I know what he is thinking: "This girl is going on thirty and she hasn't read Kertész yet!"

Virat sir, I'm getting there, slowly. Just like I teach my children about the culture that became the Holocaust.

Slowly.

ESSAY 66

Shinrin-Yoku: The Art and Science of Forest Bathing by Qing Li

I PICKED THIS BOOK BY Qing Li in a hardback edition at Wayword & Wise in 2018. The book smelled delicious, was well illustrated, and changed my stressful life for the better, making me a calmer person.

I have mentioned that I practice aromatherapy. What I also have been practicing unknowingly since 2016, and now knowingly since 2018, is the Japanese custom of Shinrin-Yoku, or forest bathing.

No, I don't mean I live in a forest, though where I live in Bandra West, I am surrounded by nature due to the fact that there is a woodland filled with nature's bounty behind my building over an expansive hilltop. No, what I mean is that forest bathing is the practice of communing with nature, especially plants and trees, in a way that refreshes and revitalizes you and makes you a more calm, sensitive and relaxed human being. It's the act of walking in the company of trees and plants– touching them, smelling the flowers, smelling the leaves, observing animals in the trees, caring for them, and walking barefoot in soil, all in an effort to communicate and be one with them.

I have mentioned before that I have a modest garden. It's the summer season as I type this piece and all my flowers are in bloom. I spend my time forest bathing in their company by thinking of them, smelling their natural aromas, touching them gently for about an hour a day to show my love to them and receive their love in return. The more I see of humans and their brutish nature, the more I prefer to love my plants and my animal friends instead.

This book by Qing Li gave me great tips and various ways of practicing forest bathing. It has really helped me control my temper and stress throughout the day. I need to only smell the scent of my magnolias and I am refreshed and ready for another hectic day of teaching, writing, and publishing.

The book has beautiful pictures of gardens, trees, forests, woods, etc., that encourage you to be filled with the spirit of the forest as you become more involved in your practice of Shinrin-Yoku. I usually listen to music, mostly Kitaro as I roam my modest garden. It is my dream to one day have a larger space for a bigger garden where these neem trees, which are babies right now, will have good soil to grow in rather than remain caged in my pots. But I don't think that is ever going to be possible at the rate at which houses are being sold in Mumbai. Maybe when I retire to the hills of Mussoorie I will be able to have a garden of sorts.

The book also mentions wonderful essential oils that can be used in aromatherapy to relax the senses.

I practice forest therapy as often as I can. I practice it in the company of my cat Trotskyna. She is a wonderful panacea for solitude. I carry her as I refresh myself near my neem trees and magnolias. Trotskyna loves my yellow ixoras and white jasmines. She loves to sniff them; she also protects my garden like a little four-legged nymph. Though my other cat, Lopez, used to destroy my pretty plants and delicate flowers, Trotskyna never harms a single green bud or twig. It's as if she is practicing forest bathing too.

Trotskyna and I have had many romps together. She adores me and yearns to spend time with me the way golden retrievers adore their masters.

I am her obsession. She is one of my only friends.

"Fiza, miss," asked one of my eight-grade students recently, "if you get married, then who will be your maid of honor?"

"That marriage is not going to happen, sweetheart," I say as I try to divert her attention.

"Still," she persists, "who will be your maid of honor if you had to pick someone?"

I didn't have to think twice.

"I would pick Trotskyna," I answer. My students laughed heartily. They were hoping that they would be one of bride's maids. My little innocent students. My sweet Trotskyna. Good old Trot!

I carry Trotskyna around the garden. We don't say a word. We are not the type to speak much.

We practice Shinrin-Yoku together. We feel the beatings of each other's hearts. It's like we were meant to be together. She closes her big gray-blue eyes as she snuggles into my chest, and I kiss her head gently feeling rejuvenated, tranquil, and energized enough to go back inside the tuition house or office-cum-writing hut to earn my daily bread.

As now, I'm getting ready to break off ties from most part of the world, my forest bathing, my Shinrin-Yoku, has become more important to me. I add to my collection every once in a while, normally those little dried-up plants that people have given up on or the eight-foot-tall climber vines that no one can deal with anymore. They make a home with me in my garden, and we practice Shinrin-Yoku together as we tend to each other and listen to the sounds that arrive on the wind.

Trotskyna loves when I add new plants or trees to the garden. She loves neem trees as much as I do. Once when she was having a bad tummy ache, she ate all the leaves of a lower branch of one of my small neem trees. After that, she was back in shape in no time, my dear little pet puss.

If you want to feel a bit calmer in your everyday life, you should read *Shinrin-Yoku* by Qing Li and start practicing forest bathing as well as aromatherapy. If you have a hectic lifestyle and want a naturalistic way to rejuvenate yourself, then this is the book for you. Do you have a garden, live near the woods, and want to connect with your natural environment in a deeper way? Then Shinrin-Yoku is the practice for you. Those of you who have been indirectly practicing Shinrin-Yoku can read Qing Li's book to expand your relationship with your trees and plants. Aromatherapy lovers will also learn from this book and those of you who spend most of your time in offices with plexiglass windows should read the part about practicing Shinrin-Yoku through aromatherapy.

I have learned a lot from Qing Li's book and continue to dip into it at intervals. Trotskyna sometimes is by my side as I do so, cozying up as close to me as possible. If there is love in the world, then it is this little something that I share with the natural world.

As I've mentioned before, I'm an existentialist, but I practice the rituals of my Catholic faith. Still, my God is only one being. He is the saint of ecology himself, St. Francis of Assisi, who in books of theosophy also goes by the name of Kuthumi. He is the only god I have. He is my muse. He guides me as I write and in everything I do. He is God, and I will always be his Mira.

I owe all my writing to him. I owe my love of nature to him. It is to him that I have sold my soul; he who has been the provider and nourisher of books to me as far back as 1989.

I will always burn in devotion to him.

Since the start of this flood of words,
I have never dammed my inky waters to you;
Sweet Francesco, my love in you be all I need,
For you alone may my blood run ink blue.

More of him later. But now the sun is setting on my horizon.

The scent of Raat-Ki-Rani (night jasmine) flowers fills the air as I type these words. Maybe after I'm finished typing, I'll go out in my garden and sit with good old Trot on my lap in the middle of the shefleras greens. I'll practice Shinrin-Yoku and think of St. Francis of

Assisi as the night bids farewell to a fragrant twilight of magnolia, jasmine, and Raat-Ki-Rani.

ESSAY 67

Book of My Mother by Albert Cohen, translated by Bella Cohen

WAYWORD & WISE LOVES TO ORDER rare books from rare publishers for their clientele. Sometimes when a great load of such books comes into the bookstore, I snatch a couple of them and save the reading for later.

It was one day in the middle of 2018 that I was rummaging through a box in my office-cum-writing hut and came across a book called *Book of My Mother*. It is an Archipelago Book, just the size of a pocketbook and short enough to finish in one night.

But I couldn't finish the book in one night.

The book was about the size of my palm. It was 180 pages, and I needed a whole week to read it.

I, the self-proclaimed book phoenix, took a week to finish a 180-page book.

The book was written by a French writer whom I had never heard of. His book however made me cry every night.

Mama.

The essays penned by Albert Cohen for his mother made me cry.

Mama, my mama.

The book is a tough one to go through, if you have not treated your mother with the love and respect she deserves. If you are that type of person, then don't read this book because it will shatter you.

Mama, my mama. My one and only mama.

In this book, Cohen will make anyone who has ever loved a mother cry, weep, and bemoan. Woe to you if you read his essay pieces when your mother is no more or, worse, if you have failed her in anyway, as Albert Cohen once failed his own dear, darling mother.

I read this book when I was twenty-eight years old. I cried because of the mother described in the book, Cohen's mother, whose whole life centered around her dear little son. I cried when he described her devotion to him, even though subjectively speaking, he didn't deserve her devotion. Subjectively speaking, I too can say that I don't deserve the love and devotion my own mama has for me – and has had since the day I was born.

Mama stood up for me when no one else wanted me. Mama stood up for her infant girl child even though she knew she had everything to lose.

"She gained you, Fiza," Rita says in the middle of one of our gossip sessions. "You are more precious than a thousand boy children and a million husbands."

"I've not been a good daughter," I mumble in reply. "I've not been perfect."

Rita sighs and tells me with innocent love, "You are not perfect. ... But you make our lives seem perfect."

Yes, like Cohen, I've not been the perfect daughter. I have a temper. I have my shortcomings. I am too silent. I'm not perfect. But Mama has loved and adored me with all her heart and soul. It is so strange, this love of a mother to her child. It is so uncanny and mysterious – how can one center one's whole life on one person?

But that has been Mama's love for me for the past twenty-nine years. In this little bookish memoir of mine, I have typed some really difficult-to-digest words, sentences, and entire paragraphs about Mama's and my relationship. But you know something? I wouldn't exchange my mama for any other mother – not for a world of books will I have anyone take me away from my mama.

I have won a lot of gold, silver, and bronze medals for my writing in my seven years as a writer. But you can melt them all, and they wouldn't match the diamond that Mama is to me. And I bet Cohen realized this too. He realized it when his mother was taken from him. I have always known love only for Mama. I've been faithful, even if it causes some deep heartaches for other people.

And the best part about my life is that I don't have just one mama, I have five: David uncle, Mechu, Mama, Rita, and Blaise. My whole maternal family have tried hard to fill the void that my papa and his family's disdain for me created. You all are perfect, but alas, I haven't been perfect!

I'm not perfect, but I'm the best there is in my category – the category of reclusive writers and readers.

"Your father was not that bad a man," Blaise told me recently when I was in a huff about something. "He just didn't have the guts to bring up a daughter in his orthodox family. He felt they would kill you."

"They did kill me," I think to myself as I wipe my hot tears and smile. "They killed his daughter, but they couldn't kill my mama's little girl."

I owe more than my life to Mama. I owe everything that I am to Mama. To think that one day we will be separated makes me sick. For what else have I known except for being always with Mama?

"Mama," I coo to her during one of our cuddles. "I want to always be your child."

"And I always want to be your mama," she says, kissing me the way she used to kiss me when I was a baby. "I want to be only your mama."

"Forever?" I ask and rest my head on her lap.

She doesn't reply.

I fall asleep.

Lullabies echo in my soul,

Tears you've dried I've never cried again;
Some things cannot be taken or weaned,
Mama's prayers of love never end.

Mama and I have been best buddies since the time I was taught the first letter of the alphabet. Our love has been going strong for twenty-nine years straight, and we don't want anyone to spoil the bliss.

The Book of Genesis says that man should leave his mother and father and cling to his wife for eternity, or something like that. I've always detested that passage, for I've never wanted to leave Mama. Never-ever! She left the world she had built, for me; how can I ever think of leaving her?

Yes, some of us have been fortunate to have angels as mothers. If you, my dear reader, have had such a mother, then read Albert Cohen's book. You will have to keep the tissue box ready, for Cohen knows how to get the tears flowing. Those who are mothers or are to become mothers, do read this emotional book about the devotion of Cohen's simple mother to her hoity-toity son. Your son may one day act the way Cohen did, and then what will you do?

For those daughters like me who, if not for their mothers would be dead, illiterate, abandoned, abused, and/or tortured, do give your mother a kiss and read Cohen's book – and always be faithful to your mother because she stood against the narrow-mindedness of the whole world so she could give you a place in the broad expanse of her ever-doting heart.

As much as I love her, never will I fathom my mama's heart. If you feel the same way about your mother, then read this book. It's meant for you to have a little cry and then to remain indebted to the womb that bore you and the arms that carried and cared for you, and made sure you were one day fit enough to read the words penned in this book.

"Virat sir, your book made me cry," I say to Virat sir as I make a visit after reading *Book of My Mother*.

"Seriously, which book?" he asks, highly amused as he shuffles through books on the table.

"*Book of My Mother*," I reply.

"One of the Archipelago books?" he asks. I nod, and he says, "They have the best stuff."

"Yes, they do." I sit down on a cane stool and go through the books in the travel section. The evening is dark and the climate hot and sultry. A number of cats roam outside with their kittens. When I leave at closing time, I will find a mother cat cleaning one of her more docile girl kittens and stroke her loving head.

ESSAY 68

What We Talk About When We Talk about Rape by Sohaila Abdulali

I WAS DRINKING LEMON ICED TEA in the café at Kitab Khana in November 2018.

Blaise and I were talking about this book that I am currently writing. He was not sure it would do well, whereas I just wanted to write the memoir.

"I like to write memoirs," I said, in between ice-cold lemony sips. "But I have not really lived that long or done that much that needs to be penned down for posterity, unless it's my ravenous appetite for books."

"Hmmm ... maybe," Blaise said, not sure whether I was making the right decision. The café was overflowing with loads of Jain people eating vegetarian food and drinking cutting chai. I wrote in my diary as Blaise ordered another round of tea. That's when Deepak saw me as he came down the stairs from the first floor.

"Hi, Deepak!" I cried, waving in a quite excited way.

He waved back and indicated that he had something new.

"I'll just be a minute," I told Blaise and scooted off after Deepak.

We passed many elderly individuals and college students as we walked by the numerous books in the coffee-table and children's section. Above us, the portraits of some great and famous writers like Mahatma Gandhi, J. K. Rowling, Sarojini Naidu, Rabindranath Tagore, and W. Somerset Maugham watched our every movement. Deepak waded through the crowd while I waddled like a fat goose behind him.

"Madam, latest," he came to a stop and pointed to the desk. I looked in the direction he was pointing to.

What We Talk About When We Talk about Rape by Sohaila Abdulali.

The book had no image, just a deep sea-blue-green cover with fluorescent writing. The writer's name caught my attention.

"This is a book penned by a rape victim herself?" I asked Deepak.

"I don't know, madam," he said truthfully, "but it is selling well."

Jagat sir, Sanju sir, and Shailesh were at their busiest attending to a large number of patrons. Sandeep, on the other hand, was on a tall stool trying to get a book from a shelf above him.

I told Deepak to keep the book for me and went back to Blaise and our tea.

"I think a rape victim has written a book about rape," I said.

Blaise nodded demurely sipping his cutting "chai."

I bought the book and would read it in a week's time every night at bedtime. I was right. The author, Sohaila Abdulali, is a gang rape survivor and activist. She had penned this book as a way to tackle some of the mixed feelings, prejudices, and misconceptions that society has about rape.

The book was hard hitting, well researched, and an enlightening read. The next time we were at Kitab Khana, I thanked Deepak for giving me this book. It was a hard book to read. No, there was no gore in it, nothing to make me faint – but imagining myself in any one of the rape survivors' shoes made me uncomfortable. I was displeased with my reaction to the book. The book was well written and tackled a difficult topic, so how dare I feel disturbed reading about what over half the women in some countries and many others around the world face[1] – actual penetrative rape, sometimes gang rape. Maybe it was because it was written in such a casual way, without a vengeful spirit. Or because it had been written by a rape survivor who had not let her gang rape define the rest of her life.

For her, the rape was just a painful chapter in her life and not the whole book.

"Why are you reading such a book?" Mama asked when she saw me reading it while I waited for my next class to arrive. "Can't you read something uplifting?"

"Ironically, this book is uplifting," I said.

Mama rolled her eyes not believing me. I have a passion for reading serious books practically all the time.

"The book is about survivors taking control of their lives and their victories over their abusers," I said.

Still, Mama cautioned me. "I wouldn't like to read a book that triggers depressing thoughts within me."

I put a bookmark in the book as my eighth-grade students entered the room.

"But we as women live with this fright wherever we go and in whatever we do," I said, facing the touch screen opposite me. "We are always afraid."

As Mama shuts the main door before heading back to her tuition class, she says, "And the situation is getting worse year by year. Democracy and civilization have gifted women nothing but pain and fear."

I place the book on the study table purposely in view of my students, teenage boys and girls. Not one of them comments on the book, where normally they are always inquisitive about what I am reading. I tuck away the book on a side stool after some time and teach history on the LCD screen.

---

[1] UN Women, New York (website), Facts and figures: Ending violence against women. Link to article on page 382.

No one seems to want to talk about rape. Not even within families and between students and teachers. Is it that taboo a topic? Is it a rare occurrence that doesn't need our focus?

Like most of India's young adults, I came to know about Abdulali in 2012 because of the infamous gang rape of Nirbhaya in New Delhi. Nirbhaya was out with a male friend and boarded a bus full of males, one of whom was a minor. She was tortured and gang-raped on the bus, and a rod was pushed through her vagina damaging many of her organs. She succumbed to her injuries after many days of fierce battle between life and death.

She wanted to live. And why not?

During that time, an old article from a woman's magazine called *Manushi* started making the rounds on the social media sites. It was an article penned in 1983 by Sohaila Abdulali, then a seventeen-year-old and a gang rape survivor. Someone had dug up Abdulali's story and shared it with other internet users. I was so touched and inspired by Sohaila Abdulali's story back then that I, too, shared the article on my Facebook timeline. Little did I know the pain Abdulali went through when this article reappeared: the amount of explaining she had to endure because most people in her life at the time didn't know she was a gang rape survivor.

Social media had brought back terrible memories for her and her loved ones. But she ended up taking up the challenge of writing a book on the subject – a subject that hardly anyone, let alone a survivor, wants to talk about. This is amazing in itself. Because, as she says, talking about it means that the pain becomes less and awareness is created.

Talking about it makes the pain less and awareness about it stronger.

And yet, is my country ready to talk, ready to have a decent conversation or dialogue about such things? Or will we be told to "get over it," and that is the way our India will turn into another Syria!

I am coming to the end of my memoir and closer to the elections. Things are getting grim for women. Eve-teasing, molestation, and rape are at an all-time high, but the Powers that Be don't want to acknowledge our reality. The government of Maharashtra is busy constructing coastal roads and underground subways, while most of the Mumbai population lives below the poverty line. Our women are losing their security and their voices, but no one cares. Those in power are just out to grab some seats in Parliament.

While reading this book, I remembered how I took my eve-teaser to the police station a few years ago. Would I be able to do that these days? Absolutely not, because here in Mumbai currently, the "eye for an eye" policy is the best policy. I can't afford to fight against an eve-teaser or someone ragging me about my body type. So I have decided to keep out of trouble – and that means keeping away from society.

But Abdulali asks us as women not to cow down before rapists.

We need to create awareness about rape; we need to talk about it. Other topics that are discussed in the book include the idea of one rape being not as bad as another, rape and sexual assault across many genders, feminists on rape, government posts being held by sexual abusers which psychologically disturb rape survivors, love, friendship, trust, and horror.

Please read this book. For those who are victims of such crimes, it is comforting to know that you are not alone. Read this book to learn the truth: that rape doesn't define you and that it doesn't deserve to control your life.

I felt terrible about sharing the *Manushi* news report after I read this book. But then again, the story of Abdulali did change me and the way I perceived rape and the "culture of rape."

As I take further steps toward my own complete seclusion, Sohaila Abdulali's book will always be by my side, and I will dip into it every time I want to get into the mind and soul of the writer and the survivors of one of the most despicable crimes leveled against women. But, yes, Abdulali is a survivor and through her prose she presents other rape victims as survivors too. Read this book, and share her message: It's not the end of the world when you are raped, sexually assaulted, or eve-teased. Life goes on. The pain lingers, but life goes on. Change the system, get justice, and change your attitude toward the thing that impales you to the floor with spikes.

Read this book to grow stronger. Read this book to know many have suffered. Read this book to know that "if not for Providence there go I."

"Need anything more, madam?" Shailesh, my brother, asks me as I come to the counter of Kitab Khana to pay the bill.

"Nothing more, Shailesh," I say. I'm dressed in a black long-sleeved cotton kurta and thick black pants with a long charcoal black nylon silk scarf around my neck.

Black is my color. Black is a happy color. Black is the color of ink.

Mama sees me trying to put the scarf over my head.

She shudders. Later she will tell me why: For in that moment, I look so much like one of her sisters-in-law. Blaise, too, looks away. But to tell you the truth, I've never felt more comfortable. I feel like it's always meant to be this way. So strange and so odious.

Some of the Kitab Khana team look. But before they can comment, I drop the scarf back around my neck like a long stole.

As we drive back home in the evening in Narayan's taxi, I recall a lecture on rape by my sociology professor in college. He said that even if a woman walks stark naked down the road, if she doesn't give her consent, you can't touch her. That is what differentiates us from the animal kingdom.

We return home. I get out of the taxi first to meet my cats, especially Trotskyna.

I find her hiding under my bedroom AC ventilator. She is petrified, and her fur is dirty.

There are six tom cats outside the ventilator waiting for her. She is terribly exhausted and hungry. Then one of them, the eldest called Golem, drags her out of the ventilator, tearing at her furry coat and dragging her under a neighbor's red car. Band and the other four cats follow him.

I move to stop them but Mama calls me in with a warning.

"The males won't listen to your call now," Mama cautions me. "They are frustrated as there are hardly any female cats in the locality. Soon two more will come along as well. Don't get bitten. Their sharp teeth can inject hard-to-treat bacteria deeply into the skin and joints, increasing the risk of serious infection."

I obey her and go in.

Trotskyna cries for me all night.

ESSAY 69

The Road and Rahul

BLAISE USED TO TELL ME that he mostly shopped for his books at a very unusual place when he was studying law and working at the Bank of India in his twenties.

"The footpath," he declared to me as we sat in the hall after he came back from work in 2013, "There are people selling books on the footpath as if they were selling toys at a fête. Back in my time there were hundreds of them at Fort. Now there are only a few near Flora Fountain close to Kitab Khana."

I was fascinated. I wanted to try buying from the footpath.

This was just after I had left my job at a regular ICSE school where I taught English and history. We drove with Narayan to the "footpath bookshop" and Blaise, Narayan, and I got out.

There were stacks of books on the footpath near a stinking gutter. There were people browsing under the heat of the hot summer's sun. The road book sellers looked scary. They stared at us as if they were going to hound us.

"So, what do we do? Browse?" I asked Blaise in a frightened whisper.

"Er, let's go over to the good-looking guy with a smile," said Blaise, pointing to a young man a few steps away from us. "He seems friendly enough."

"We still have time to go back home," said Narayan.

We glared at him and gestured for him to follow. Trust Narayan to chicken out when the going gets tough. The good-looking bookseller had had his eyes on us the moment we parked nearby the road.

As we neared, he got off his stool and asked amiably, "Madam, what do you want?"

"Er," I stuttered, "how about some books on history or literature?"

The young man nodded and went to the back of his mound of books. He came back moments later with the most incredible books I had ever seen:

- ✓ Old fiction novels from the nineteenth century
- ✓ Old fiction books from the early twentieth century
- ✓ A series of books of the writings of Indian nationalists
- ✓ Letters of various writers like Tagore, Tolstoy, and Kingsley Amis
- ✓ *The Outline of History* by H. G. Wells
- ✓ A detailed foreign biography of Sant Kabir
- ✓ Julius Caesar's complete writings in a leather-bound cover
- ✓ Treatises on Islamic history ...

You name it, he had it – and at dirt-cheap prices.

He stood pridefully over the erudite collection he had presented to us. "Say what you want and I'll give you a bargainable price."

I held H. G. Wells's *The Outline of History* to my heart, which was beating very fast. At that gesture he nodded and went a bit deeper into his treasure trove and came back with an H. G. Wells omnibus as well as a paperback of his rare writings.

I took them one by one.

"Say," he said with immense satisfaction, "Isaac Asimov? Ray Bradbury? Their letters? Their biographies? Their personal correspondence? How about the history of science fiction? How about the history of science itself? Psychology? Are you interested in psychology too? Say, madamji, say!"

At this point I was absolutely confounded and near fainting. "What is your name?" I asked him.

He smiled a very handsome smile.

"Rahul," he said. "You can call me Rahul."

And that was it. With knowing Rahul, I came to know how to get the things I wanted at bargain prices. He introduced me to the other footpath booksellers, some barely literate like him but who knew what we bibliophiles wanted, inside out.

From then on, I made bimonthly visits to the footpath booksellers to get something new and not-so-new. I was always greeted pleasantly, especially by young, dashing, and charming Rahul. He knew his business. He had learned my tastes.

"Today, what will you want, say," he greeted me as I descended the taxi with Narayan. "Say, just say and I will get the best for you."

I wish I had more males asking me this question. Then maybe I would have been married by now!

"How about the old published books of Ruskin Bond?" I ask as I browse the books on display. "And then you can get me an old collection of short stories and maybe something on alchemy?"

"Done." He goes rummaging behind. His assistant gets me a stool to sit on and another for the books. Rahul comes back with stacks of books, some of which I select and some of which I keep for another time.

"*Chai peeyegi*, madam?" he asks. It's very gentlemanly of him, but I say no though I'm dying for one. I say no when I'm with Blaise. But when I am alone with only Narayan, who is very lenient with me, I always take chai. Rahul knows this and appreciates it.

I spend long hours scanning through books as Rahul and the other footpath booksellers lay them one by one on my stool. Whenever I stop by, Rahul calls out that, "Madamji has arrived," and immediately I'm a celebrity of sorts. Pedestrians watch with wonder and awe as stools and chai, and sometimes even umbrellas are produced to keep either the hot sun or rain off me.

Rahul is my main man, the one I am loyal to. His is the only area where I can sit comfortably, knowing I'll get the best service not only from him but from all of the booksellers in that area.

Blaise is plain suspicious of Rahul. Mama finds him cute.

"If only he was educated, I would have happily strung him like a garland around your neck," Mama said once as a joke. "He is so devoted to you. His face lights up whenever he gets a glimpse of Narayan's taxi."

"Or her purse," says Blaise with a huff, and I tweak my nose with false pride.

Blaise is overprotective. The footpath booksellers are swell friends, and Rahul is the best of them. Blaise buys good books from them too. Rahul and the footpath bookseller gang have been there to help out whenever we have been in dire need of a specific book.

I remember one incident very clearly. I was researching for one of my magnum opuses (yes, I have many) and I needed to study pornographic literature. Who came to the rescue but good old Rahul?

Blaise didn't allow me to get out of the taxi for this bargain. I was to be in the taxi and the books would be handed to me one by one by Narayan – erotica books and porn books, that is.

I was feeling so ridiculous but they made me comply. Rahul was most amused with my odd selection. Blaise kept on saying the whole thing was for research but Rahul kept a dignified silence as he handed one erotica book after another. I selected quite a few, and we headed back home.

"The things you make some of us do," Blaise scolded me in the taxi as he wiped the grime of the road off his hands. "That Rahul fellow will not be forgetting this in a hurry."

"It's just erotica," I said, exasperated with all the nonsense. "Why can't I buy my own erotica books?"

"Because you are a good girl, and good girls don't read erotica!" Blaise declared.

I face-palmed and Narayan, shaken by all those female nudes on the covers, said nothing the whole way back home.

But when I went back next month to Rahul, things were as usual. The stools came out, chai was offered, and Rahul stood there with a winsome smile that has not once been a leer in the past six years. "Say, madamji, what books would you like to read and buy today?" he says.

"How about al-Qaeda's history?" I ask as I sit down and place a book called *The Bin Ladens* by Steve Coll on my lap. "Or the Taliban or any other Islamic extremist group?"

He laughs an innocent laugh.

"You've got some strange taste in books, madamji," he says. "But I like girls who read. They use their brains and then make our Mumbai better. The others –"

He leaves off on that and goes back to his stack of books in the inner portion of the entire horde of books. He comes back with at least thirty books on the al-Qaeda. I pick what I need, and he shows me some books about the rise of Jihad culture, the Taliban, and the history of the Kashmir issue. The last one is a rare edition bound in red leather.

From the conversations I've had with him, I know that Rahul is not educated but has taught himself to read in order to identify the title of books which he sells. However, he knows how to calculate the price of my purchases using Vedic mathematics. He flips through the books when he is not working and researches them as well for better customer service.

Rahul is fun-loving but an absolute businessman. He may not have a license to sell his books, but that doesn't stop him. He has been providing me some of the best books I've ever read, right there on the footpath near the open gutter with towering buildings of colonial India flanking us.

I've sat down and shared a cup of chai with him. I've seen him work with the other footpath booksellers. I've seen his two pets, two stray puppies who adore him and are most comfortable in the company of books and book lovers. They are as lively as their master. They are full of spirit.

Sometimes Rahul takes me into the inner part of the seven-foot-tall book mound. That's where all of the best and rarest of books can be found, saved for a genuine book connoisseur, not for a crazy book lady like me. I've had loads of fun rummaging through these books and working my way to the heart of the mound.

"Feels great doesn't it?" he asks me as he takes my hand to bring me to the center of this huge igloo of books.

"Feels like heaven," I say twirling around like an obese ballerina. "I smell books."

"Say," he questions me, placing his strong hands on his narrow hips, "which books do you want from here?"

That day, I select a variety of books on literature. The sun sets and smartphone torch lights are switched on in the road of Flora Fountain as Rahul, using Vedic mathematical skills of addition, totals up the bill. I am happy that once again Rahul and the footpath booksellers of Fort area have provided me the books I desired.

I thought that nothing could change that.

I was wrong.

In 2014, things started to change.

Rahul was given a notice to move the pile of books away from the curb. He was also asked to cut down the number of books in the mound to a great extent. I remember the day the authorities destroyed the mound of precious-precious books. They scattered them across the road. Rahul was not smiling that day. He was a broken young man, living in a world that didn't understand the service he was providing to his customers.

"What happened?" I asked him as I got out of Narayan's taxi and came running toward the strewn books and a very heartbroken Rahul. He laughed to himself as tears welled up in his honey-brown eyes. Blaise and Narayan tried to help, gathering some of the scattered books.

"What happened?" I implored him to tell me.

Through a choked voice, all he said was, "Say. What can I get you today?"

He was chivalrous. He wiped his tears and got the books I'd asked for.

I was numb.

The e-book avalanche hit the road booksellers of Mumbai Fort area the same way it did the other bookstores. Rahul still sells books with the others on the road, but he doesn't get as many buyers as he used to. Everyone finds it easier to buy and read a Kindle book than go through the trouble of rummaging books on the road.

But the road booksellers still have their regulars. And I am one of the regulars.

I'll never give up on the road booksellers. They have been loyal to me, and I never ditch anyone who has given me good books to read.

I love browsing, looking at one mound and then another. The road booksellers know I will pay good money, so they trust me with their secrets: I've been given the rarest of rare books, some of them banned in Mumbai, as well as in the whole of the Indian subcontinent. I have earned a name for myself – the good madamji, the Pathan.

Strange that they call me that. I don't remember telling Rahul my name, let alone my surname. But when he and the other road booksellers look at me, there is warmth and genuine happiness in their tired eyes. Tired because they have been trying to sell books all day in the heat of the tropical Mumbai sun. Tired because they haven't had a bite all day. Tired because people have started becoming indifferent to books, reading, and everything bookish in general. Tired because sometimes they have to present the customer with a great number of their books, yet the person goes away without purchasing a single book, and then they have to put them all back again. Tired because they can see, with their own eyes, a one-time prosperous book-selling business burning to the ground.

"What do you want, daughter?" asks one of them, exhausted after the ranting of an irate customer. I tell him to relax, have a bite to eat or take chai but he insists, "No, daughter. Tell me, what do you want?"

I answer feebly, "World War Two books, fiction and nonfiction, as well as anything new."

He nods and climbs up a pile of many books to the topmost part of the eight-foot mound. I can't bear to look, he is so tired that he is bound to fall, but ...

"Here, daughter," he says handing me a leather-bound series. It's a first edition and a biography of Winston Churchill. "Just come from an old Parsi gentleman's library. He loved to read foreign books."

Most of the books on the road have been sold to the booksellers from the vast libraries of various bibliophiles, dead or alive, who don't need them anymore.

"Would-would you," the road bookseller has been exerting himself in an effort to find the books I want and now he is panting. "Daughter, would you also like to buy these?"

I look at what he has. I balk.

The Unabridged Writings of Imam Khomeini by the University of Iran.

"Daughter," he asks out of breath. "Would you like these?"

He sells them at a ridiculously low price and won't take more.

"At least you read, daughter," he says as Narayan helps him place his books back. "Your father is blest to have such a learned daughter."

As he says this, he points in the distance to Blaise, who is in serious conversation with Rahul over business. I shake my head.

"He is not my father," I say, "he's my godfather."

"Where is your father, daughter?"

"He abandoned me when I was baby because I was a girl."

I look down at the pavement. He does as well. We stay quiet for a while.

"What would I not give to have a daughter like you!" he says wiping the sweat with his sleeve smelling of the open drain. "I would have given you all the books in the city."

"You have no children?" I ask him softly, like I am eight years old again. He looks away, anger is written all over his face.

"I only have a son; I wish I had a daughter."

I buy more books and then move on to the next mound. As I walk down the road of books, I meditate on the statue of the seated Dadabai Naoroji, a moderate freedom fighter of our country and an integral part of the Congress Party in India. He sits on his chair with a soft touch to his features while all around him, the road booksellers sell their books.

Some of the road booksellers flock to the Ashish Book Fairs whenever they are held at Churchgate. I've seen many elderly gentlemen pouring over the coffee-table books and paying great sums to get them for their customers on the road. Customers like little old bookish me.

I once observed an elderly Muslim gentleman with a bent back going through some rare books from Princeton University. The books were on Islam. He was the quietest man at the book fair, but he had a wallet full of bank notes. The Ashish team had to pack the books in two boxes.

That was in 2006. At that time, I vowed that one day I would earn enough money to buy as many books as he had at one go. At the last Ashish book fair, I took home four boxes. I hope to do the same if not better for the rest of my days.

"Say, madamji, when are we going to see you next?" asks Rahul last month when I went to the road.

I look back from the open door of the taxi and laugh.

"Not so soon this time. I'll be busy writing a book."

"About what?" he asks skeptically. Perhaps Rahul doesn't trust my writing capabilities. Neither do I.

"I'm writing a book about bookstores and libraries," I answer.

"Hey, and what about all of us?" Rahul raises his hands in the air. "Don't we mean anything to you?"

He folds his sinewy arms, showing off his bulging muscles derived from lifting all of those mounds of books.

"Yes, you all will be in it too."

"Don't lie!"

"I'm serious," I say.

Rahul rolls his eyes. "I'll believe it when I see it."

Then I take my leave.

"Now where?" Narayan asks me as I close the taxi door.

I sigh.

"Now home, Narayan."

He starts the taxi, and we zoom past the long line of road booksellers, still bargaining, still serving.

ESSAY 70

My Office-cum-Writing Hut

IT WAS THE YEAR 2016 when I incorporated my publishing firm, Fiza Pathan Publishing (OPC) Private Limited.

It all happened so quickly. I never knew just how time flew by. By June 2016, I was on the lookout for an office to store my publishing firm's books. It was then that the tailor who rented a well-kept shanty just a few steps away from my kitchen window in the Wadi was leaving the place for better prospects. My trusty electrician and well-wisher, Ashok Sawant, asked me if I was interested. The property belonged to the Jadhavs, and if I was interested the owners would allow me to rent the place.

I was ecstatic. Blaise was not so sure. Mama was not liking the idea at all. Rita was most bothered about the coconut tree growing in the middle of the shanty. Mechu was optimistic but asked me to check it out. David uncle, the wisest among us, said only these words: "Close to home."

And David uncle won.

I started renting the place. It is 250 square feet, and it struck me that this could be the place I've been looking for all through my twenties, a place where I could write peacefully. Blaise and the rest agreed with me.

Everyone in the Wadi was most excited. They had not seen me that often and didn't know of my business credentials. We began to plan the layout of the shanty, which we had taken to calling "the office." With the help of Ashok uncle, Jadhav uncle, Jadhav's elder brother who owned this property, Narayan, Blaise, and a whole lot of other people, we designed a place in which not only books would be stored but where I could write and read, as well as conduct my business.

For those of you who think that things like this don't happen in a hurry in Mumbai, I say, you don't know what kind of a person I am. It took only a few weeks to set it all up. By September, I was at work in the office-cum-writing hut of Fiza Pathan, which I have been talking about all the way through this book. These very lines are being typed in this office-cum-writing hut, which has been my refuge since 2016. The most peaceful place, the place where my books are.

So, we got working. We divided the place with a partition wall. One side was for storing books with an office table and chairs for business. In that area Blaise or my co-author and colleague, Michaelangelo Zane, works. There are steel bookshelves and racks on the wall where our consignments are at the ready. There is also a watercooler for preparing instant coffee or tea while we are busy at work. Michaelangelo Zane loves coffee and so do I, but I prefer black Earl Grey tea while writing. Blaise doesn't like to take any beverage here. He goes back home where Rita prepares hot regular Nescafé or Tata tea with a lot of milk and sugar for him.

In that area, there is a place where we keep our mops and brooms as well as a cupboard for our teacups and coffee mugs. The room these days is stacked with many consignments as well as our own private book collections in various boxes – Michaelangelo's, Blaise's, and mine.

On the other side of the office is my haven. The place where I spend my days and nights typing, writing, and reading when school is out for the holidays. I've paid a lot of attention to this area because, for once in my life, I wanted to create a working place for myself with my tastes for curiosities, plants, bric-a-brac, flowers, reed diffusers, and of course BOOKS all around me to put me into the writing mood.

It took only a week or so to get it all done. We bought steel racks installed them all around this area. The men fixed the bookshelves themselves and watched in awe as Blaise, Narayan, Michaelangelo, and I started placing books on the shelves, a sample of my humble and modest collection.

I then brought some old and new curios and set them up on the sturdy bookshelves as well.

Believe it or not, there is a real coconut tree growing from the floor to the roof above in the office. Around that coconut tree, I have made a sort of temple to nature and the religious people and enlightened masters who have influenced me. I used to grow areca palms, white balsam, green indoor money plants, yellow-green money plants, china grass, ribbon grass, cacti, yellow-green schefflera, and so much else. I placed in this very green garden the statues of the orange-clad Mira Bai with her Veena, who perpetually waits for the coming of her Lord, the Hindu God Sri Krishna. Next to her, a few centimeters away, is the statue of a black Buddha under a wooden Bodhi tree, the tree where he attained enlightenment.

Damiyanti, our maid, used to look after the plants on weekends while I watered and trimmed the plants, and checked the soil, on weekdays. The day Damiyanti met with an accident and became homebound, I had to bring the plants and cacti out to my main garden as I could not afford to care for them as well as she did with my heavy workload. They now are growing well in the garden outside of my home.

These days, imitation plants and flowers are kept where originals used to be. Since they are imitation, I also keep some books piled up there; it makes the area look very attractive. The imitation plants look so real that people cannot tell the difference.

"Is that real, *kya*?" one delivery boy asks another when they arrive with our consignments.

"*Pata nahi bhai*?" says the other, equally confused. "But this madam seems to have a heck of a lot of books."

"She is making a library, *kya*?" the other asks as Blaise hands them a generous tip. "So many books can't be just for one person, can they?"

Blaise, Narayan, and I laugh sneakily, and they are off, a day's work done well.

I am very fond of curios and curiosities. But since we live in a small 1BKH, I never ever had a chance to create a space of my own. With this place, I managed to create a writing hut full of wondrous stuff that inspire me whenever I am searching for a story to type.

These are a few of my little curios:

- A stone bust of William Shakespeare
- A plaster of Paris statue of an angel presenting me a book
- Plaster of Paris and rubber curios of Tintin, Captain Haddock, Professor Calculus, the Thompson twins, Snowy the dog, Nestor the butler, and Senora Castafiore with a pet parrot in her hand
- Plaster of Paris and rubber curios of Asterix, Obelix with his menhir, Getafix with his pot of magic potion, Dogmatix with a bone in his mouth, and Cacofonix ready to strum a tune on his harp
- A statue of pigeons with a nest of yellow eggs in a peepal tree
- A set of dogs, some with blue backpacks on their backs
- A marble statue of an angel reading a book
- A bust of Shivaji Maharaj
- A statue of Swami Vivekananda
- A cobbler of India at his work
- A vegetable seller in a poor cloth saree
- An Indian umbrella man mending an old black umbrella
- A red transparent bowl of fake red chrysanthemums
- A statue of Jesus Christ meditating in a cross-legged position
- A statue of an angelic girl strumming a guitar

- A globe showing the political world
- A 1956 Olympia typewriter that can still type
- A statue of a young mother with her infant on her lap
- A ship in a glass bottle
- A gold-plated Feng Shui relic and a lot of other wondrous curiosities that mean a lot to me

They look wonderful, and I have placed them all in their appropriate positions with the help of Narayan, our Man Friday. We have floor-to-ceiling bookshelves, which are a dream come true; a dream I have had ever since I walked into the BSS library under the care of Mrs. Ratnaswami and Aruna.

I have not left any open wall space. Every nook and cranny I've filled with books on bookshelves and racks made of steel. On the walls upon which I could not hang shelves for one reason or another, I've hung pictures of St. Francis of Assisi and other themes. The entrance to the office is guarded by an altar to the Sacred Heart of Jesus and the Immaculate Heart of Mary.

There is a fountain of St. Francis of Assisi, flowing water creating the sound of a running brook that is peaceful and calming.

"It's Fiza's miracle fountain," Blaise tells Ratan uncle when he comes for a visit. "The statue at the center sucks up water from below."

"You mean osmosis?" asks the ever practical Ratan uncle.

Blaise nods and they look around inspecting the books.

It was Fr. Bento, our dearest Fr. Bento, who blessed and who every year blesses the office for us with a prayer and holy water.

"Lord," he prays in his anglicized bass voice, "your Word is worshipped here. Bless our dear daughter Fiza who has made this place a home to your Word and to her favorite saint, the saint who has stood by her through it all, St. Francis of Assisi."

Yes, this place in my temple devoted to "The Word" and to the only God I love without strings attached, St. Francis of Assisi, my Francesco. He was with me when I was a toddler and has remained my favorite version of God.

"I want a statue," I told Mehmood from St. Paul's in 2016, "of St. Francis of Assisi."

"For a church," asked Mehmood.

"You could say that," I answered, and he booked a statue for me three feet high.

That statue was blessed with holy water by Fr. Bento Cardozo. It is Francesco with his birds, arms stretched open, and I've placed this statue, this homage to the only God I have in the middle of all the books racks overflowing with books, books, and more BOOKS!

I sit by him as I write on a small, round wooden table in a comfortable armchair. When I've finished the work for the day, I sit on a recliner beside Francesco and read my many books or my Kindle. I have collected many statues of St. Francis of Assisi, but this one is my favorite. Whenever I enter the office, the first thing I do is run into this statue's arms and kiss him on his lips.

He will be the only man I will ever kiss, forever.

"Don't kiss him," Blaise once told me in the beginning. "He is divine."

I laughed.

"What's the use of a God who doesn't like to kiss his lover? And besides," I say in a naughty tone, "he is a great kisser."

Blaise shakes his head in disbelief. I give Francesco another warm kiss – warm as the blood in my veins that only yearns for His "Word."

There is one last section in the office. It's placed near the divider. It starts with a rack of bookshelves, but instead of books, this time, they are full of some of my award certificates and medals. Above them are five framed pictures of the writers that have had the greatest influence in my life. From left to right: Ruskin Bond (the writer from the Hills), Dr. B. R. Ambedkar (Babasaheb), R. K. Narayan (The Grand Old Man of Malgudi), Munshi Premchand (the reason I love Hindi literature), and lastly William Shakespeare (who gives me my bread and butter as I teach his plays to students at my tutorial). Next to it is the stand of our LOGO – Freedom With Pluralism – along with "Chota Shanbaug," the smallest bookshelf I bought from the

Strand bookstore on which I've displayed all the books I've printed and published in the past seven years.

All of this put together is what I call my office-cum-writing hut.

I don't have a yellow door like Roald Dahl had in his place of writing, but it has a white door with my name etched in a gold plate outside – Fiza Pathan, Director of Fiza Pathan Publishing (OPC) Private Limited.

I have bolted all the windows. I cannot see the outside world at all as I work in this little modest kingdom of my own ... my office-cum-writing hut.

ESSAY 71

My Office-cum-Writing Hut 2

I LEAD A VERY QUIET LIFE IN THE bustling city of Mumbai, the city that never sleeps.

I drink my BRU Gold lukewarm coffee late in the day and then, with laptop bag on my shoulder, walk to my office-cum-writing hut to get to work.

There, I write or type until it's time to teach a class. I leave some of my things behind if I know I'll be able to come back later and continue to type or write.

I am a writer who works whenever I get time to do so. I have discipline, a working pattern, and I don't make a fuss about things. I can't understand these writers who make excuses about not being able to write for the following reasons:

- Not in the mood
- The setting is not right
- The muse is not with them
- They are experiencing writer's block
- They can't just write at any time
- They can only work at a particular time
- They need a certain environment

All of these things make me laugh out loud because I have such a hectic job that whenever I get even one hour to write anytime, day or night, I go without a fuss to my office-cum-writing hut and do it! I don't have the luxury to make the above excuses. I have a very-very-very tight schedule. My muse is St. Francis of Assisi, or Francesco, and I just touch his feet before starting or kiss him or give him a quick hug, and then it's on to work.

I have typed and written most of my work after September 2016 here in this office-cum-writing hut. If given a chance, I would live here but Mama will kill me if I think of doing so – she'll miss me and my silly bookishness.

This place is heaven. I could spend the rest of my life locked up here with food and water being delivered to me via a special flap door!

"You are like one of those old eighteenth- or nineteenth-century writers," Blaise says to me over coffee. Mama's there too with us. It's the weekend. "The ones who spent hours in cold garrets writing away."

I muse over that idea as I blow over my hot coffee drink.

Blaise finishes his coffee and sets the mug down. He asks, "What are you planning on doing next?"

"Seclusion," I say.

"What?"

"Seclusion," I repeat as my mama wets her dry lips anxiously. "I want to cut myself off from society and social life. I want to spend every waking hour at my work teaching, writing, and reading. If I go out, it will only be to bookstores, libraries, or book haunts for business purposes or to buy more books. Otherwise I don't wish to get out of either my house or my office-cum-writing hut forever."

"No!" Mama screams.

Blaise looks at me with a glazed expression. He asks totally shocked and pained, "Why are you doing this to yourself? You are only twenty-nine."

"I've seen enough of life and I don't want to have to do anything with it. Besides," I say with an impish grin, "life seems better when it's written down in a book."

"That's enough!" Mama rises to her feet. "I don't want you to do this."

"I have been doing this for as long as I can remember," I answer.

They think it over. They look at each other. They know I'm right.

"You really don't have any friends, Fiza?" Mama asks, astonished. "Someone who you can trust and go out with or ..."

"I have no friends, Mama," I say flatly. "And now I love books so much that I don't need humans. Humans are boring; books are much better."

"What about us?" Mama asks, looking frantically at Blaise and then me. "Where do we stand?"

I look at her tenderly.

"Mama, you all along with our Parsi friends, Michaelangelo Zane and Fr. Bento, are the only ones who I care for. To you all I'll be a daughter. To you I will allow myself to open up. Otherwise the world is a showroom full of everything I don't need."

The world has rejected me,
Only Francesco and his "Word" has accepted me.
The open wound feels better with this biblio balm,
Otherwise everyone has dug into its deep palm.

I then finish off my coffee and go to brush my teeth. Mama and Blaise sit still. Pensive.

Yes, I have begun my life of seclusion. I'm more than happy here in my home, the tuition house, and the office-cum-writing hut.

Especially in my office-cum-writing hut.

I can write or type here for hours on end. I've often typed here for eight hours at a stretch, one thousand words per hour on my Dell Inspiron 11. If I write with ballpoint pen in a spiral-bound notebook, then it is two thousand words per hour.

When I'm tired because of the continuous typing or writing, I get up and walk around the writing hut. I browse through my books, set some aside for later reading. Arrange some here and place something correctly there, while the Francesco fountain fills the bookish atmosphere of the place with the sound of running water.

Most of my Ashish books are here on the bookshelves, along with books from Kitab Khana, Wayword & Wise, Trilogy, Title Waves, Granth, the roadside books, Strand ... but mostly Ashish books.

My cats come to visit me often here in this office-cum-writing hut. Lopez likes to play "catch me if you can" while Trotskyna just loves the chilled AC atmosphere. I have two ACs in this office. I like to live in a chilled atmosphere of around 18 degrees Celsius coming from two powerful air conditioners.

I write in my diaries here. There is one diary that I will leave to the boy I loved and still love from school. It's all that I wish to say to him but can't in this life. There are other diaries for some other people who have tried to pry open the lock of my soul, a cupboard full of the rarest books, but I've never given them the key. All they will have from me is my writings to them, that is if they wish to read them.

Here is a list of some of the books on my shelves, which I'm typing randomly here. Have you read any of them?

- *The Golden Treasury* by Francis Palgrave
- *London* by Edward Rutherfurd
- *My Brilliant Career* by Miles Franklin
- *Sinister Street* by Compton Mackenzie
- *The Visitors* by Mary McMinnies
- *The Angel in the Corner* by Monica Dickens
- *That's Fourpence You're Eating! A Childhood in Perth* by Frances Rimington
- *Melissa* by Taylor Caldwell
- *Letter from a Stranger* by Barbara Taylor Bradford
- *Flowers for the Judge* by Margery Allingham
- *The Egoist* by George Meredith
- *Across Five Aprils* by Irene Hunt

- *The Classic Slum* by Robert Roberts
- *A Story About One Big Family* by Pavel Beilin

These are one of the many reasons why I am going into seclusion. These I have read and hope to read once again.

Here is yet another list of the books on another rack; do these ring a bell?

- *Ulysses* by James Joyce
- *A Group of Noble Dames* by Thomas Hardy
- *Gandhi: Naked Ambition* by Jad Adams
- *Nine Lives* by William Dalrymple
- *The Fun Stuff* by James Wood
- *The Raj at War* by Yasmin Khan
- *Girl in Translation* by Jean Kwok
- *Noonday* by Pat Barker
- *Queer* by William S. Burroughs
- *Silk* by Alessandro Baricco
- *Sex Is Forbidden* by Tim Parks
- *Death by Water* by Kenzaburō Ōe
- *Hell's Angels* by Hunter S. Thompson
- *My Life with the Taliban* by Abdul Salam Zaeef

These might have been a bit more familiar to an Indian reader, I'm sure.

No, I'm not going to list anymore because once I did this and somebody wanted to come over and check the titles out themselves when I actually don't want to see anyone evermore – keep out of my office-cum-writing hut!

I'm done with society. I'm done with people. I'm done with body shaming and the whole lot of people who say they wish to talk to me but only land up talking on and on about themselves.

I'm going to teach my students but remain elusive totally. If I'm not teaching then here will I be, in this writing hut. In fact, whenever Mama says that "Fiza miss" is busy or gone out most of the time means that I'm holed up in here typing like crazy.

Yes, I won't stop writing or publishing, but I want to be as "hard to get" as possible. I'll be active on social media, because it's one of the ways indie authors sell their books. I can't stop that, or I'll go broke!

It's just this thing called life. It's failed me. People have failed to live up to the expectations they have of themselves, let alone my expectations of them. People talk too much, and everything what they say is said in a book, so why even bother to "catch up" with anybody. We are not going to be very truthful with one another – we won't show our coffee mug stains on the pages of our past or present.

That's why I like it here, in my office-cum-writing hut. I can be myself and, frankly, I have got enough books in here to last me till World War III and after that even, not to mention my until now, faithful Kindle and electricity supply.

When I am alone here, I pray to Francesco. Maybe in another plane of existence I would have been a Franciscan nun. Maybe I would not have gone through the hurting years where I lost my vocation ... Or maybe I haven't lost my vocation?

I pray to Francesco to keep me reading all my life. To allow me to help my family out. To be able to be faithful evermore to His "Word." And I feel that when I am here, I can do it all. This is my place of power. Yet it's not my power, I can tell you that, it's the power of the books. ... They live ... they are alive ... they live in me.

Whenever I'm in a tough situation, I look up at my five writer mentors: the five men who have shaped my bookish life in more ways than one.

Otherwise, especially when I'm free, I open my recliner, get it next to Francesco, get a bottle of water or a cup of Earl Grey tea and it's reading time all over again – like it was in the beginning, is now and ever shall be, books without end – Amen!

Mama doesn't think I am wise to go into seclusion. But she accepts that I am a much happier person when I am there.

"Your father would not have understood you," Rita tells me during one of our gossip sessions. "Because you are so many people in just one person, that it is tough to see what is really going on in your mind, heart and soul."

Ready for some more books from my shelves here? Let's have another go:

- *A Hero of Our Time* by Mikhail Lermontov
- *A Million Little Pieces* by James Frey
- "Red Wind" by Raymond Chandler (short story)
- *Red Earth and Pouring Rain* by Vikram Chandra
- *Ivanhoe* by Sir Walter Scott
- *Long Walk to Freedom* by Nelson Mandela
- *The Tiger in the Smoke* by Margery Allingham
- *A Kestrel for a Knave* by Barry Hines
- *Ziska* by Marie Corelli
- *Nightmare Abbey* by Thomas Love Peacock
- *Ho Chi Minh: A Life* by William J. Duiker
- *Lucky* by Alice Sebold

I read for hours if possible, here, in my little heaven, just like I used to do many years ago in the BSS library. I can still hear Aruna's dusting and Mrs. Ratnaswami scolding a child for being late in returning a book. My papa was there then, and now where he is, I hardly know. Yesterday has turned a page and tomorrow seems grim by the looks of what is happening in the world. My real papa is deluded. Mama is getting old. The summers are getting hotter and yet, if there is bliss, it is this.

Sometimes Michaelangelo Zane sits here and writes or types. He is a silent fellow and a workaholic. He doesn't speak much. Reads a lot. And he loves to smoke and drink, which he can't do when he's here in the office. He chooses Nescafé instant coffee instead and smokes outside Tertullian Road.

There are dictionaries and thesauruses galore here, so I am never short of words to write. Yet, I'm only vocal when I write or teach. Otherwise I'm silent as Nana's grave in St. Francis of Assisi Church. I feel after every book I type or read, that I've lived many lives in this body. A body that others look down upon because it is obese. This obesity has given me a pulmonary disease – I'm always short of breath. But when writing, I'm never been short of words, stories, and new conceptualizations. My imagination hasn't failed me yet, and it works very well in this writing hut, with the smell of lavender wafting in the air thanks to my reed diffuser.

I've been to so many bookstores and libraries in my search for a home to write in. It is ironic that at the end of it all I had to look no further than eight steps from my home to this place ... and yet, for those steps to be taken took over twenty-nine years. Twenty-nine very long years!

Ready, one last time? This time you'll remember:

- *Ayn Rand and the World She Made* by Anne. C. Heller
- *The Children of Men* by P. D. James
- *Black Like Me* by John Howard Griffin
- *The World Set Free* by H. G. Wells
- *The Red Badge of Courage* by Stephen Crane
- *Headbirths, or, the Germans are Dying Out* by Gunter Grass
- *If This Is a Man* by Primo Levi
- *She* by H. Rider Haggard
- "The Gold Bug" by Edgar Allan Poe (short story)
- *Kim* by Rudyard Kipling

Blaise tells me my office time is over. It's over before it even began. But I've just started reading such a wonderful book; must I shut it so soon?

The Wadi boys play their game of cricket, the women in sarees fill their water at the water tap, and a toddler rides upright on his cycle, ringing the bell for the first time in his life; that's why he cannot get enough of it. After I'm done here, I've got a class to teach. So, I'll pack up and leave, after kissing Francesco goodbye. This night is short, but I'll write another essay tomorrow.

I've placed a fragrant white magnolia (Champa) flower at Francesco's feet. The sun is setting; it's time to go.

But wait, it's not over. Maybe if luck favors me, I have to travel to at least one place before the door of my office is shut upon society and its hypocrisy forever.

The story of this book phoenix has not yet come to an end.

ESSAY 72

Ruskin Bond

OF ALL THE WRITERS WHO HAVE influenced my writing style and my life, only one is yet alive and doing very well.

He is the writer on the hill, India's beloved Ruskin Bond, eighty-five years young. He lives in India with his adopted family, in the hills of North India, in a hill station called Mussoorie, in the Landour area.

Before I die, I wish to one day meet this mentor of mine who has given me such a fondness for the hills that even though I've never set a foot in North India, let alone Mussoorie, I wish to retire there one day, with all my books.

Ruskin Bond has been a favorite author from the time I was a wee thing in summer frocks and red underwear, airing my hinder parts under the fan as I read the tales of the hills.

I've always had such a tight schedule that I have never had the time to go to Mussoorie, Landour. And now with David uncle and Rita so ill, frail and helpless, I don't think it will be possible to go out of the city any time soon.

But I must meet Ruskin Bond.

I need to touch his feet, kiss his cheek, and give him a tight hug before I go into seclusion.

No, I'm not being batty. Ruskin Bond will live a long, happy life and will continue to write his stories, novels, novellas, sketches, and essays forever and ever AMEN! And he will be India's favorite writer forever and ever and ever DOUBLE AMEN! And I TRIPLE it for good luck, since all things go in threes.

"You are mad, Fiza," Mama told me last summer (in 2018) when I begged to go to Mussoorie to meet Ruskin Bond. "You are not going anywhere. You have classes to teach, and I'm not sending you alone with Blaise, as he is a silly man!"

"I'm not silly!" Blaise retorts while he secretly stuffs salty wafers down his throat in the kitchen. "But I'm not going alone with Fiza. You, Philo, will have to come with me."

"No," Mama declares sternly with an icy stare. "No, Blaise, I cannot go to Mussoorie because I have tuitions throughout May."

"Then I'll go bloody alone!" I yell, quite angry.

At that, Blaise, Mama, Rita, and David uncle stare at me together. And they laugh.

"What's so funny?!" I cry like a cat whose tail has been caught in the closing door. "I can look after myself quite all right."

"Yes," Mama mimics my tone. "Like the way you pounded that eve-teaser and took him to the police station."

"It is ridiculous!" Blaise scoffs as he crushes the wafers and munches on them. "You are too young to travel alone. And good girls don't travel without an escort. Besides," Blaise adds with a chomping of his full mouth, "you will be robbed."

"You will be raped," Mama adds face-palming herself.

"You will be kidnapped and sold as a prostitute in Afghanistan," Rita adds, as if not wanting to be left out.

"You'll get lost at the airport itself," Mechu adds as she looks at me over her horn-rimmed glasses, "and you won't be able to get on the plane."

We all start arguing like wild cats. Lopez (the actual cat) hears our shouts and thinks she better make herself scarce and come back later for the remaining tea and coconut cake.

In the middle of this cacophony, David uncle says, "I'll pray that he comes to Mumbai soon. Otherwise, this lot will never let you go."

"But David uncle, I want to see Mussoorie," I plead like a three-year-old.

Later, Mama says, "We'll go for three days. Blaise, you, and I. We will keep Narayan in charge of ailing David uncle and Rita. I would have had them sent to Mechu's house but Mechu's husband is not well at all."

Then, as I'm going to bed, Mama says, "I promise you, Fiza, we will make sure you see your Ruskin Bond before he dies."

"Don't talk like that," I shoot back.

"Sorry?"

"I will go and meet him before *I* die!" I throw the words back at Mama. She holds on tight to her holy oil.

"Don't say such things, Fiza," she says. "He has lived his life, he ..."

I pretend to be reading a book and turn the other way.

❋

We have not made it to Ruskin Bond's Mussoorie even this year, 2019.

I don't blame anybody. Circumstances have made it difficult for us to meet him. Besides, he rarely meets fans these days, my Ruskin Bond, and what if we go all the way to Mussoorie and he happens to not be home and at some literary festival or other?

But I would still like to go to Mussoorie one day and meet Ruskin Bond there.

I want to meet his adopted family: Rajesh, Binya, and their children, Siddharth, Shrishti, and Gautam. I would like to meet Prem, Mukesh, Dolly, and the whole family.

I want to walk on the roads of Mussoorie with Ruskin Bond and have him show me all the places he has mentioned in his book, especially his place of power–Pari-tibba Hill. I want to see the cherry tree that he himself planted near Pari-tibba. I want to walk with him, hand in hand if possible, to the school where the children of Prem studied, just the way Ruskin Bond used to walk hand in hand with

Rajesh to school, making up a story of an ever-hungry leopard who ate a great number of people.

I want to visit the bookstore where Ruskin Bond signs books and meets his fans. I want to buy his books there and have the greatest prolific writer of India, the writer of the hills, sign my book. I want to walk with him on his usual walks, keeping track of every flower on our way.

I want to sit in, and take in the smell of, his bedroom-cum-study room. I want to smell his bookcase, see the creeper growing right into his room there, and look outside his window that he has always spoken about. The window where one gets to see the most beautiful part of Mussoorie and the cloud formations in the sky.

I want to sit on his cane chair, or at least gaze upon it in wonder.

I want to see more photographs of him when he was my age. He looked oh so handsome; if I were living back then, I would have surely married him! He especially looks handsome in a suit.

I want to speak to him, to tell him how much his books have meant to me, how I have grown to love the hills and would like to retire there with my books once my duties in this life are complete.

Dearest Ruskin Bond, my dear Owen – I know you have hated that name – my dear, dear, dear Rusty Ruskin Bond, tell me more about your father and how it came to be that you wrote so much that it touched the heart of little old me and made me feel so Ruskin Bondish!

The day I finally meet you, Ruskin Bond, will be the greatest Ruskin Bondish day ever!

You write such wonderful poetry, Mr. Bond. I cannot compete with it. But here is a little something for you from me:

When the story seems hard to believe,
When the pen begins to run its ink away.
When you feel given more than you receive,
When you hear the tale and it's the same;
Then you will be with me on a hill this side,
Then you shall say it was all meant to be me.

Then I will get on the windy breeze for a ride,
Then I shall say that our story was meant to be.

Adieu Rusty, till we meet someday in Landour.

ESSAY 73

The Joy of Books by Eric Burns

I SHALL END THIS LITTLE MEMOIR with one last book review. The review of a book I found on the road in Rahul's mound.

"Books *ke bare mein hai.*" He picked it up one day in 2013 and showed it to me as it rained cats and dogs. A terrible wind was blowing, and Narayan, who hadn't brought an umbrella that day, was soaked to the bone. I took the book and laid it on the stool while we all huddled together in the shade of a tarpaulin. Blaise was getting fidgety. He didn't want to be so engulfed by books.

We left when the rain stopped.

I read the book that same year. It was with a book phoenix's love that I read it. I love the part when the writer introduces us to his favorite childhood book and then, toward the end, he introduces his own child to the same book.

Although this book was published in 1995 and the author is a bit slanted where the advantage of technology in the reading process is concerned, I liked the book and gave it a five-on-five because, for me, any well-written book about the love of reading and the testimony of a diehard fan of the reading life is a book I appreciate.

Though I have other views about how technology has in a way been very beneficial in the whole reading, writing, and publishing process since 1995, it still was a fascinating read with a lovely bibliography section which I looked into the moment I finished the book somewhere in April 2013, just after my twenty-fourth birthday.

I still have that book with me today. I saw it in my "Read" cupboard (yes, I have a "Read" cupboard. In fact, I have several "Read" *cupboards*, do you have a problem with that?).

It's a wonderful book about how the reader and the writer are related. It's also part memoir. It was one of my best reads in 2013. And, when I was finished the book, I obtained the titles on his suggested reading list either from Amazon or at my other regular haunts.

Life and books sure have changed since 1995. And they're going to change again even after these words have been written and the appreciation for Eric Burns's fantastic tribute to books in written form is over and done with. My windows may be barred and shut tight in my office-cum-writing hut, but I have got good ears. I can hear the Wadi boys going home after their games to sit in front of the TV and watch some good old IPL cricket. Lopez is sitting on the doorstep, keeping guard of God knows what, and the last of the Wadi women are filling their buckets with water from the tap next to my hut. They have been doing this ever since I was born and even before that. Some things change and some things never change, and some things need to change.

But Eric Burns teaches us book lovers to have pride in our passion for the written word. He tells us that, yes, maybe we are a bit different, but we are a powerful set of people. And I personally believe that as long as there are readers and writers on this earth, exercising their freedom of speech without unnecessarily hurting the feelings of others, there is still hope for this world.

I am in complete seclusion. But I have a voice. Even if you don't hear it, you'll see it written down in these words – my joy for books and the bookish life.

The Joy of Books by Eric Burns marked the first of many books on books and reading and writing that I would read straight through my twenties. It influenced me to a great extent and inspired me to write this book. I haven't been a very serious reader because of my hectic lifestyle. Last year I only managed to read exactly one hundred books; I was aiming for two hundred! I'm not the wisest of the lot, and I don't pretend to be, either. Just like Ruskin Bond always says, I've got my "humble craft" and as long as it can keep me together, body and soul, and earn me some cash, I'm happier than happy.

Today seems like a really Ruskin Bondish day. Maybe I'll read a Ruskin Bond book when I get home; it's been a while.

Or maybe I'll find out what's wrong with Lopez and where Trotskyna has gotten herself to.

Or maybe I'll light a scented candle and practice some aromatherapy. Or maybe I'll do a bit of forest bathing in my modest garden while the cats are having an evening romp.

I'll maybe play a bit of music and think of that BSS boy of long ago. He may read these words one day in spite of my attempts to keep his identity a mystery. Maybe I'll be lucky and meet him someday soon, maybe at Kitab Khana, Wayword & Wise, Title Waves, Granth, Crosswords, St. Paul's, Ashish, or on the road with Rahul playing with his two puppies, who now have grown into dogs.

Or maybe I'll stay here in my office-cum-writing hut for a while and go through the books.

Books, hasn't it always been the same?

Books.

Books are all I need.

Books.

The Joy of Books.

Books.

Bibliography

Abdulali, Sohaila. *What We Talk about When We Talk about Rape.* New York: New Press, 2018.

Acharya, Prabhaker. *The Suragi Tree.* Ahmedabad: MapinLit, 2006.

Blatty, William Peter. *The Exorcist.* 40th anniversary ed. New York: Harper, 2011.

Bond, Ruskin. *The Blue Umbrella.* Rupa Publications India, 2014.

———. *Landour Bazaar.* Rupa Publications India, 2018.

———. *The Room on the Roof: 60th Anniversary Edition.* New Delhi: Penguin, 2016.

———. *Puffin Classics: Vagrants in the Valley.* New Delhi: Penguin, 2016.

———. *The Sensualist.* New Delhi: Penguin, 2016.

———. *Maharani.* New Delhi: Penguin, 2017.

———. *A Handful of Nuts.* New Delhi: Penguin, 2009.

———. *The Lamp is Lit.* New Delhi: Penguin, 2017.

———. *Scenes from a Writer's Life.* New Delhi: Penguin, 2017.

———. *The Beauty of All My Days: A Memoir.* New Delhi: Penguin, 2018.

———. *The Night Train at Deoli and Other Stories.* New Delhi: Penguin, 2016.

. *Rain in the Mountains: Notes from the Himalayas.* New Delhi: Penguin, 2016.

———. *Lone Fox Dancing: My Autobiography.* New Delhi: Speaking Tiger Publishing Pvt. Ltd., 2016.

Brooks, Kevin. *The Bunker Diary.* London: Penguin Books, 2013.

Burns, Eric. *The Joy of Books: Confessions of a Lifelong Reader.* Amherst, N.Y: Prometheus Books, 1995.

Carroll, Lewis, and Hugh Haughton. *Alice's Adventures in Wonderland and Through the Looking-Glass and What Alice Found There/* Lewis Carroll. Ed. and with an Introduction and Notes by Hugh Haughton. Centenary ed. Penguin Classics. London: Penguin, 2003.

Chattopadhyay, Saratchandra, and Sreejata Guha (Translator). *Devdas*. New Delhi; New York: Penguin Books, 2002.

Cohen, Albert, and Bella Cohen. *Book of My Mother*. 1st Archipelago Books ed. Brooklyn, NY: [Minneapolis]: Distributed by Consortium Book Sales and Distribution: Archipelago Books, 2012.

Devi, Phoolan, Marie-Therése Cuny, and Paul Rambali. *I, Phoolan Devi: The Autobiography of India's Bandit Queen*. London: Little, Brown and Co., 1996.

Divakaruni, Chitra Banerjee. *The Mistress of Spices*. 1st Anchor Books ed. New York: Anchor Books, 1997.

Faustina. *Diary: Divine Mercy in My Soul*. 3rd ed. with revisions. Stockbridge, Mass: Marians of the Immaculate Conception, 2000.

Flynn, Gillian. *Gone Girl*. First paperback edition. New York: Broadway Books, 2014.

Genova, Lisa. *Still Alice*. New York: Pocket Books, 2009.

Goins, Jeff. *You Are a Writer: (So Start Acting like One)*. Tribe Press, 2014.

———. *Real Artists Don't Starve: Timeless Strategies for Thriving in the New Creative Age*. Thomas Nelson Publishers, 2017

Jadhav, Narendra. *Ambedkar: Awakening India's Social Conscience*. New Delhi: Konark Publishers, 2014.

———. *Outcaste, a Memoir*. New Delhi; New York, NY: Viking, 2003.

Kang, Han. *The Vegetarian*. Translated by Deborah Smith. London: Portobello Books, 2015.

———. *The White Book*. Translated by Deborah Smith. London: Portobello Books, 2017.

———. *Human Acts*. Translated by Deborah Smith. London: Portobello Books, 2016.

Kazantzakis, Nikos. *God's Pauper: St. Francis of Assisi*. London: Faber, 1990.

Kertész, Imre, and Thomas Cooper. *The Holocaust as Culture*. London; New York: Seagull Books, 2011.

Lahiri, Jhumpa, Ann Goldstein. *In Other Words*. First edition. New York: Alfred A. Knopf, 2016.

Li, Qing. *Shinrin-Yoku: The Art and Science of Forest Bathing*. London: Penguin Life, 2018.

Lovecraft, H. P. *The Transition of H.P. Lovecraft: The Road to Madness*. New York: Ballantine Books, 1996.

———. *The Best of H. P. Lovecraft: Bloodcurdling Tales of Horror and the Macabre*. New York: Ballantine Books, 1987

Mander, Harsh. *Fatal Accidents of Birth: Stories of Suffering, Oppression and Resistance*. New Delhi, [India]: Speaking Tiger, 2016.

Narayan, R. K. *The English Teacher*. London: Vintage, 2001.

———. *The Bachelor of Arts*. India: Indian Thought Publications, 2007.

———. *The Vendor of Sweets*. India: Indian Thought Publications, 2007.

———. *The Painter of Signs*. India: Indian Thought Publications, 1973.

———. *Talkative Man*. India: Indian Thought Publications, 2007.

———. *Malgudi Days*. India: Indian Thought Publications, 2000.

———. *The World of Nagaraj*. India: Indian Thought Publications, 2003.

———. *Mr. Sampath: The Printer of Malgudi*. India: Indian Thought Publications, 1997.

———. *Salt and Sawdust*. New Delhi: Penguin India, 2006.

Pathan, Fiza. *CLASSICS: Why and how we can encourage children to read them*. Mumbai: Fiza Pathan Publishing, 2017.

———. *The Love That Dare Not Speak Its Name: Short Stories*. Mumbai: Fiza Pathan Publishing, 2017.

———. *Amina: The Silent One*. Mumbai: Fiza Pathan Publishing, 2018.

———. *NIRMALA: The Mud Blossom*. Mumbai: Fiza Pathan Publishing, 2018.

———. *The Reclusive Writer & Reader of Bandra: Essays*. Mumbai: Fiza Pathan Publishing, 2018.

Pawar, Daya, and Jerry Pinto. *Baluta*. First English language edition. New Delhi: Speaking Tiger, 2015.

Rehman, Waheeda, and Nasreen Munni Kabir. *Conversations with Waheeda Rehman*. New Delhi: Penguin, Viking, 2014.

Revathi, and A. Mankai. *Our Lives, Our Words: Telling Aravani Lifestories*. Sexualities. New Delhi: Yoda Press, 2011.

Seltzer, David. *The Omen*. New York: Signet, 2006.

Stoker, Bram. *Dracula*. Dover Thrift Editions. Mineola, N.Y: Dover Publications, 2000.

Thomas, Scarlett. *The End of Mr. Y*. 1st ed. Orlando, Fla: Harcourt, 2006.

Wohlleben, Peter, and Peter Wohlleben. *The Hidden Life of Trees: What They Feel, How They Communicate{u2014} Discoveries from a Secret World*, 2016.

Yousafzai, Malala, and Christina Lamb. *I Am Malala: The Girl Who Stood up for Education and Was Shot by the Taliban*. First edition. New York, NY: Little, Brown, & Company, 2013.

Zevin, Gabrielle. *The Collected Works of A.J. Fikry*. London: Little Brown, 2014.

Websites:

UN Women, New York (website), Facts and figures: Ending violence against women, accessed November 20, 2019, https://www.unwomen.org/en/what-we-do/ending-violence-against-women/facts-and-figures .

Index

ABOUT THE AUTHOR

Fiza Pathan has a bachelor's degree in arts from the University of Mumbai, where she majored in history and sociology, gaining a First Class. She also has a bachelor's degree in education, again with a First Class, her special subjects being English and history.

Fiza has written thirteen award-winning books and short stories, which reflect her interest in furthering the cause of education and in championing social issues. In over seventy literary competitions, she has placed either as winner or finalist.

Last year she placed in fifteen literary awards, chief among them: 2018 Digital Book World Winner Best Book (Short Stories); 2018 Digital Book World Finalist Best Book (Social Issues); Killer Nashville 2018 Silver Falchion Award Finalist Best Short Story; 2018 IAN Book of the Year Awards Winner – Outstanding Fiction LGBTQ; 2018 Montaigne Medal Finalist (Part of Eric Hoffer Award); 2018

Shelf Unbound Competition for Best Independently Published Book – Notable Indie; and 2018 Dan Poynter's Global E-book Awards Winner (Silver Medal).

This year she has placed in the 2019 IAN Book of the Year Awards – Finalist General Non-Fiction; 2019 Global E-Book Award – Honorable Mention Memoirs (Non-Fiction); 2019 Purple Dragonfly Book Awards – Honorable Mention in Chapter Books (three awards) and Memoirs; and 3rd Place/Honorable Mention in the 2019 90-DAY ALPHA/OMEGA "BEGINNING TO END" SHORT STORY WRITING CONTEST.

She lives with her maternal family and writes novels and short stories in most genres.

Amazon links:
https://books2read.com/u/3LpMNX
Personal website https://fizapathan.com/
Blogs at https://insaneowl.com
Twitter handle @FizaPathan
Company's websites:
https://fizapathanpublishing.us/
https://fizapathanpublishing.org/

www.ingramcontent.com/pod-product-compliance
Ingram Content Group UK Ltd.
Pitfield, Milton Keynes, MK11 3LW, UK
UKHW041859190726
13854UKWH00002B/987

9 788194 055815